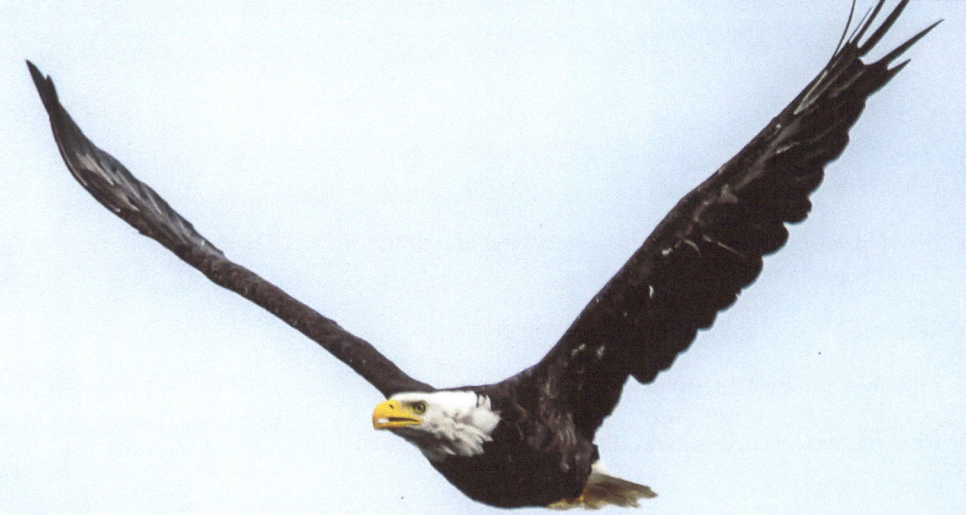

Ever Onward

Adventures Across America and Into the Sky

Text and Photography by David Schneider

ISBN: 978-0-9838967-8-4

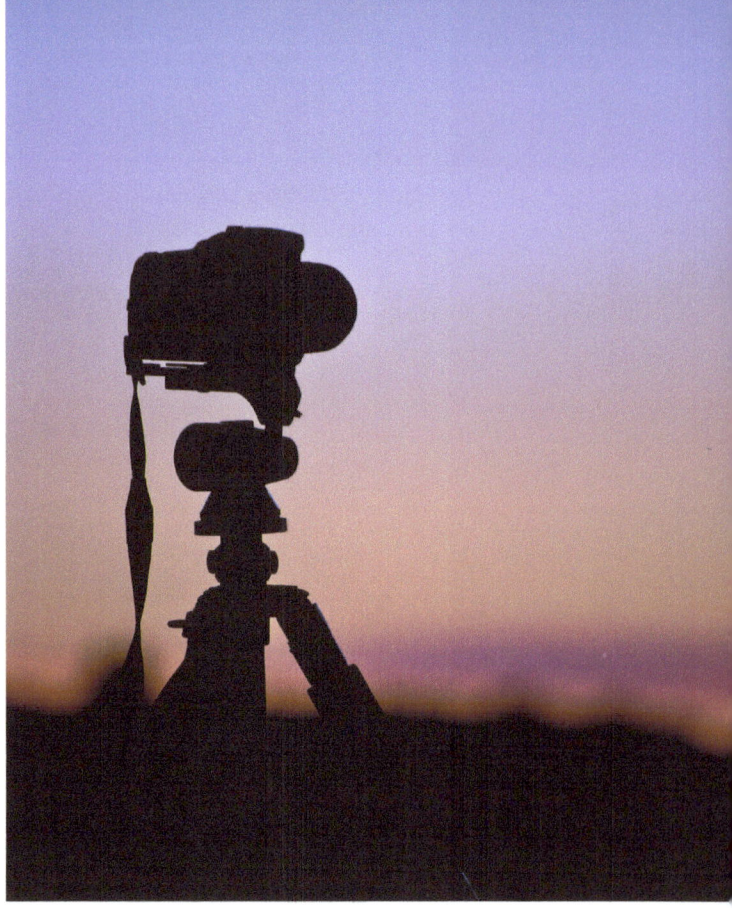

Text and Photography by David Schneider

Edited by Bobbie Christmas

Created, produced, designed, and printed in the United States

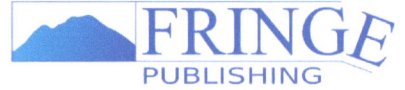

An imprint of Fringe Innovations, LLC

For more information about our books, write Fringe Publishing, PO Box 67555, Albuquerque, NM 87193, call (505) 750-4PIX, or visit www.fringepublishing.com

Contents

Preface

The scene was dark—pitch black described it aptly. I made my adjustments to no avail, trying every technique I knew. I had to hurry, for moments like that one were what I lived for, yet everything I tried didn't make a whit of difference. A sense of unease bordering on panic replaced my typical calmness. I could not miss making this photograph! At the last moment I remembered a critical step I had forgotten. I removed the lens cap from my camera and made the perfect photograph.

I need to step away from the camera more often. Just not today.

Ever Onward is my fourth book. It was difficult to decide which stories to include and far more difficult to tell others, "Next time." Since *Unbounded Chronicles*, my adventures have continued, some more successful than others; par for the course. My life has had its share of challenges. Both my parents have passed, a difficult time for me, but also a time to reconnect with my childhood beginnings in the best possible way. It saddens me to realize my parents can't read these stories, especially since my parents set me on my path of discovery.

COVID-19 descended on us, which curtailed my explorations, but not my spirit, and although I wrote this book during the pandemic, the road ahead still called me, louder day by day.

My life is blessed in many ways too, and it is on those blessings that I focus. My children, Blake and Jessica, will be able to read my stories, and maybe they will inspire my offspring on their own journeys. Mary Beth, my partner, will read them too, and she'll learn the details of incidents I've studiously avoided telling her.

It's my pleasure, then, to share these stories with you. Let's head ever onward.

Western Parks

The National Park System preserves and protects our wild lands for all to enjoy. Iconic viewpoints and amazing adventures are to be had, if only you know where and when to look. Those parks are among my favorites, and a new story can always be found within their boundaries.

Despite, or perhaps because of, my wanderings across our country, my heart belongs to our National Park System, which highlights the beauty and grandeur of our country. The parks feature some of the most diverse ecosystems anywhere in the world and protect precious, unique places we must preserve for future generations. Although I photograph everywhere, I always find my way back to them, and I always find a sense of calm inside their borders. Passing an entrance sign to one of these parks makes me smile, and whatever worries I might have had are left there. The parks are timeless. The passage of time is measured not in seconds and minutes but in years and decades. The photographs made within them are timeless too.

It's fitting, then, that we begin our journey in our national lands.

Glacier National Park in Montana holds special significance for me because of my childhood. There I first encountered a bear in the wild, and that singular moment has stuck with me ever since. I was in my early teens, young enough to enjoy still being a child and old enough to be on my own a bit and explore without anyone telling me what to do. I took full advantage of that opportunity.

Every year Mom and Dad took a summer vacation and dragged me along. I know they carefully planned each vacation down to the last detail. Dad knew how many days off work he had, how far we could travel in a day, and how many days would be best at each stop, all of which gave him a good sense of what we could see. Glacier National Park was a prime destination for my parents, and they were eager to visit. I had absolutely no clue about anywhere out west, and to me, one park seemed as dull a destination as the next. Besides, summertime was a time for me to play with my friends, and given the choice between a boring park and spending idyllic summer days with my friends, well, it wasn't a hard choice. All I cared about was how long we would be gone and which highly entertaining things I would miss by being forced away from my friends. To say that my parents had to stuff me in the car was an understatement, and I think my dad's entire plan was to get out of the driveway and drive fast enough that jumping out of the car was no longer an option. I considered doing it many times.

The dreaded day came, and as expected, my parents crammed me into the back seat and drove away. I spent the rest of the trip to Montana sulking, and although I cannot remember the particulars, I am sure I let my parents know my considerable displeasure at their fiendish plan.

As an aside, I later apologized to my parents for the misery of summer vacations I put them through. Their perseverance in taking me lit my desire and passion for our national lands, and I owe them an eternal debt of gratitude.

At any rate, after days of driving, we eventually arrived in Glacier National Park. My parents situated our small fourteen-foot travel trailer, into which Mom somehow managed to pack our entire house, and settled in. My parents proceeded to "camp," which meant they sat in folding chairs, pulled out a year's worth of magazines and books, and read. The arrangement did not sit well with me. Oh no, not at all. I tolerated that behavior for all of five minutes. "I'm bored," I announced to see what would happen, not expecting any results. Without hesitation or glancing up my parents told me, "Find something to do."

I did. The entirety of a national park surrounded me; I was young enough not to realize the difficulties I could get into and old enough to be able to do it anyway. I scrounged up a trail map and decided to see all the trails. I figured that I could accomplish it in a morning, maybe early afternoon, tops, not realizing how staggeringly big, at 1,582 square miles, Glacier National Park is. I set off down the nearest trail, happy to have found "something to do."

I have no idea how long I walked or how far. It could have been a half mile; it could have been many miles. I don't know where I was, but I remember the trail as plain as day. It was wide and easy walking. Tall pine trees rose on either side of me, so there weren't any views to speak of. I hustled down the trail as quickly as possible, since the goal was to hike the trail, not take in any of those pesky scenic sights. I trotted along as best as I could. Up ahead of me was a bend in the trail, wholly unremarkable and precisely like the thousand or so other turns I had already made. What was a little different, though, was the huge bear coming around the next bend on the same trail. The bear stopped. I stopped. We regarded each other carefully, probably not more than one hundred feet apart. I promptly did what everyone tells you not to do, not that I had listened in the first place. I turned and ran. In hindsight it was not a bright thing to do, and I was lucky the bear had no interest in me. Knowing what I know now, my first encounter with a bear in the wilderness could have gone poorly indeed. Whew!

When I got back to the trailer, Mom and Dad asked me what I did. I told them I was out hiking, and they went about their afternoon. Not until years later did I tell them what actually happened when I was hiking, which was fortunate, because they would have put a stop to it. The fact that they didn't stop me was good because about that time I found my deep love of the outdoors and nature and, yes, even bears. I continued to hike, albeit far more carefully, and I was hiking because I realized the many things to explore and encounter. I had sights to see and bears to meet. The national parks were spectacularly scenic places to be, and I had to be in them. That remarkable original event started my love for the park system, its inhabitants, and the wonders it contains.

When vacation was over, my parents stuffed me back in the car. As before, I threatened to jump out. Who wants to go home and play with friends when the great outdoors awaits? Dad resorted to the tried-and-true plan of driving fast enough that I couldn't jump out, although as before, I deeply considered that option.

Not until many years later did I go back to the magic of Glacier National Park. I had dim memories of various places in it. I could remember Going-to-the-Sun Road well enough, although not the particulars of it. I faintly remembered Logan Pass. Now and then I saw something I almost recognized. With adult eyes I searched for the trail where I met the bear, but I have no idea where I was hiking as a child. Glacier still had a surprise for me; a welcome home gift, if you will.

That crisp fall morning was my first in the park since I went back, and I decided on Going-to-the-Sun Road as an excellent way to get myself orientated in the park. I traveled up and over Logan Pass, this time enjoying the scenic views instead of wishing I was home with my friends. I headed down to the other side, and something in the bushes on the slope caught my eye. As fate would have it, the thoroughfare offered a convenient place to pull over, which is not always possible on that road. I stepped out and intensely scanned the bushes, which were rustling. I had my camera ready. I crouched down and patiently waited, still and quiet.

A grizzly bear walked out of the bushes farther down the slope. She saw me, but as with the bear many years before, she had no interest in me. She was more concerned with the luscious berries all around her. How do I know the bear was a female? Oh, that's easy. Her cub tumbled down the hill behind her. Momma and her cub foraged on the hillside, occasionally sparing me a glance. I enjoyed the moment. My childhood experiences came flooding back, and I knew without any doubt that I was where I belonged. Glacier welcomed me back in her own way. That time I knew what not to do.

Prowling Glacier is significant because it takes me full circle. To re-experience a cornerstone moment from my past, this time with camera in hand, was exhilarating. All those earlier emotions came back to me, connecting me to my past and reminding me of my future.

The bears moved off into the brush, and I moved on down the road, all the richer for the experience.

Going-to-the-Sun Road bisects the park and offers the only way to move from one side to the other. As the name implies, it seems like you are climbing to the sun, especially since there isn't a level section of the road. Oddly, the road's name came from nearby Going-to-the-Sun Mountain, not the fact that it seems to go up forever to meet the sun. The roadway is narrow and

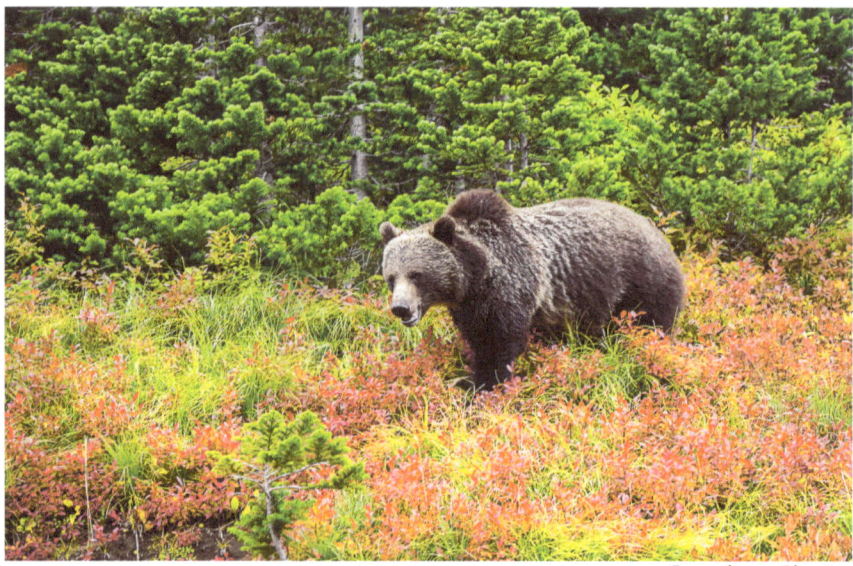
Prowling Glacier

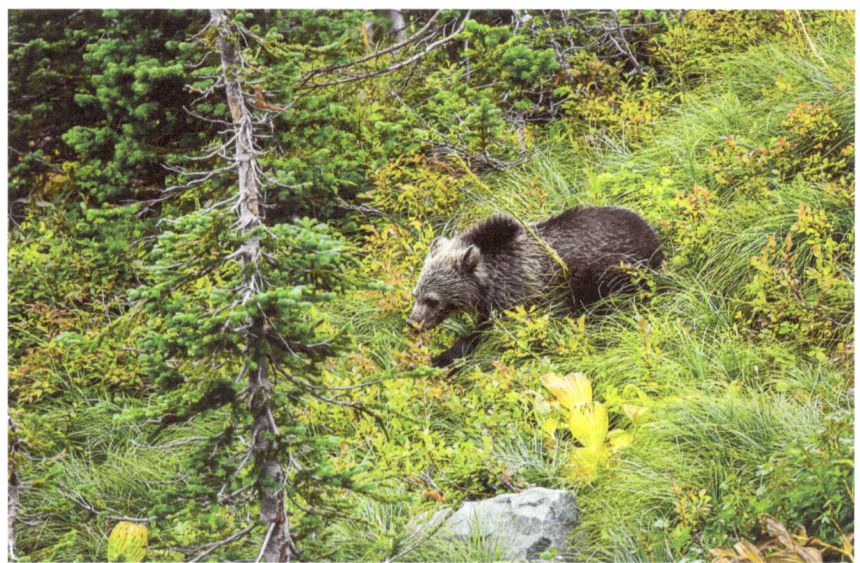
Glacier's Cub

features steep drop offs, but unless you have an intense fear of heights, it isn't an overly scary road. Come to think of it, the way some people drove on it was frightening, but that's another story. The road is a treat to drive on, and every turn of every section offers panoramic views.

As in many places, the views change depending on the time of day. Dawn is one of my favorite times, which is when I made *Glacier Morning*. Rain clouds accompanied me during most of my time in the park, and I wondered if the sun ever shines in Montana. Now and then I was rewarded with a glimpse of the sun, reminding me that it was still there. The combination of clouds and rain makes fabulous photographic opportunities, so I did not complain in the least. Well, I didn't complain too much.

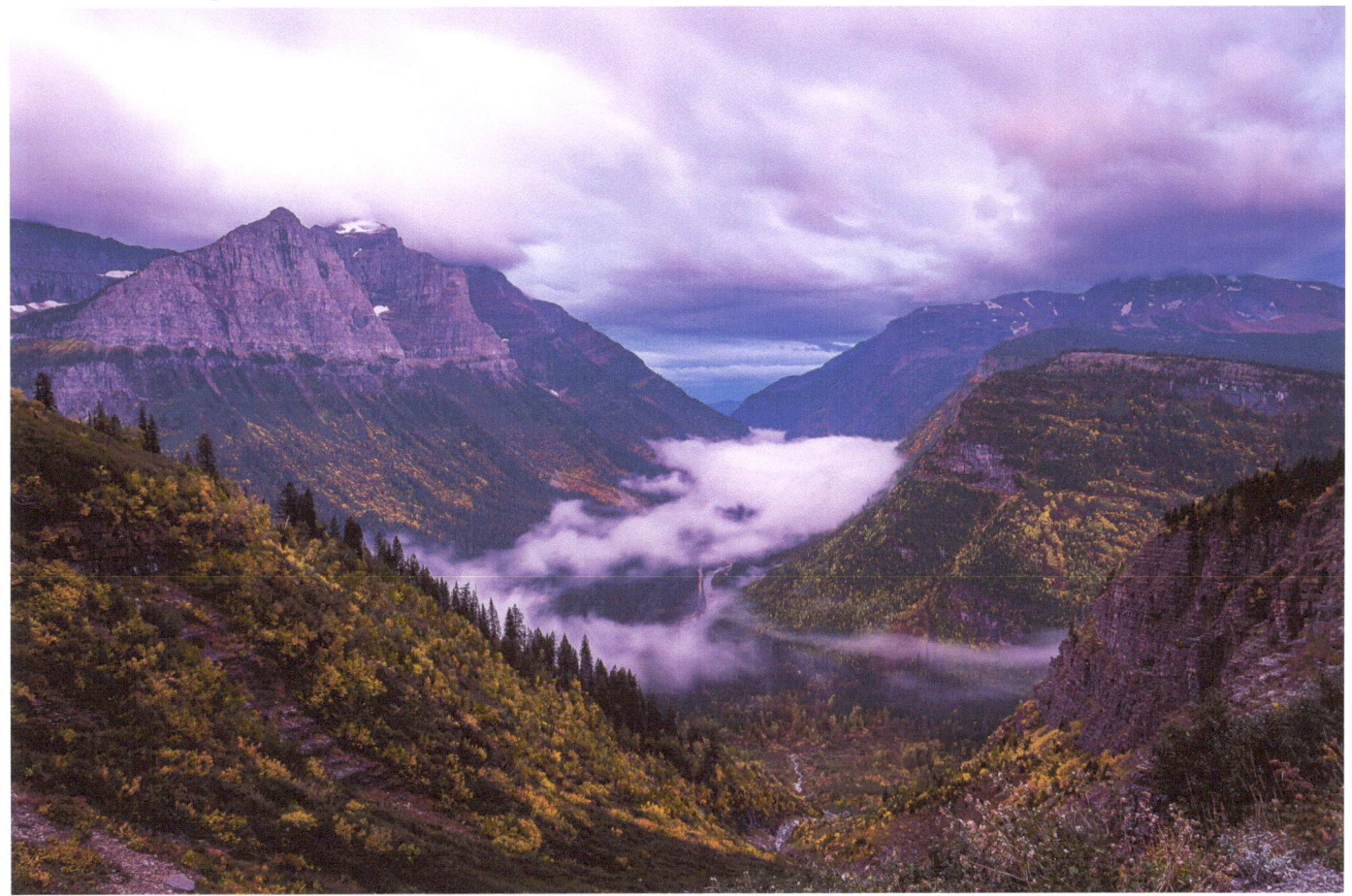

Glacier Morning

One of those cloud-and-rain combinations came together and allowed me to make another delightful photograph. I was on the east side of the park near Many Glacier. The morning had been socked in, and my watch was the only way I knew it was morning; the sun was nowhere around. Still, nothing stopped me. I explored all around, both by vehicle and by foot, although I kept coming back to one area. The combination of rock faces and water, fall colors, and the looming mountain in the background intrigued me. I knew in my heart a photograph was there, but the low, heavy clouds precluded making one. I was in no hurry, so I simply waited to see what might happen. I didn't look at my watch either, for doing so was a sure way to make time slow down if not stop altogether. Eventually the sun found some chinks in the cloud's armor, and before I knew it, Sol tossed a sporadic ray of light out here and there. I took full advantage of one of the rare sunbeams to make *Many's Storm*.

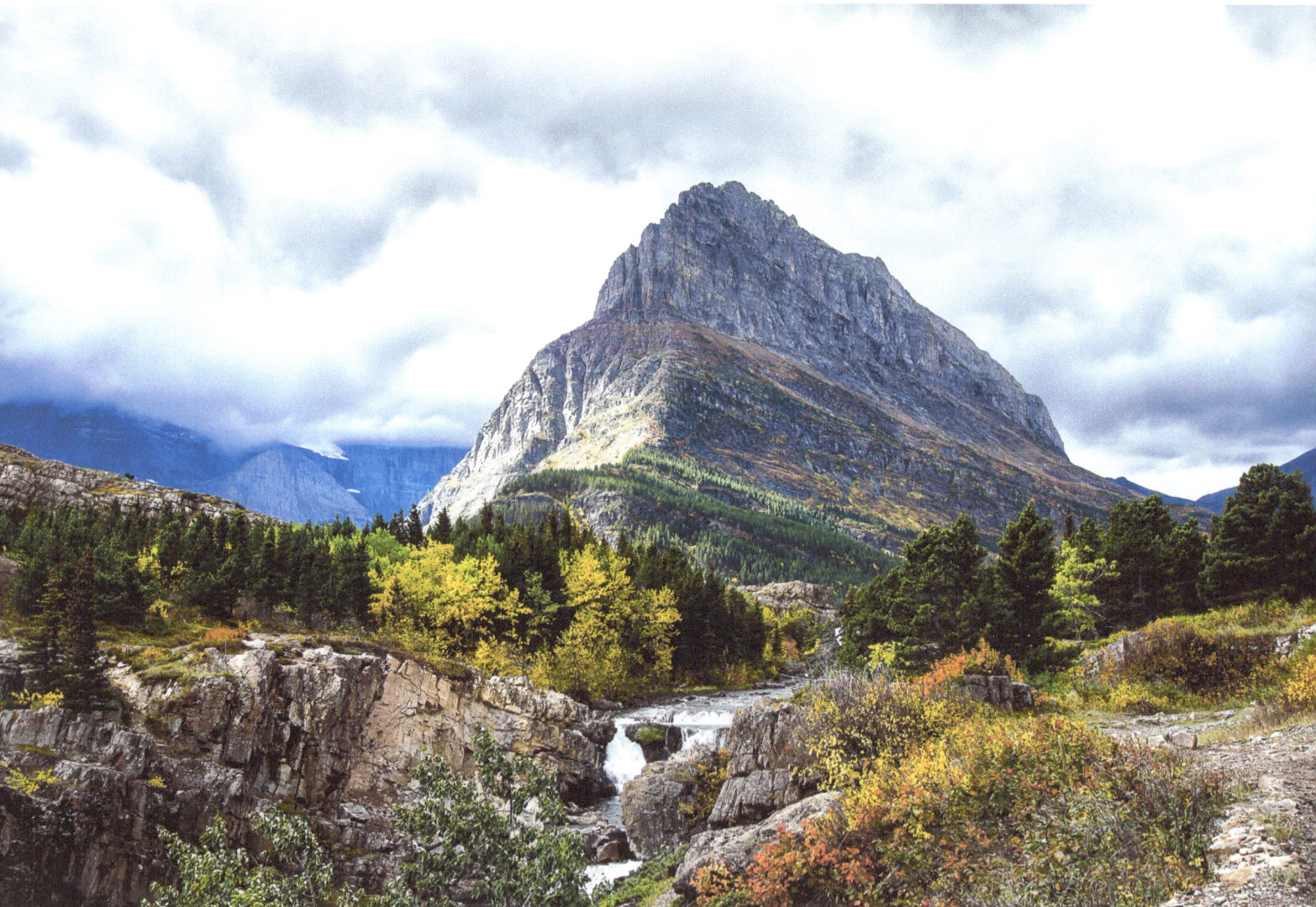

Many's Storm

I am pleased with how it came out. I adore the play of colors against the cloudy and fierce skies above. It reminds me of the forces of nature at work in Glacier National Park and the duality of storms and beauty. We'll see more of this interplay in the chapters ahead.

Going-to-the-Sun Road had one last unexpected treat for me on my most recent visit to the park. I was headed back up it from the east side toward Logan Pass when I glanced to my left at the mountains. Much to my surprise a young bighorn sheep was standing at the edge of one of the pull-outs. Most bighorn sheep spend their time high in the mountains, where they look like small white dots rather than sheep and defy a photographer's lens. Carefully, and without undue commotion, I parked, grabbed my camera, and crept to within a reasonable distance. *Glacier's Bighorn* is the result of that encounter, and it was as if Glacier wanted me to know that it had more than grizzly bears to offer.

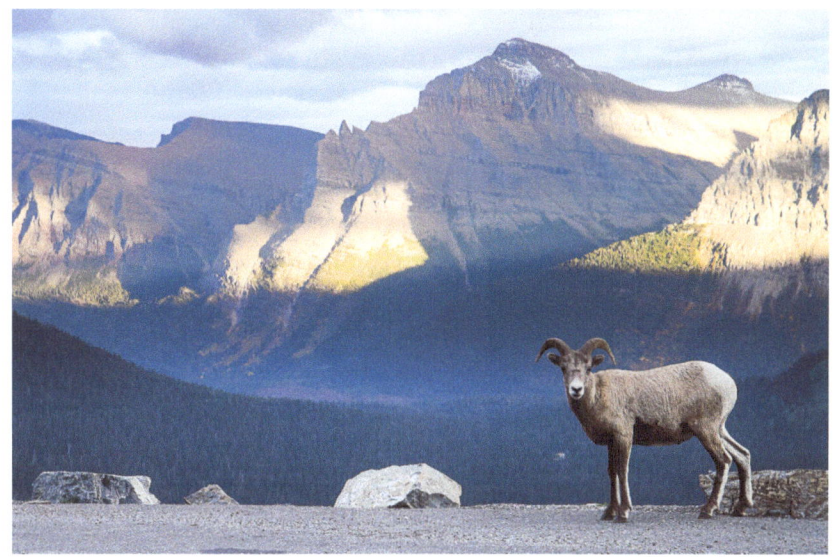

Glacier's Bighorn

Glacier National Park is not the only park to have bighorn sheep, though. Many of the western parks feature them, especially Yellowstone National Park. Yellowstone is another of my all-time favorite parks and another with strong childhood memories. My parents took me there several times, although unlike Glacier, I have specific memories of specific places. We stayed at Fishing Bridge Campground near the center of the park. It was one of Mom and Dad's favorite campgrounds anywhere, and we once spent an entire vacation in one campsite. It was quite the experience to go back to the same campground restaurant, forty years later, and sit at the same stools and order the same shake. Some things never change, although I think the server was new.

Ram Snack

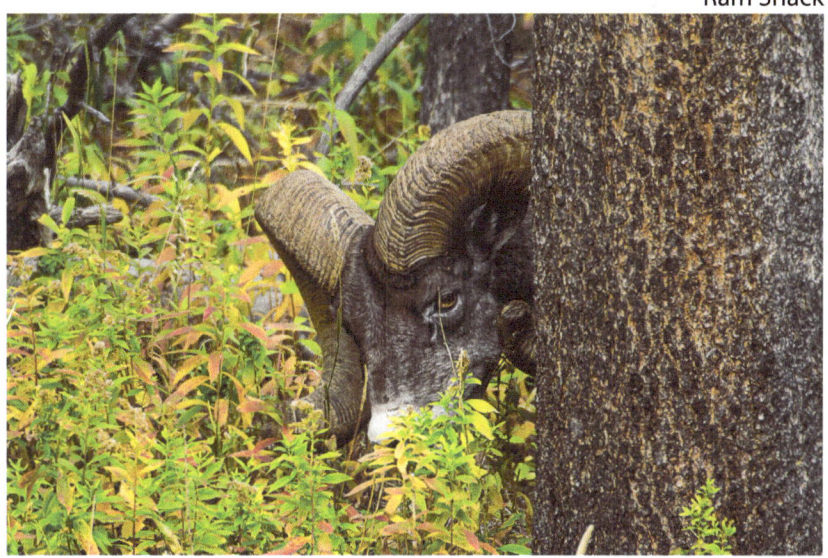

I find it always delightful when I encounter bighorn sheep. This fine ram was grazing in a small hollow, and although he knew I was there, he wasn't overly concerned with me. I wanted to create close-up photographs of wildlife on that particular Yellowstone excursion, and this bighorn certainly fit that criteria. I watched and photographed him awhile, and we eventually said goodbye and went our separate ways.

Another splendid close-up photograph from Yellowstone is *Resting Bison*. On that warm fall day, what leaves remained on the trees were a deep golden brown. The summer grasses, long dried out, were ready for winter, and the park was preparing for the heavy snowfalls soon to come. Why not enjoy the warmth of the sun when you can? This bison, resting comfortably, was in no hurry, content where it was. I made this photograph and then moved on, lest I disturb its rest. Disrupting a bison always leads to trouble, and I saw no need to stir things up.

Bisonic Intensity

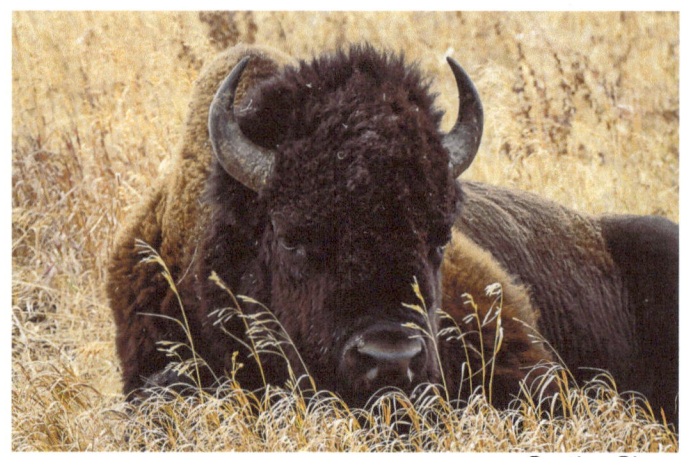

Resting Bison

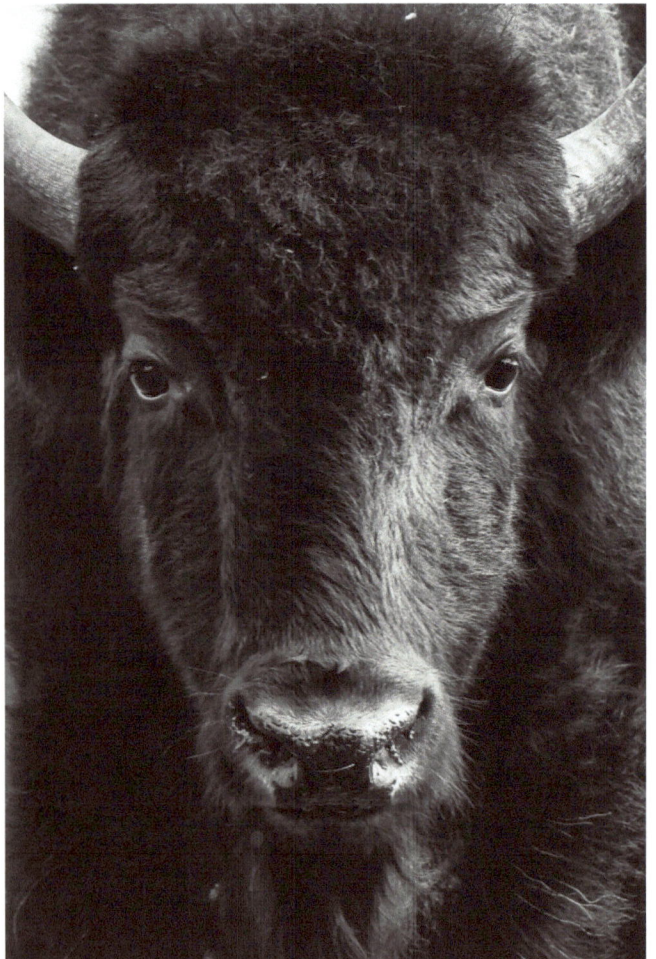

Not every bison I photographed was resting. The one in *Bisonic Intensity* fully engaged with what I was doing, which was more than a little unsettling. To be clear, I was a healthy distance away from the bison. Bison may look slow and lumbering, but they are not. They are quick and agile and can run, especially toward you, far faster than you expect. Plus, they are quick to anger. Given their size, their agility and temperament calls for healthy respect.

Yellowstone, as with all parks, has strict distance rules with the wildlife, and adhering to those rules is beneficial to you and the wildlife. Too many people have learned that bison have a straightforward method of dealing with unruly humans: knock them down or maybe gore them once or twice to get the point across. With that information in mind, I stayed well away from this bison and remained aware of my surroundings.

The bison and I regarded each other carefully, although for differing reasons. I was looking for the best possible photograph; it wondered what I was doing, and if, perhaps, it should also be doing something. I didn't linger, though, or make any sudden movement. I made *Bisonic Intensity* and then cleared the area. The bison watched me go and then turned back to foraging through the grasses.

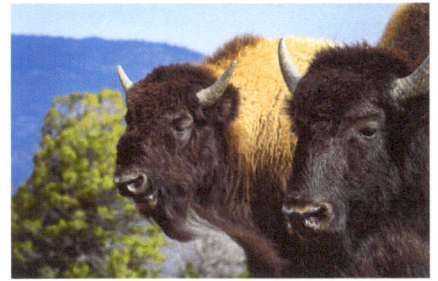
Double-Barreled Bison

I was almost ready to depart Yellowstone, but one more bison opportunity presented itself at the last moment.

I created *Double-Barreled Bison* in the same general area, which is down a track far away from the main road. I like this area because it is relatively unknown and doesn't see as many humans as other, more popular areas. It's easy to miss the road, and most cars whiz by it without a second glance. Naturally I use it whenever I can, and this time I spotted bison alongside it. These two bison were on the move. What their destination was, it was hard to say, and indeed, only they knew. I like the photograph I made, though. It shows the bison's power and spirit.

Let's head south out of Yellowstone into Grand Teton National Park, another of my favorite locations. People often ask me my favorite place to photograph, and I struggle to answer. It isn't that I can't, but instead because as soon as I think of one, I think of a more beloved one, and then another, and so on. I am instantly tongue-tied, since so many places spring to mind, and the answer is impossible. Always near the top of my list, though, is Grand Teton National Park in Wyoming.

The Tetons are always "on the way," and I'll make any excuse at all to visit. If I head to Texas from New Mexico, I might well decide the Tetons are on the way, and I need to drop in and see what is happening. Mary Beth, my partner, used to look at me like I'd completely lost my mind when I did it, but she has come to understand my deep love for the park. Now she just looks at me like I am crazy, which is an improvement, so I am happy. At any rate, I'll visit the Tetons any chance I get.

I've been in every nook and cranny of the park, time and again, year after year. Like the previous question, I don't have a favorite place within the park, but some areas draw me back. Mormon Row is one of those places, and I have a great story from there that I'll save for an upcoming chapter. For now I'll start at a small forest road just off the main highway that runs through the park. Nothing is special about the road itself, but if you park and thrash through the weeds and brush, you'll come to an excellent view of the Teton Mountains. From that secluded road I made *Teton Stronghold*.

Teton Stronghold

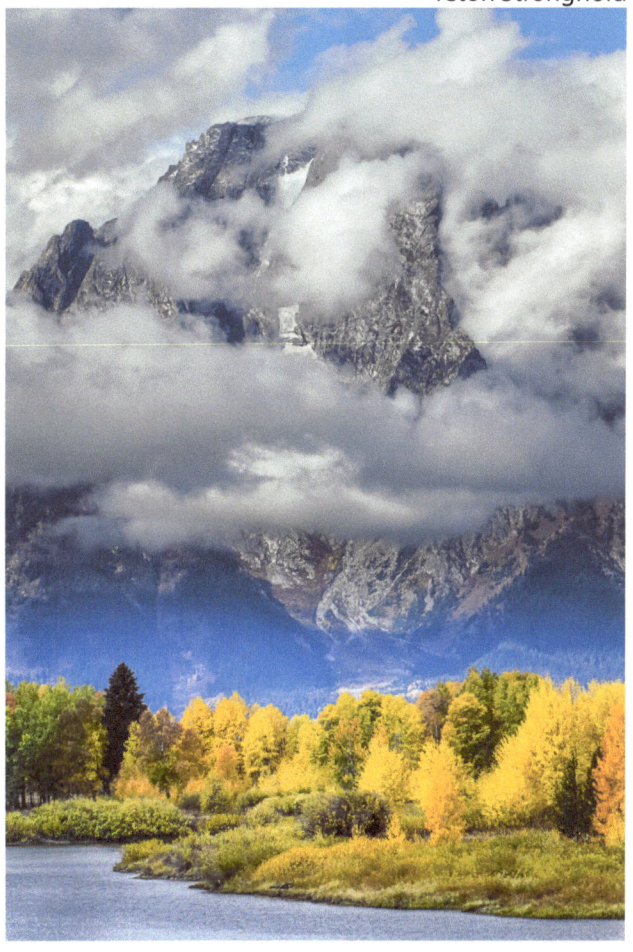

I spend an enormous amount of time scouting locations. I'll find an out-of-the-way place to park and then look around. I'll follow the wispiest of trails, just to see where they might lead. Most of the time I know the answer will be "nowhere," yet I am compelled to find out. Now and then a path leads to a photo-worthy view like *Teton Stronghold*. I might take years to find the right moment to create the perfect photograph, but I am in no hurry. Many times I'll head to my favorite places just to see what might be going on. The continual process of exploring and rechecking is how I increase my knowledge of the parks. I am lucky I can remember where those places are, and Mary Beth is no longer surprised when one moment we're cruising down a highway and the next we're randomly on a previously unseen dirt road deep in the woods because I want to see how a location looks at the moment. I can't remember the color of the shirt I wore yesterday, but I can remember the exact place to turn off the highway. Luckily I'm a storyteller and not a fashion designer.

The Tetons look phenomenal at any time of the year, and winter is no exception. One crisp winter afternoon Mary Beth and I drove along Highway 191, the main route through the park. I forget the exact temperature, but I know it was

Teton Afternoon

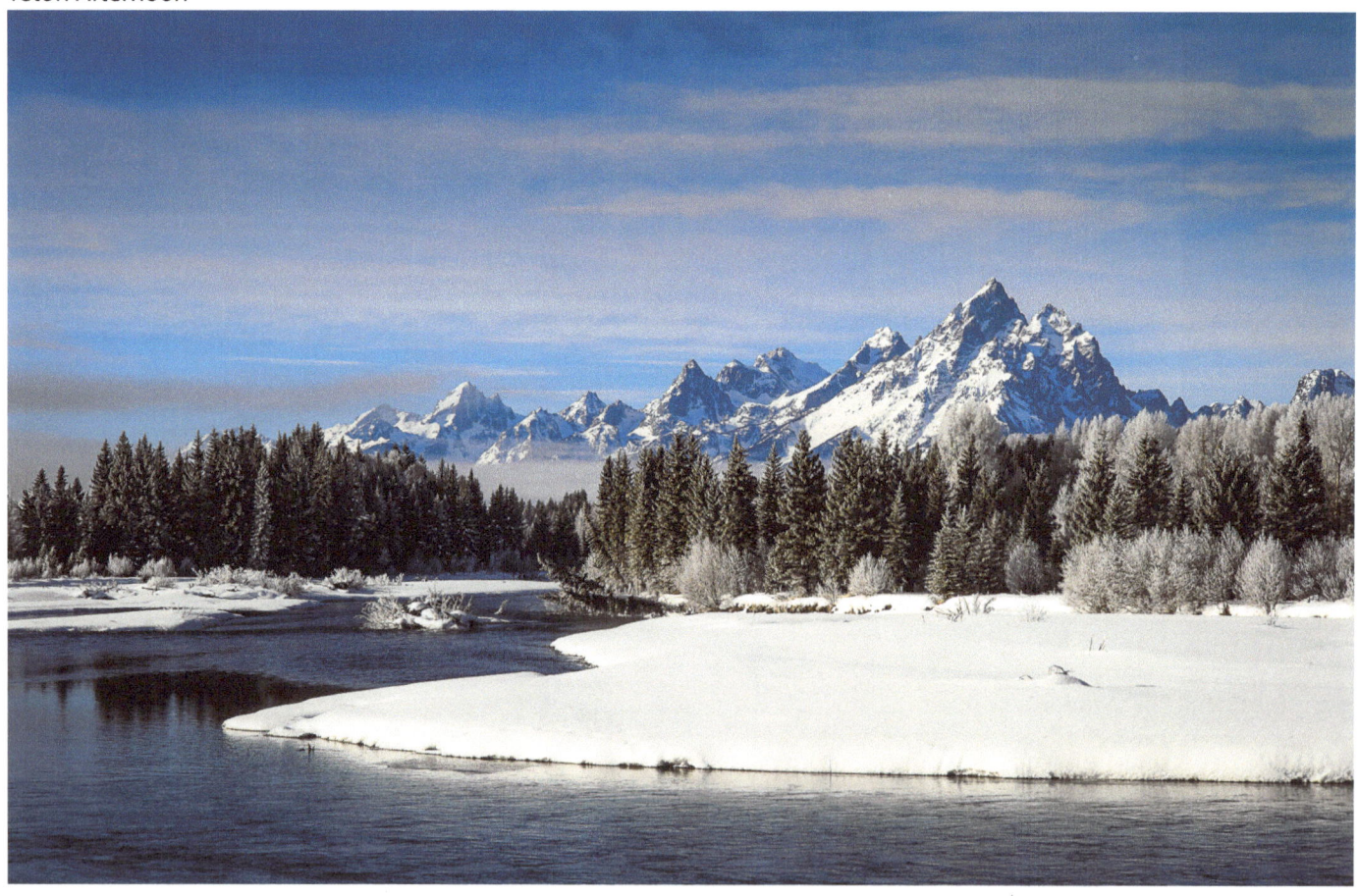

darned cold. While I drove, I looked all around and realized that the winter scene before me was becoming better and better. I frantically looked for a place to pull over, but the road was narrow and the snowbanks high, and pulling over was impossible. Before Mary Beth fully realized what was happening, I stopped in the middle of the highway. I opened the door, grabbed my camera, and scrambled up and over the nearest snowbank. I was gone.

The scene around me held my full attention, and I wasn't going to let minor details, such as nowhere to pull over and frigid cold, deter from me making *Teton Afternoon*. I stood sans jacket, shivering and teeth chattering in deep snow, determined to make the photograph. As time slipped by, I realized that not grabbing gloves or a warm coat was a severe mistake. I had gone that far, though, so I tromped around until I found the perfect spot for the photograph. My fingers grew more numb by the minute, and it took all my concentration to make the photograph. I made my way back to the road, pushing my way through the snow back to the highway. I realized that my plan was perhaps not as well thought out as it might have been. No car. No Mary Beth. No warmth. Uh-oh.

After a few long minutes, however, she drove by and stopped for me. Later she told me she hopped into the driver's seat and cruised up and down the highway waiting for me to appear while trying not to be too angry at me. She was "mostly sure" she was going to stop. That incident was not my first and likely not the last, but I made the photograph, and that's what counts. Luckily she understands. I think.

The inhabitants of the Tetons, unlike me, are ready for the cold. Winters in the Tetons can be fierce and the cold intense. They take getting used to. A marvelous case in point is this pair of red foxes in the snow on a bitter cold winter day. I encountered, then observed, these foxes for a few hours, and this sequence is one of my all-time favorites. I was well prepared for the cold this time, and good thing, because I was out in it for a long time.

Much of the Tetons is closed during winter, although you can still move around some areas of the park. It was in one of those areas that I came across the foxes. I first spotted the male not far away and had the time and sense to have donned proper cold-weather gear. I crept across the snow, hid behind a large snowbank, and settled in to watch the wild canine. He went about his fox business, whatever that was, much to my delight. He knew I was present, but I was no threat to him, so he carried on. Finally he settled down on the snow, curled up, and looked straight at me. I was able to make one of my all-time favorite photographs, *Fox Curl*. I am proud of all my photographs, but this one is priceless to me. I was able to compose the photograph flawlessly. Every time I look at *Fox Curl*, I am reminded of that priceless moment.

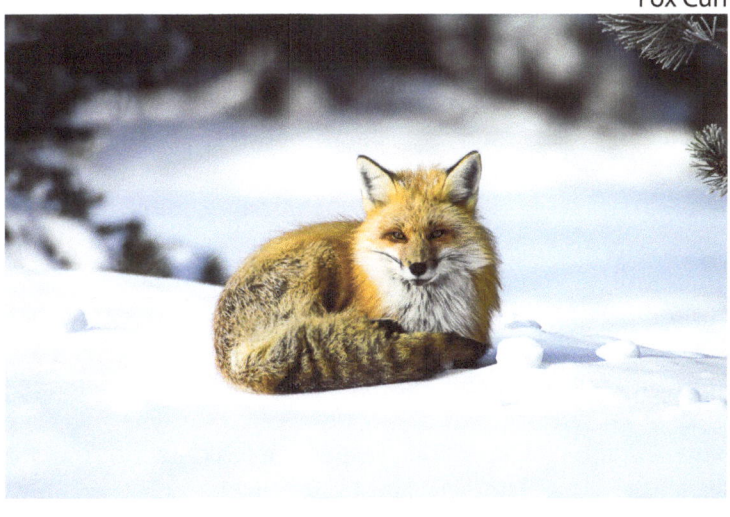

Fox Curl

Things went even better when a female came into the scene. Like the male, she was aware of me but paid me no attention and went about her day, also doing fox stuff. She wandered about, sniffing this, glancing at that, and generally prowling around. I made *Fox Stride* during that time.

Finally both foxes came together, nose to nose, and I was able to create *Fox Kiss*, which was the crowning achievement of the encounter. All told I spent several hours watching the foxes, and despite my preparations, was once again shivering and as cold as I had ever been. Still, what felt like hypothermia was a small inconvenience for the results.

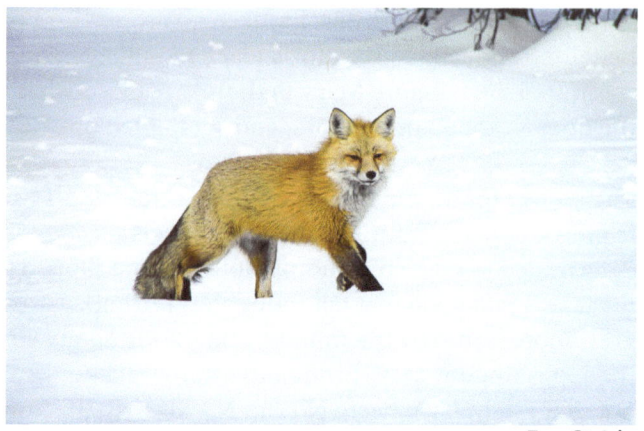

Fox Stride

I had been chatting about my favorite places but digressed. Let's finish Grand Teton National Park with another of my favorite locations, Oxbow Bend, which is about as simple to reach as possible. All you need to do is pull into the parking lot from the paved road, and you've arrived. The only difficulty is dodging the tour buses. If you are unlucky, two or three full buses will stop and disgorge their passengers. One moment you are standing alone and enjoying the tranquility, and the next, you are in the middle of a large crowd of people, most of whom are chattering loudly and trying to get a selfie. Some people even try to take the selfie in front of the main feature, but it's interesting how many don't. Trying to create a photograph amid the pandemonium is pointless, so the best thing to do is guard your equipment and wait. The buses don't give their passengers long to enjoy the view, and after a few minutes, everyone dutifully troops back onto their designated coach and peace descends again.

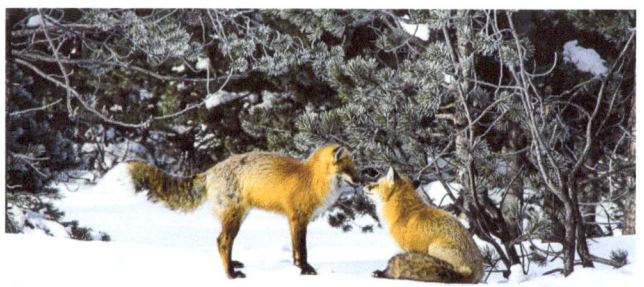

Fox Kiss

It might not seem like it, but I don't mind the buses. Everyone should see our national parks, and buses are an excellent way to visit and have a quick introduction to each park. Yes, they hold many people, and yes, all those people end up crowding around you. For those on the tour bus, though, it's a good experience, and the tours bring the parks to everyone. I adapt and stay out of the way, which is harder than staying out of the way of bears and bison.

One crisp fall morning I was loitering at Oxbow Bend, hoping for something magical. The clouds were low and thick most of the morning, obscuring my view of Mount Moran, the predominant mountain towering over the Snake River. Now and then I caught a glimpse of the peak, but nothing I could turn into a reasonable photograph. The fall colors were bright, and I hoped against hope that the scene would work out. I needed a scrap of sunlight, a clear view of the

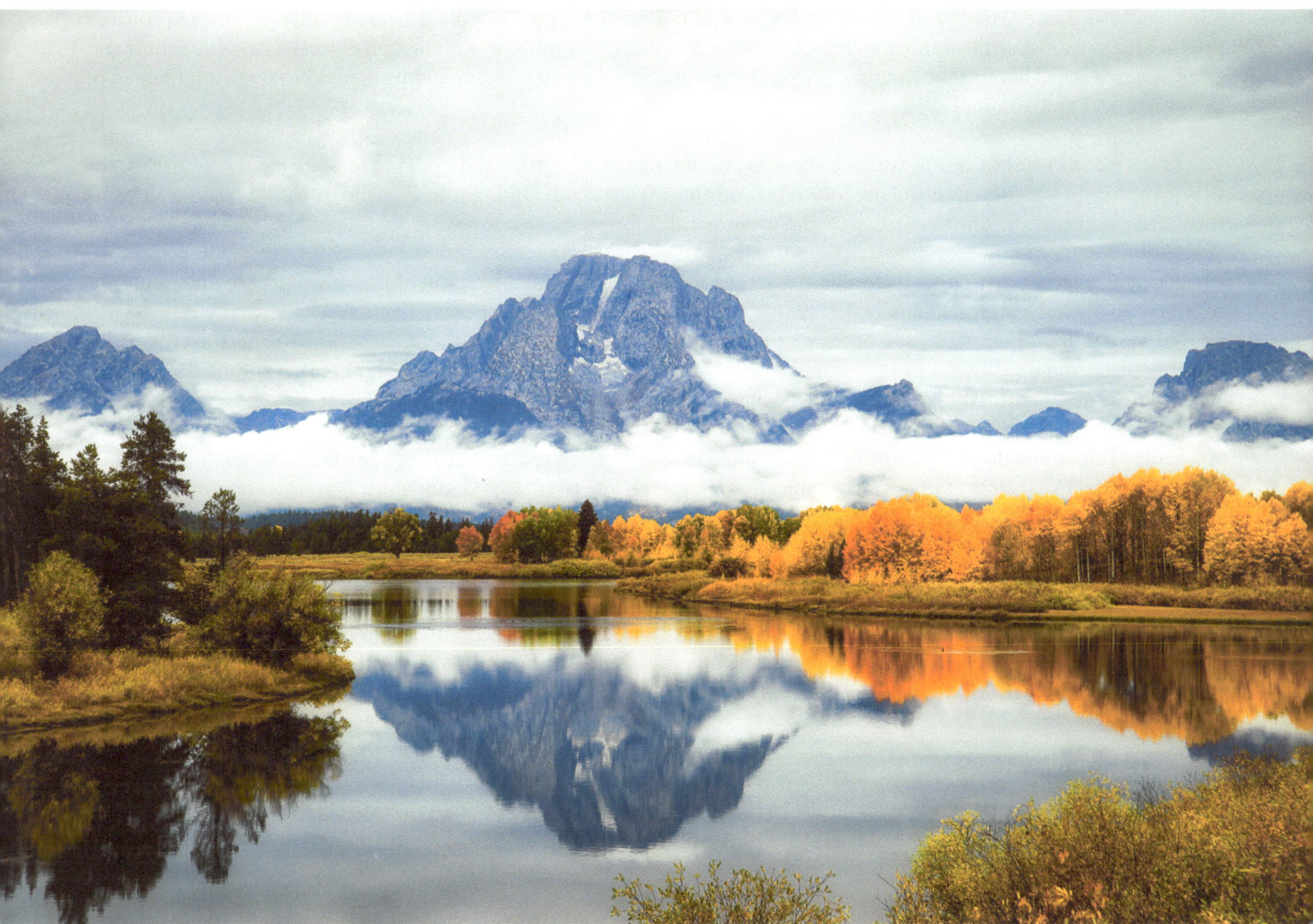

Oxbow Fall

mountain, no wind to stir the waters, and no tour buses. Although a lot to ask for, I was stubborn and willing to wait. The morning wore on and the clouds shifted but never entirely lifted. For one brief moment, though, all the conditions I desired came together. The light wind dropped to nothing and the waters of the Snake River turned to glass, creating a clear reflection. The sun broke free behind me, lighting the scene ahead of me. The clouds revealed the top of the mountain for a moment. And the parking lot was virtually empty, letting me move around the area to find the perfect composition. *Oxbow Fall* is the result of that moment.

Shortly after I made *Oxbow Fall*, I heard the squeal of brakes as tour buses pulled in. More than a hundred tourists flooded the area just as the wind reengaged. The clouds rose higher, once again completely obscuring the mountain, and the sun ducked behind the clouds. I kept smiling while I packed up my gear and headed off into what remained of the morning. I had accomplished my goal.

Not every place I want to photograph is as easy as pulling into a parking lot and dodging tourists. Some require extensive planning and preparation and are located far off the nearest road. Hiking into the wilderness is always an adventure, and it was time for me to journey to and explore The Subway.

I had long wanted to visit The Subway and Archangel Falls in Zion National Park. Unfortunately people need a permit to hike into those locations, and permits are not easy to come by. Getting a permit that lined up with my travel plans proved harder than it should have been, so I miraculously obtained a permit and then worked the travel logistics around the permit date. In the end the arrangement worked out fine. I should have thought of that solution in the first place, but sometimes the simple answers elude me.

Archangel Falls aren't the largest around, and by some measures, the site doesn't even count as a waterfall. It's more of a gentle cascade. Regardless of the exact classification, water flowing over the red sandstone is an inspirational sight and one I had wanted to witness for the longest time.

Many iconic photographs from our national parks are taken in readily accessible locations. For example, I made *Oxbow Fall* a short distance from a parking lot off a paved road. Accessibility does not take away from the difficulty of making a magnificent photograph, however. To make one, you still need the right conditions to line up, including the most critical factor: the weather, which is seldom predictable. Archangel Falls and the Subway, conversely, are more challenging to photograph, and you can't just drive right up to them. Far from it.

Once you have a coveted permit, you're on your own to get there and back in a single day. That task sounded simple enough; it's an eight-mile round-trip hike, which I can easily accomplish in a day. The "easy" part stopped there. I knew that a small trail led to the Left Fork of North Creek, after which no official, or any, trail existed. I would have to find my way by following, or wading in, the waterway. On top of that, the beginning had an ultra-steep descent, which meant a nearly unsurmountable ascent at the end. The hike was going to be challenging.

I arrived at the departure point before dawn. I wanted an early start to have as much time possible at the falls and The Subway. I had plenty of water and snacks, so I was good to go. I loaded my camera gear, which was heavy enough to start with and would feel like it doubled or tripled in weight by the time I walked back. I double-checked all my preparations, and I jauntily set off down the wisp of a trail.

Finding my way to the first significant part of the adventure, the initial descent, was straightforward. Many people before me went that way. The footing was easy, the slope gentle, and it was a pleasant pre-dawn walk in the wilderness that I thoroughly enjoyed. Before long I made it to the initial descent, a series of sharp and short switchbacks down a four-hundred-foot slope. The steep slope had little in the way of footholds, and while not sheer, it felt like it. The descent was a slippery scramble, the rocks were loose, and it was a challenge to make it down safely. Once at the bottom, I carefully recorded my GPS location. That spot, the only way up the slope for miles in either direction, was utterly unremarkable, and I couldn't find any indicators at all. You would think that all the people passing through there would have left a trail or something to mark the way out, but such was not the case. The pathway going up blended right in, and unless you knew where it was by your GPS, or were lucky enough to see a small sign that was supposedly there, you could easily miss it on your way back. I never did find the alleged exit sign.

Once at the bottom, I took a good look around, got my bearings, and headed up the river. You would think there would be a trail there, but there wasn't. There was no formal route whatsoever, but I didn't need one. All I needed to do was head upstream until I reached the falls. How a hiker accomplishes this task is entirely up to the hiker. You can try walking in the creek, which I did at times. You can try walking beside it, which I did as often as I could, but every few feet, I reached a barrier of some sort. A deep pool might block the way. Boulders forced me to climb them. Branches and bramble prevented me from proceeding easily. A large downed tree forced me to choose a different path. More ways than I ever would have imagined impeded my progress. When I encountered an obstacle, I had to decide how to tackle it; over it, around it, under it, or through it, whichever I thought was best. I did a lot of backtracking.

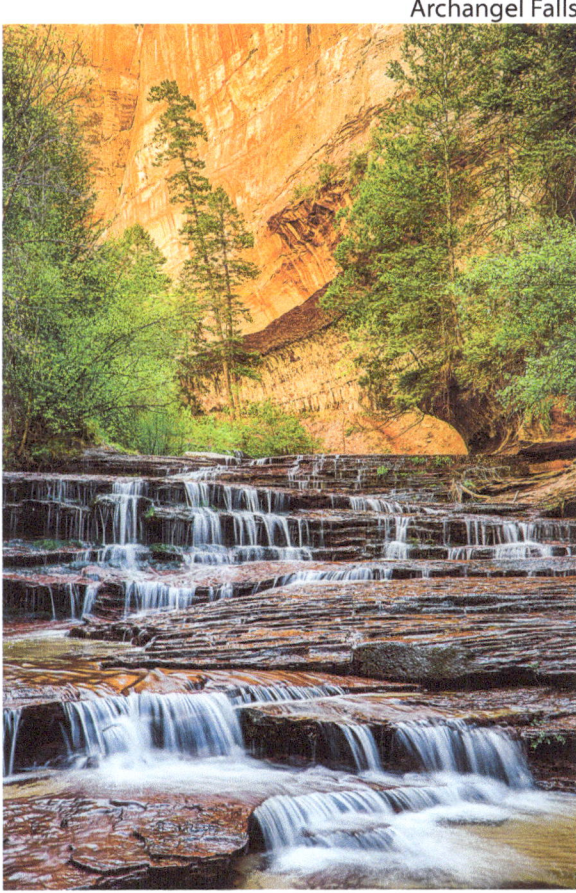

Archangel Falls

Because there wasn't a marked trail, I was left on my own to figure out each hindrance, which formed a serious challenge. Every barrier represented time, and time gradually grew against me. I scrambled, hopped, crawled, waded, and pushed my way through the obstacles, expending energy on each one. I did not realize how exhausting it would be and how many problems I would encounter. I lost track of how many times I had to backtrack down the creek because I ran into something I could not get through. Sometimes I had to retreat quite a way. One time I had to backtrack a quarter mile, which cost me dearly in time. To make it more interesting, I went in April. Typically April is a pleasant time of the year and ideal, but the river water was piercingly cold because of the melting snowpack, so being in it more than a few moments made me shiver and fear hypothermia. I had prepared for the hike, but I wasn't truly ready for it.

Every once in a while I was able to traverse a section easily. I relished every one and made up time when I could. I mostly counted my blessings and wondered what was up ahead that was going to slow me down next.

After two or three weeks—no, months, nay, years—heading upstream, I finally reached my first goal: Archangel Falls. What a sight it was! The river spread out, and water flowed across the wide sandstone steps. Sunlight bounced off the far canyon wall, reflecting bright and brilliant orange. The reflected light also gave the trees an ethereal backlight. The entire scene captivated me, and I took off my pack to explore and enjoy the area. The Subway was only a half mile ahead, which helped relax me and let me take my time.

I lingered quite a while, taking all the beauty in and letting myself experience that small wonder deep in the wilderness of Zion National Park. I had more to see, though, so I pushed onward. I saw no possibility of going around the cascades, so I headed right up the middle. Doing so bothered me, for it seemed disrespectful and even sacrilegious. I tried to stay to the edges as best I could, but I still didn't feel right. I kept looking around, half expecting a ranger to appear out of nowhere, telling me to get out of the river. None did, and I continued my solo adventure upriver.

The last half mile was a treat and far more relaxed than the first three and a half. I made excellent time to The Subway, my final destination. I needed to find a way to traverse one final slope. The walls closed in around the watercourse, so I had to go up the watery incline. Unfortunately moss and slime made the slope slippery, and I had no handholds or irregularities to use. I had no choice but to try my best to scramble up. My heavy pack made it quite the challenge, and it took me several tries, but at last I made it.

Over countless centuries the river has diligently carved its way through the rock, almost forming a tunnel. The opening at the top is only a couple feet wide and far less, in some places. The gently curved walls complete the illusion of a subway, and I almost anticipated a subway train to come barreling by at any moment. Like the cascades, I needed to walk in the water, and doing so felt odd once again.

Subway Pools

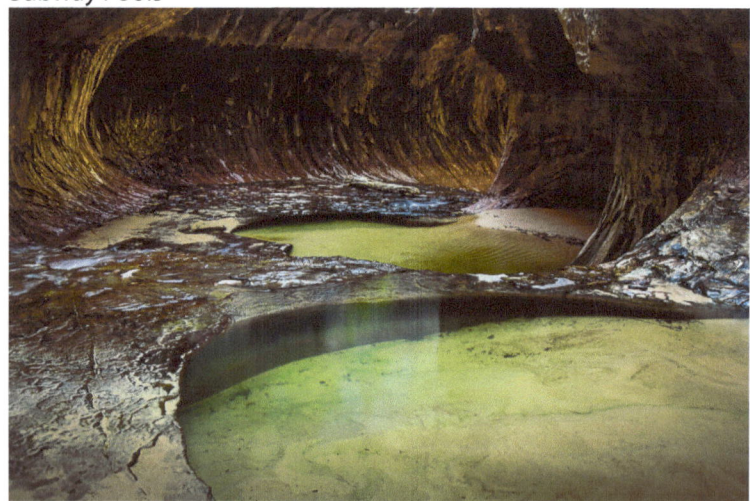

The pools constitute another striking feature. A couple of them are quite deep, and the water reflects an otherworldly green. The pools seem to glow in the dim light, as if I had stepped onto a different planet. As with the cascades, I took my time and enjoyed the area and its photographic opportunities.

These photographs are precious to me because of the effort required to create them. It's a shame we can't drive to a nearby parking lot, hop out, scamper down a flight of stairs, and enjoy The Subway. Because we can't, however, these photographs are special.

There is another way to reach The Subway from farther upstream. It's called the "top-down route" and requires canyoneering skills, which I don't possess.

Canyoneering involves a combination of hiking, rappelling, sliding, and more and must be done in a harness and with ropes. Perhaps one day I'll be able to make that trek, and I look forward to it. Instead I turned around and headed out the way I came.

Going back was slightly more manageable. For openers I headed downstream and slightly downhill. I remembered many of the barriers and how to circumvent them. I made decent time, although I was tired by the time my GPS told me I was at the exit point. I looked around, and for the life of me I couldn't see the path up and out. I pushed through some low bushes, and there it was. Whew!

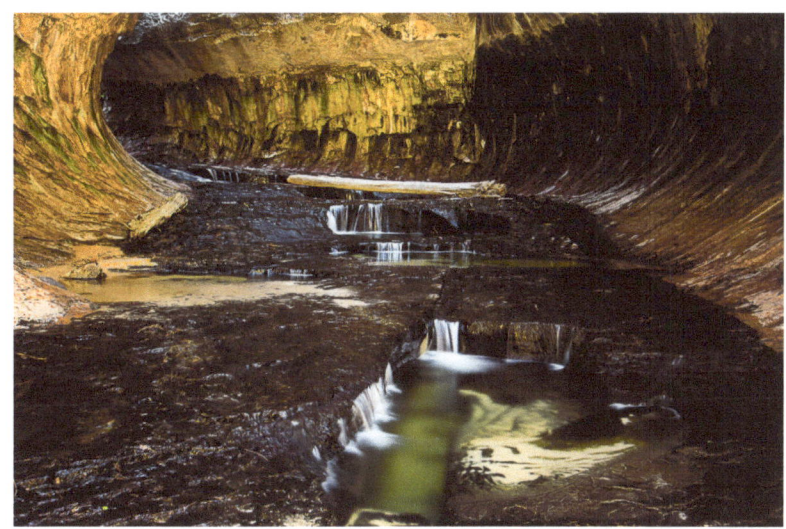
Subway Falls

Next came the hardest part of all, yet there was nothing for it but to do it. The prior steep descent became a four-hundred-foot grueling and torturous climb. I crawled up that slope with the last of my strength and willpower. The difficulty going down paled in comparison to the climb out. I measured my progress in precious inches, provided I didn't backslide. I stopped at every turn and rested, panting, trying to catch my breath and hoping for more strength. My breath came back. The strength did not. I reached out, grabbed dirt, or if I was lucky, a small rock, and pulled myself forward. One more foot up. One less foot to go. Several times I backslid a couple of feet and had to start again.

Eventually, after an eternity, I reached the top and found the path from that morning. I somehow found the energy to stand and move a few feet up toward the parking area. Foot by foot, again, I measured my progress, although even on the easy path, I frequently had to stop and rest. I'll never forget how happy I was when I was close enough to unlock the 4x4. The sound of the door locks opening was the most joyous one in the entire world. I stumbled forward, opened the door, and hung on it, happy to have something hold me up. Wheezing, panting, and wondering how much I overdid it and what those consequences might be, I performed the Herculean feat of changing out of my hiking boots and into my tennis shoes. I sat in the driver's seat and resisted the temptation to sleep or pass out. I started the car and headed out.

Remember earlier when I mentioned I would make my schedule fit this excursion? I didn't point out that I was due back in Albuquerque the next morning. I was on the wrong side of the park, so all I had to do was drive through the entire park, which contains 231 square miles, and then drive more than five hundred miles home. Hoo boy! I didn't count on the hike being quite so hard on me, that's for sure.

I did make it back, safe and sound, and I did meet my commitments, but I wished I didn't have to. I do what I need to, though, and I keep moving, ever onward, to new adventures.

Coastal Oregon

Oregon is a photographer's paradise and offers opportunities throughout the state. The whispering waves of its coastlines and the guiding lights of its lighthouses call to me. Towering sea stacks, daring fishing vessels, and gray, foggy mornings are just some of the tales waiting to be shared.

Heading off into a new adventure is always an exhilarating feeling. The thought of what lies ahead is exciting to contemplate, and the promise of a thrilling new story is enticing. Some expeditions are low-key and qualify as a journey more than anything else. Such has been my explorations of the Oregon coast. The quiet scenes reflect beauty and power, majesty and grace. Time spent observing and composing is of the essence, and patiently waiting until it all comes together is the key to photographic success.

The sweeping Oregon coastline is more than 350 miles of rugged peaks, tranquil harbors, and soaring vistas. It is hard to pinpoint any one place or view as my favorite, although I go back to certain spots time and again. For example, I adore the town of Bandon and make a point to stop there as often as possible. Impressive sea stacks, which are enormous rocks, stand alone in the water and make excellent photographs. I can, and have, watched them for days on end. I know it sounds like I expect the rocks to pick up and move suddenly, but I am observing the tides, the changing light and sky, and the moving clouds. A pretty scene quickly becomes dramatic, and sometimes a once-in-a-life time opportunity fades into a fantastic memory.

As in the case everywhere, if you don't like the weather, wait five minutes, and it will change. This axiom is as true on the coastline as anywhere else. Perhaps unlike other places, though, this area of the country is known for its rainy days. Unlike in the Southwest where thunderstorms quickly come and go, the rain here can settle in for quite some time.

On one of my first trips to the coast, I drove through a small town, a typical, everyday town. I saw a group of children playing in a park, kicking a soccer ball around, and chasing each other. Their squeals of delight echoing across the grass were music to my ears. I saw a couple of dads standing and chatting with each other. Other people with not a care in the world walked along the sidewalk with groceries. A few older children were riding bikes. The sense of community was unmistakably strong, much like being inside a Norman Rockwell painting. Oh, did I mention it was steadily raining?

In that town the rain meant nothing, and residents went about their day as if it were sunny. I thought about that experience, and from that point on adopted the same stance. Rain would mean nothing to me while I photographed, and I would pay it no attention. Another similar experience further reinforced the point. I was photographing in Silver Falls State Park on a different rainy day, a weekday, and I had the park virtually to myself, an unexpected treat. I took my time photographing various waterfalls when I heard a commotion in the distance. It sounded like large trucks driving in. I heard the dull roar of engines and the high-pitched squeals of brakes. Ominously I heard the unsettling sound of many doors opening. A few minutes later a few thousand school children tumbled and rumbled down the trails at full tilt. That day, of all days, was field-trip day, which was probably why the park had been empty. Anyone from that area would have known about that day and avoided it. By now you've guessed that it was pouring rain, a fact that did not seem to register on the kids or teachers. They all acted as if it was a perfectly sunny day, and they enjoyed their field trip with abandon. Was there really a thousand children? Probably not, but it certainly seemed that way. The experience helped me understand that being in the rain is not a big concern, and it's amazing what children can teach us.

Oregon has a tremendous amount to offer a photographer, and it is hard to know where to begin. I'll start in one of my favorite places: Bandon and its sea stacks.

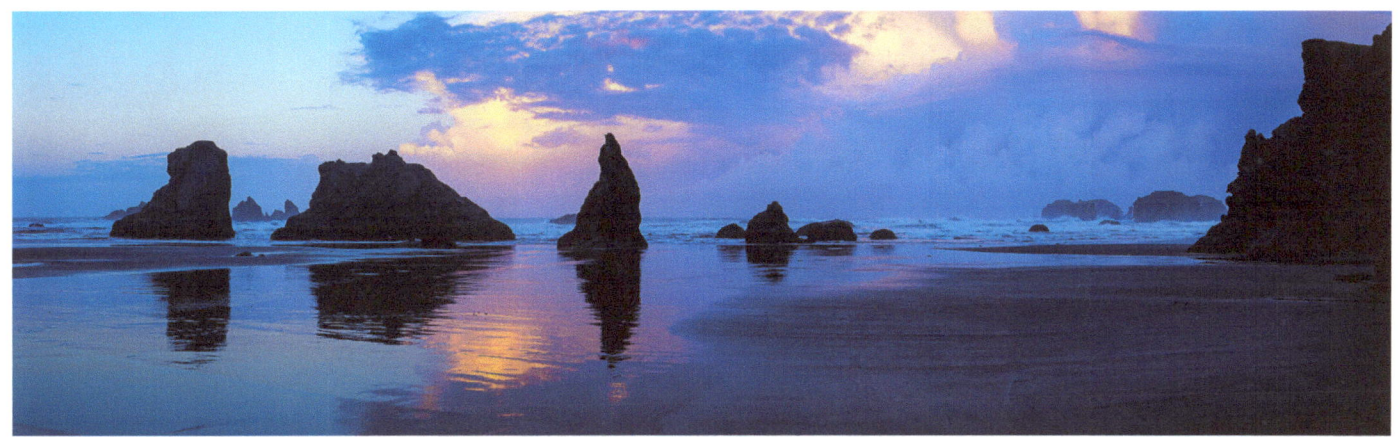

Bandon's Introspection

These large standing rocks conveniently reside on the beaches of Bandon and are beautiful themselves. Some sea stacks sit in the tidal zone, surrounded and then abandoned by the tides, while others are farther out, forever hugged by the ocean. To top it off they are surrounded by tall bluffs, which gives me endless opportunities. I can photograph them from up high as well as from the beach. Both dawn and dusk work equally well, and if the day is overcast or cloudy, sometimes the middle of the day works out too. I can spend, and have spent day after day sitting and watching those rocks.

One of my favorite hotels is in Bandon. It isn't a four-star hotel by any means, nor are its rooms large or luxurious, but it has charm. More importantly, the rooms overlook the wide sandy beach and the sea stacks. I readily hear the ocean call; the constant droning of the waves comforts me through the night. I make it a point to stay at that hotel whenever I can and make sure I leave plenty of room in my schedule to stay as long as possible.

Silhouetted Stacks

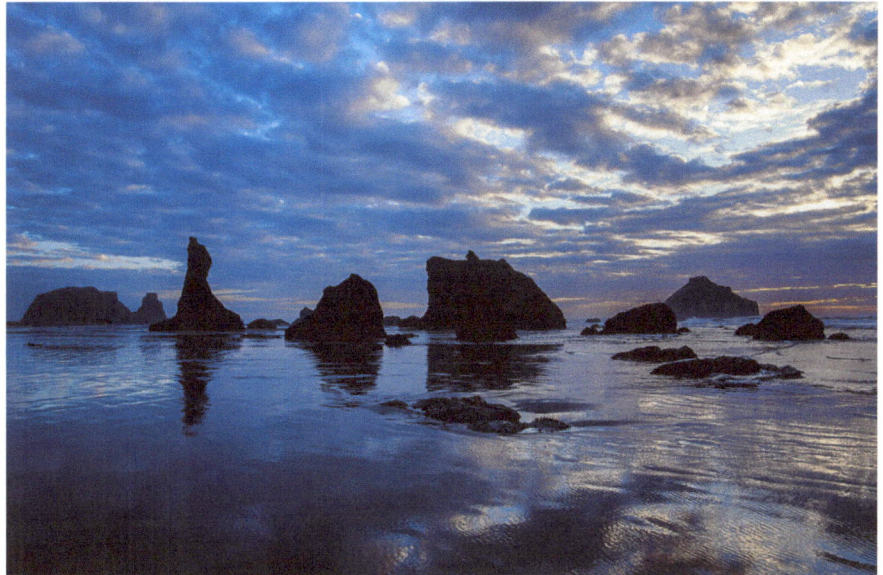

The sea stacks have a personality all their own, which changes from day to day. Every time I visit them, they present a different mood, and pulling myself away isn't easy. Although I know these rocks well, I am never quite sure how they will look on any given day, and finding the answer is always a delight. The result can look more like a painting than a photograph.

The beaches of Bandon are my favorite ones of the entire Oregon coast, but sea stacks are not the only thing to find along the coast. Oregon has eleven lighthouses, some of which beg to be photographed.

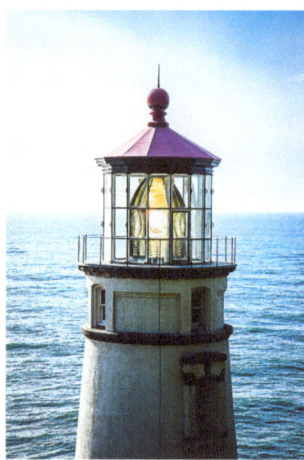
Heceta's Light

Lighthouses are critical to the marine traffic that passes by them, both today and yesterday. Each light has a unique flashing pattern that identifies it. Mariners observing it can tell exactly where they are. Strategically placed lighthouses beside treacherous areas also offer warnings. Even though some of the towers aren't overly tall, their ideal positioning allows their lights to pierce the darkness far out to sea.

The importance of the light stations, especially the early ones, cannot be overemphasized. Back in the late 1800s, well before today's GPS systems, those lights were the only reliable way for a seafarer to know a boat's position, especially in bad weather. Seeing the light orientated sea captains, keeping them on course and away from the hazardous shoreline.

Keeping the light going was no easy task, either. The lightkeeper and his family had to live at the station. Lightkeepers were responsible for maintaining and repairing the light and keeping it lit and operating. The lightkeeper had to carry weighty cans of oil up to the top of the tower, often up a narrow, steep, and winding staircase. I've been up some of those stairs, and they are no fun to ascend with a camera. I can't imagine what it must have been like to carry heavy oil cans up them. Some of the lighthouses are tall, with many narrow stairs, making the task even more challenging and demanding.

Although the life of lightkeepers was lonely, the lightkeepers took their jobs seriously. They understood how important they were to the ships sailing by, and although it might have been enjoyable to see the tall masts pass by, the keepers were happy that the masts didn't crash on shore. Lightkeepers kept detailed records and logs. Today we can look at those journals and maybe even read a few entries, but the time and care it took to create them was extensive.

When I visited those light stations, I thought at length about the lightkeepers and their challenging chores, and it influenced my photography. Each light, and thus each family, lived far away from the community, assuming there was a nearby community in the first place. By definition the existence was a lonely one, or at least isolated. The work was demanding and not something the keepers could skip for a day or two if they didn't feel well. The safety of ships was literally in their hands, and the price they paid for not keeping the light operating was high. I admire all the people who lived and worked in lighthouses. We hear tales about brave captains who piloted their boats through dangerous adventures, yet we don't hear about the lightkeepers who kept those captains and their boats safe. The early days of the lighthouses are the ones that interest me the most, so I attempt to frame them showing their power over the ocean, yet also emphasize their isolation.

Eventually electricity came to the stations, making life substantially easier for lightkeepers. Later still technology advanced to the point that the stations were automated, changing the nature of them forever. Although at the end of an era, many stations still operate today, and some are open to the public, keeping their spirits alive and well. Given the romance and stories behind lighthouses, I suspect the lighted monuments to another era will persevere a long time. I am drawn to them and make sure to visit as many as I can when I am on the coast.

Some lighthouses are even more picturesque than others, and Cape Blanco is near the top of that list. Sitting atop a small grassy knoll, the white building and tower replete with the red roof and red cupola make a postcard-perfect scene. When I was growing up, this lighthouse is the one I imagined whenever I thought about lighthouses. That day in real life, I had the privilege of photographing an icon from my childhood, and I was as thrilled to photograph it as I was to see a postcard of it so many years earlier.

The tower stands only fifty-nine feet high, which doesn't seem all that high, but it is one of the highest of the Oregon coast stations. It is built on a cliff, as many are, so its light is visible miles out at sea. Best of all, it is still active.

Interestingly, though, this particular photograph drove me a little bit crazy. Approaching the lighthouse, I could see how iconic it looked and was already creating the perfect image in my mind. I had an ideal setting, a beautiful day, and excellent conditions. All I had to do was step back, position the lighthouse against the vast ocean, and make the photograph. What could go wrong? I found the best angle, walked down the slight hill so I could fit the light station in the frame, and, hey! Wait a moment. The knoll, the one I walked down, blocked my view of the ocean. What a problem! Never mind. I moved a little to the left. The hill, unfortunately, sloped down on all sides, so the left side had the same problem. It was an impressive view of the station,

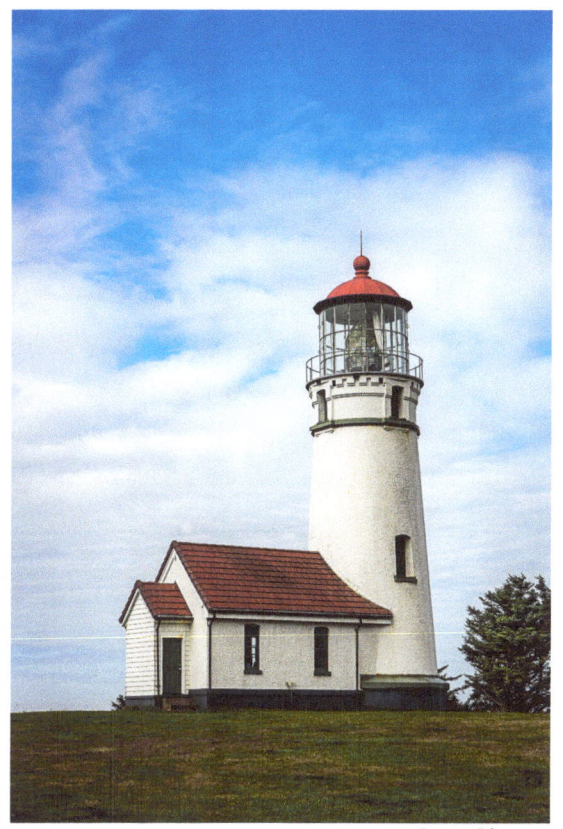
Cape Blanco

but I couldn't see the ocean. Luckily for me all I had to do was move to the right, at the base of the hill, and that would be that. Except it wasn't. It dawned on me that making that photograph was far more challenging than I anticipated.

In the end I could either view the ocean or I could put the lighthouse in the frame, but I had to choose between the two. Flying a drone, a solution to the entire affair, was not allowed, so it was not an option. Thanks to that beautiful, grassy hill, I could not position the ocean behind the lighthouse, so I had to settle for the available view, which I still adore. Until I pointed it out, maybe you didn't realize the ocean wasn't there.

There is, however, another solution to ensuring you see the ocean behind a lighthouse. Go to a different one! Let's visit Heceta Head Lighthouse, which is also stunning.

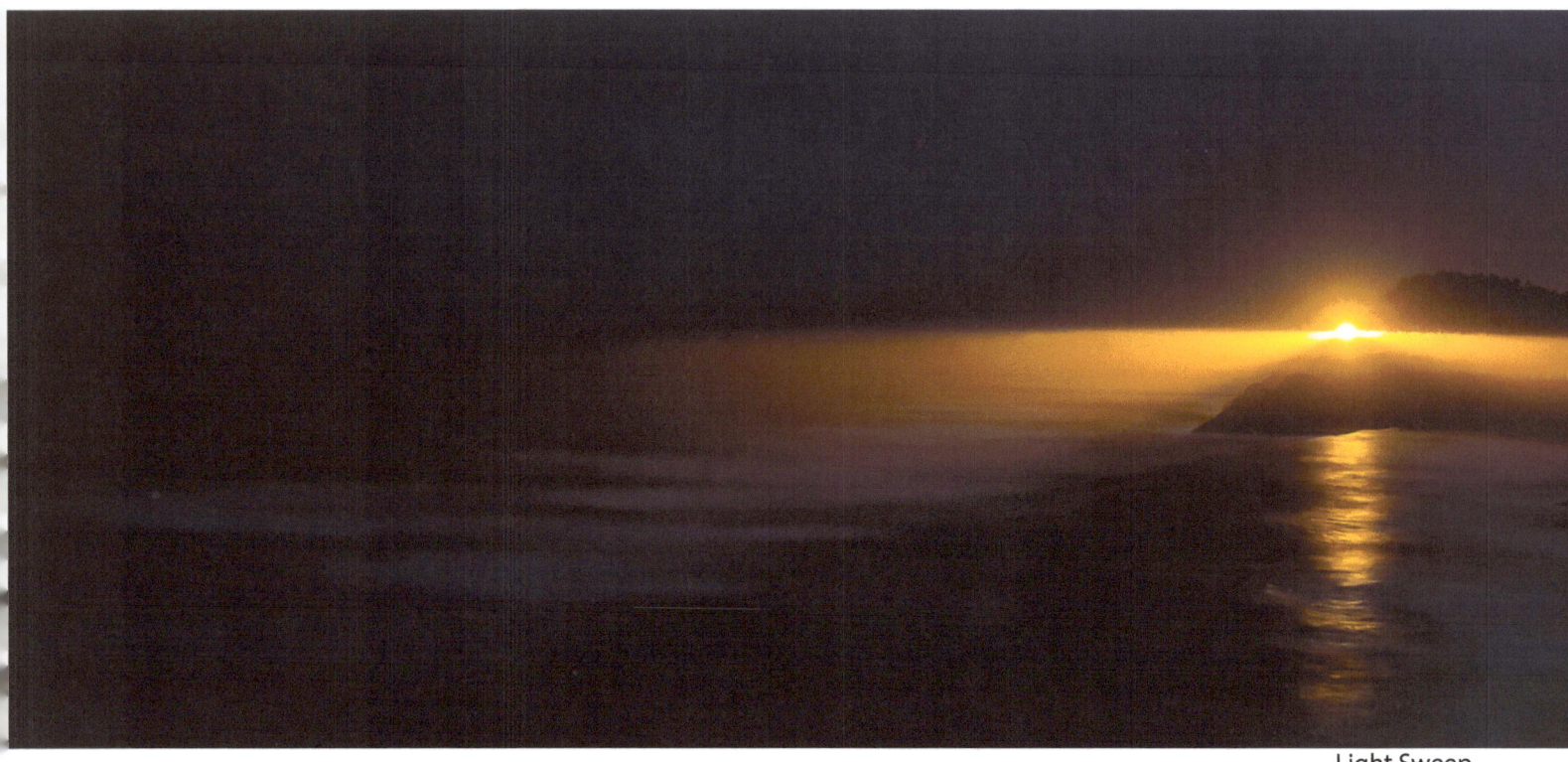

Light Sweep

The night is pitch black, and thanks to the clouds, even the stars are asleep. As for the moon, it's nowhere to be found, leaving us bobbing alone on the inky black sea. Off in the far distance we faintly hear the waves break against the shoreline, but we can't be sure how far away it is. Although we think we know where we are, there is no guarantee of accuracy. We sail on, with everyone awake keeping a sharp eye out, lest we are closer to the rocks than we think. We continue creeping forward and hoping we are safely on course.

There it is! Cutting through the blackness, a tiny dot of light winks at us and then blinks out of existence. We hold our breath until we see it again and then measure the seconds. We count "One, two, three," up to ten, until the light appears again. The pattern repeats. We know for certainty we are at Heceta Head, and our course is true. We keep an even sharper eye out for the rocks we know are near us, and we confidently make our way past the light and up the coast. We spare a glance back to wave goodbye to the now-distant light, already beckoning to the next travelers and safely guiding them on their way.

Even though I imagined that story when I made *Light Sweep*, it was predawn, and the darkness felt absolute for nine out of every ten seconds. The sweep of the light lit the sea up ever-so-briefly, and it was easy to imagine what it must have been like in the late 1800s. Piloting around the light stations must have been scary yet comforting at the same time.

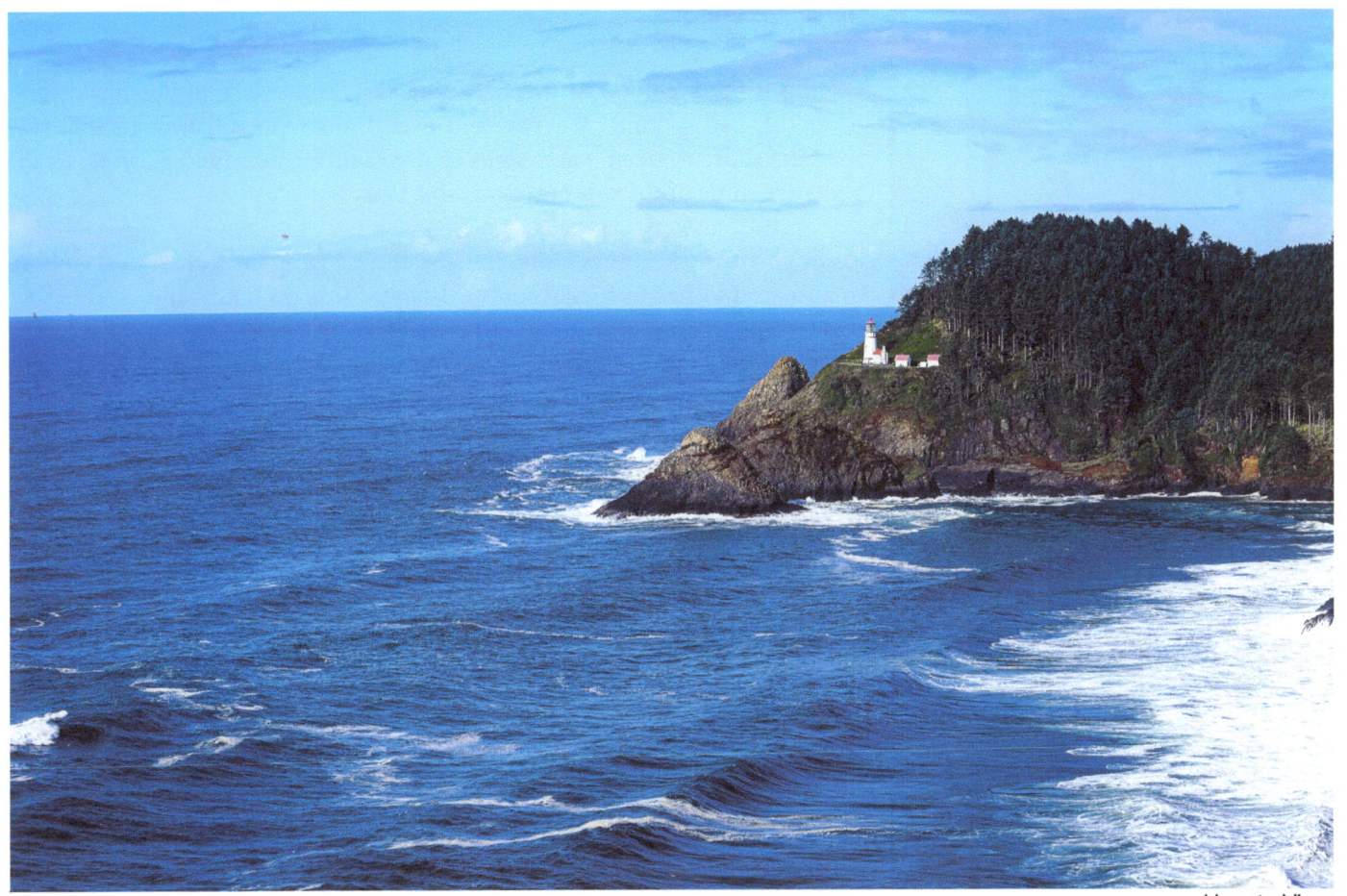
Heceta View

Heceta Head is impressive in the daylight. Its fifty-two-foot tower seems small when set against the broader backdrop, but its light is powerful and effective. It's easy to see why Heceta Head is a popular photo spot, and like Cape Blanco, it appears on countless postcards and calendars. Still, that fact doesn't lessen its appeal to me.

Heceta B&B

If you ever want to experience what it is like to run a lighthouse, or at least sleep near one, the old lightkeeper's residence has been converted into a bed and breakfast by the U.S. Forest Service. The Forest Service doesn't offer many accommodations, and certainly not bed and breakfasts, making this one unique. The fully restored residence is far from civilization and a short walk from the light station. It creates the opportunity to go back in time and experience life from the perspective of the lightkeeper.

We're going to leave the light stations behind, though, and explore another essential and eminently photogenic aspect of the coast: harbors and fishing.

Crabbing (Teal)

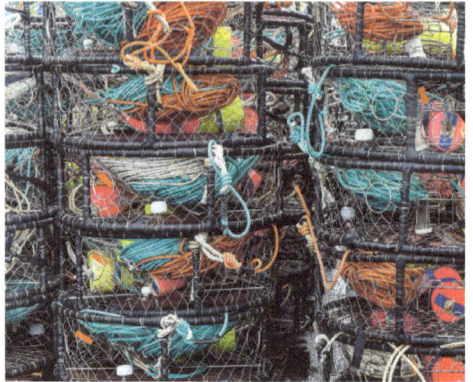

Fishing is the lifeblood of the Oregon Coast, and every harbor has fishing boats that call it home. You can find everything from small boats that stay near the shore to deep-water ships that go out for extended periods. Crabs boats are some of the most recognizable vessels.

Throughout my journeys along the coastline, I've spent a great deal of time in and around harbors. Although I usually focus on landscapes and nature photographs, something about boats and fishing vessels, in particular, grabs my attention. I don't know why, exactly, that ships have this hold over me, but I adore the ocean. Even so, I don't care to be at sea, not in the least, as we'll see in Alaskan Frontier. Being on dry land suits me fine, but every harbor compels me to check it out.

From Astoria in the north to Winchester Bay in the south and all the harbors in between, I find something beautiful to photograph. Sometimes I find a treat, such as this vignette from Newport Harbor showing the F/V *Winona J*, the red boat, which a season of the TV show *Deadliest Catch* featured. I'll admit it is a thrill to find a vessel I've watched on TV. The letters F/V mean fishing vessel. Such abbreviations help identify ships throughout the world.

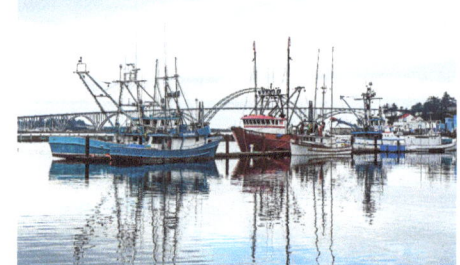

Newport Harbor

Is it that dangerous to be out on these boats? It most certainly is. Often television hypes up the drama or edits the programs in a way that distorts reality, especially on reality TV shows. Producers need good ratings, and what better way to get them than creating drama and tension? *Deadliest Catch,* however, accurately portrays the dangers of fishing. Crossing the bar is one of the journey's riskiest parts, both coming and going.

The bar is where a river meets the ocean, and each harbor has one. The confluence of tides, waves, winds, and the river current combine in one place, creating a problematic portion of water to cross. On windy or stormy days, crossing the bar can be challenging and treacherous, even for larger vessels. Boats can and do founder on the bar, and the results can be catastrophic. The memorials at the harbors are a silent testament to how dangerous the bars are. Luckily, despite gloomy skies, *Noah's Ark* smoothly crossed the bar and headed out on her voyage. I waved to her and watched her disappear into the distance on her way to the fishing grounds.

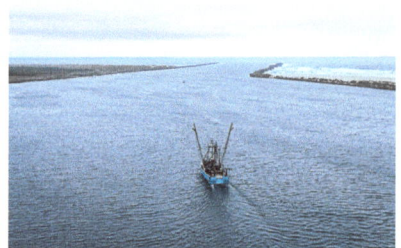

Noah's Ark

Once you are inside the bar, though, everything changes, and in an odd coincidence, the bar contributes to harbors being calm and tranquil.

One morning I was at Salmon Harbor, which is just outside of Winchester Bay. The morning fog was so dense that I had to drive slowly so I could find my way, and even walking was more challenging than you might imagine. Walking around the docks was a surreal experience, since it seemed to be just a dock that stretched into infinity and me. I could hear the sounds of boats readied for sailing, but couldn't see anything. I continued to wander the docks, though, soaking up the experience.

As the morning wore on, the fog began to lift. It wasn't as if a puff of wind came by and blew it out, but it dissolved so slowly it escaped notice. Bit by bit I was able to see farther down the dock and a nearby boat and then another and another. Before I realized it, I could see all the ships in the harbor, which allowed me to make *Salmon Harbor*. I adore the vibe of this photograph; it feels gritty to me, yet it has majesty as well. When looking at it today, I can still hear the morning sounds as the fishermen prepared their boats for their journey.

A few hours later, the fog was gone and so were most of the boats; it was a completely different feeling, and I am glad I made the photograph when I did. It represents how magnificent a still harbor can be on a chilly, foggy morning. It depicts the entirety of the Oregon Coast in my opinion: moody, powerful, compelling, and misty.

After being in the rain so much, I decided I needed to up my game and commit to photographing in it, specifically storms. Maybe even violent storms. Let's explore that, shall we?

Salmon Harbor

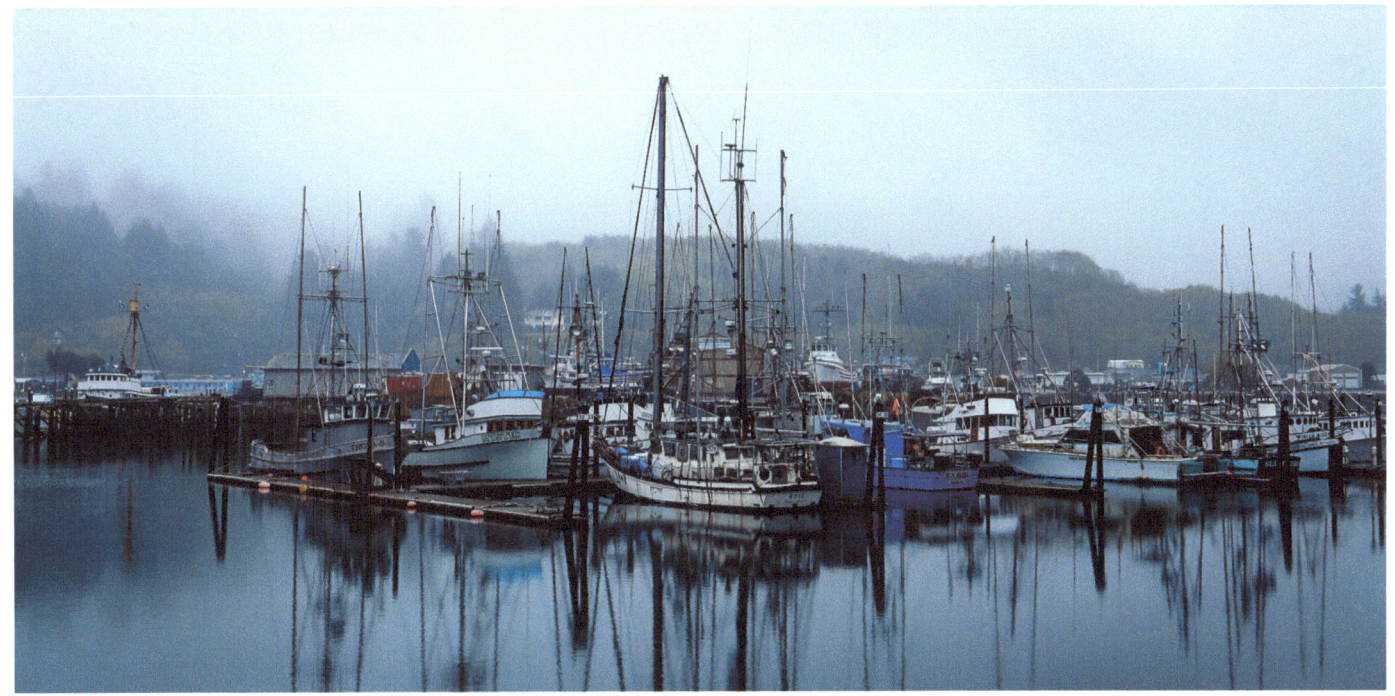

Stormy Weather

"Rain, rain go away" is not a phrase I ever use, for rain means clouds and stormy weather. As we shall see, there is a difference between a rainy day and a storm, and that difference makes dramatic and compelling photographs. It also means the possibility of electrifying encounters.

Each of us has objectives and goals we hope to accomplish. Some of these goals are mundane, such as purchasing milk at the grocery store today. Some of our goals are extraordinary, like photographing a tornado today. My refrigerator had plenty of milk, which left me only the tornado option. The question became this: how can I pull it off while still being safe?

The idea of photographing a tornado was not a new one for me. I had wanted to photograph a twister for a long time. Every spring I told myself, "This is the year" with the firmest of all convictions. Every fall I said to myself, "Next year is it" with equally firm intentions. The seasons and years slid by at an alarming pace without my having created a tornado photograph. The biggest dilemma I faced was, "How do I do it, exactly?" This question, above all others, vexed me, and I pondered it frequently.

I knew I could watch the weather, wait for a stormy day, and head to wherever other storm chasers seemed to be going. On the surface it was a grand idea and completely foolproof. The reality turned out to be quite different, though. A lot, and I mean a staggering number of people are storm chasers. A select few know the exact conditions they are looking for, and they have a good idea of where and when to be in the correct location. They have years of experience to help them make sound decisions. The vast majority of less-disciplined storm chasers end up with variable results. Many amateur storm chasers believe they can predict where a tornado will break out. My comment is not derogatory. I've met many of those people. They have confidence in their abilities and sometimes have results to back up their assertions. Most amateur storm chasers have a decent to firm grasp of the weather fundamentals necessary to predict a windstorm, but they don't have the experience or fully understand the nuances to fine-tune the possible touchdown spot and stay as safe as possible. It's not easy to correctly position yourself beside a moving, unpredictable storm.

Social media plays into storm chasing as well, in a couple ways. Immediately before and during an event, people chasing the storm take to social media, letting others know where they are going. Others see these postings and head in the same direction, often creating crowds at a storm that may end in a tornado, but commonly it does not.

At the day's end we see only the best of the best photographs. They are the photographs everyone talks about, the ones that make the evening news or high-profile websites. It then appears to a casual observer that it's easy to photograph a tornado. The reality is quite different. Of all the photographs made across all the storms in all the states, only a couple are worthy. They are the ones showcased on TV and the Internet. Therein lies the rub. I am a single individual and must pick a single storm in a single location. I don't get to pick and choose after the fact. I need to make my decision well before the event happens. And I have to keep myself safe. I can't trust the crowds of people heading to a storm to be right, and even if they are, they might lead to the wrong side of the storm, and then safety becomes an issue.

I wasn't idle all those years before I headed out. I knew in my heart I needed help to achieve my goal, which meant working with professional storm chasers instead of trying a do-it-yourself approach. I researched, talked with people, and put together a solid plan. I became friends with a top-notch team of storm chasers who let me ride with them. More accurately, I hopped into their vehicle when they weren't looking, and by the time they noticed me, it was too late. Or something like that. In any event, I had a seat with a bona fide storm-chasing team. This year was going to be the year, and it sure beat a trip to the grocery store. The milk could wait.

Storm chasing is an odd business. Long periods of boredom are followed by, if you are lucky, a few moments of pure exhilaration. Or terror, depending on what side of the storm you are on. Talk about feast or famine! That arrangement was right up my alley, and I was up for the challenge. Storm chasers have differing objectives. Some have the necessary equipment and strive to put themselves in a tornado. While those teams make excellent videos, I didn't want to photograph a raging storm from the inside. I intended to image it from the outside, which is a safer option. The team I worked with met all my goals, photographically and safety-wise. Notice how I keep harping on safety? It's a real thing and something many amateurs overlook. People can, and do, perish while storm chasing, although ironically, many of the fatalities are from traffic accidents and not the storm itself.

Each day started the same. We woke up and gathered for breakfast. We pored over the weather news and tried to figure out the broad, general area where tornados were most likely. Those areas became our targets. Next we read the more detailed weather discussions to confirm the initial targets. The National Weather Service provides excellent forecasts that get better all the time. The service can predict with some certainty when a small area is likely to experience severe weather and can list the probabilities a tornado might occur within that location. The forecasts are reasonably accurate and enough to form the day's general plan. The challenge for storm chasers is to narrow a broad outlook down into a specific time and place where a tornado might happen. Nothing beats knowledge and experience, although even the best don't always get it right. Remember, I was trying to place myself, a single person, in front of a tornado before or as it formed. Further, I needed to be somewhere within a few hundred miles of where I was in the morning. Making these things happen was not an easy feat. Not in the least.

Our morning target had to be reachable from where we were at the moment. Next, there had to be a strong likelihood the storms would produce a tornado. The right combination of lift, sheer, moisture, wind direction, and speeds had to line up, at least enough to get us to move in that direction. By the time we had enough coffee, we had settled on that day's target. It was time to load up the gear and head out.

This part sounds exciting. It isn't. Not by a long shot. We sat in a vehicle rolling down the highway with nothing to keep ourselves occupied other than telling each other the same story we told the day before and look at the current weather. The more we looked at a forecast, the more we wanted to change our minds and select a better target. Perhaps we should head to the next county. Maybe we should try for twenty miles to the east of this morning's destination. No, fifty miles west. Or south. Or north. The wheels turned and the miles rolled by, and the only exciting thing likely to happen was us finding a restroom when the coffee became a pressing matter.

Hot, delicious coffee at breakfast is an enjoyable thing. An hour later with nowhere to stop, the coffee idea is not quite as good. I never did learn that lesson.

As we crept closer to our ever-shifting target, we switched from the earlier forecasts to local radar and looked for signs that a tornado was forming. We slid from the possible to what was happening around us at the moment, and our excitement built. Sometimes we stopped for a few moments and waited for a situation to develop. The waiting was one of the hardest parts of the chase, especially when we knew a tornado may be imminent.

You might think our vehicle sported a turning radar dish, a million antennas, and other high-tech gear. It didn't. Cell phones replaced much of the specialty gear. Many researchers have all the super high-tech items, but that gear is expensive. Budget restraints weigh on us all in the end, and cell phones offered everything we needed, especially the accurate radar apps. Silence descended when we all peered at our screens, looking for the ideal setup. Conversation became short, clipped sentences. Instead of the previous day's recycled stories, we talked about heading toward this city or that road or intersection. Everything became about storm motion and path. We held our breath and waited to see a red box appear on our phone's map, marking a tornado warning. That process was the first step in reaching our ultimate goal.

If all went well during a chase, someone would say, "Tornado warning," indicating that the National Weather Service had issued a warning. We paid the most attention to the boundaries of the tornado warning area. We wanted to be immediately outside that box and ahead of the storm. If we were too far away, we wouldn't be able to see much of the tornado, and if we are too close, we couldn't see it because we would be in the storm. We had to find that delicate balance in the moments the tornado was forming. We had to be right. A typical twister doesn't last long, sometimes only a few seconds, so being completely accurate was crucial. There is no "almost" in storm chasing. You are right or you aren't. You aren't right most of the time, but the few times you make the correct decision pay off.

We peered intently at the radar images, trying to divine exactly where the storm was going so it would meet us. "Storm chasing" implies that we chase the storms. It's a marvelous phrase, but not descriptive of what happens. Storm chasing involves deciding where and when the storm will be and then being there before that moment. If you're chasing the storm, you're too late. To catch it, we had to be ahead of it.

At some point we settled on where we thought we needed to be. Part of the final discussion was about safety. Tornados are unpredictable. They can twist and turn at any moment, making you suddenly far away and can as quickly put you directly in harm's way. Every location we selected had to have alternative escape routes for that very reason. One road in means only one way out, which in turn means we would not have any options should we need them. Safety always reigned supreme. Some storm chasers like to put themselves into the tornado proper. Some are prepared for the conditions they will encounter and have a strategy for handling and surviving it. Most do. Some do not.

Speaking of the dangers of storm chasing, it's worth repeating that the most dangerous thing we faced was traffic. As we worked out where the tornado might be, it was a guarantee that others had done the same. Experienced storm chasers know how to drive in those conditions. Many less-knowledgeable people hurtle down the highway as fast as they can while looking at the clouds. They do not look at the road or what might be in it. Some people park on the road, and some people drive faster still. The closer a tornado gets, the more dangerous the situation becomes. By the time the tornado arrives, ironically enough, it is not the most important thing going on. Traffic is. You have to keep a keen eye out for everyone else, because they are most certainly not watching out for you. People drive like lunatics around a tornado, making an already dangerous situation even more precarious. I was glad I was not the one driving.

We headed toward our selected target and kept an equal eye on the traffic, the radar, and the sky. Quite often you can see a tornado forming. You look for the wall cloud, a section that drops down from the main storm clouds. It appears quickly and looks like someone slid a drawer out of the clouds. Tornados form from the wall cloud, and once you see one, you know a tornado could form. Sometimes it does. The funnel cloud drops from the wall cloud and heads to the ground. In the blink of an eye you are encountering a tornado.

You might think that you can photograph a tornado from any side; after all, swirling wind is swirling wind. Such is not the case, and usually there is only one side you can safely photograph. The rule of thumb is that you must be southeast of the tornado, looking northwest at it. Although it is possible to photograph a tornado from any angle, you will not likely succeed unless you position yourself correctly. Generally tornados move to the northeast, so you don't want to be there. If you are north of the tornado, the rain will likely obscure your view. If you are west of it, you are looking at it while it moves away, and rain will likely block your view. Your best bet is to be southeast and let the whirling dervish drift by you as it heads northeast.

Position yourself correctly, and at some point the tornado will sweep past you. If you are lucky you have a good look at it before it becomes rain wrapped. As the term implies, rain surrounds tornados, blocking your view of the storm's core. Often tornados appear for a few moments and then become obscured. One can pass by you or dissipate, and then you can decide to stay on the storm and reposition or you can see if more promising prospects are nearby.

After each day's chase, we found a place to stop that looked like it had a hot shower, a comfortable bed, and breakfast in the morning. The cycle repeated, and we tried to think of a new story to tell each other while we looked for the next tornado. Or restroom, whichever came first.

The day I made *Tornado Encounter* followed that script exactly. The morning was clear and bright when we woke up in Abilene, Texas. The local forecast didn't look promising, but there was uncertainty, and thus potential, in southern Oklahoma, so east we went by way of Fort Worth and then north on Interstate 35. We checked the forecast along the way, and no other opportune targets appeared. We sped on, in a do-or-bust mission toward Oklahoma. Around mid-morning, as we crossed the state line into Oklahoma, the forecast began to degrade. The threatened storms were not going to appear, and our target area was breaking down. Over by Wichita Falls, however, the situation looked far more interesting. We changed course and sped west.

Before long we reached Wichita Falls, but our target was shifting, leading us farther south. We followed a hunch and headed southwest to Seymour, Texas, arriving around lunchtime. The skies were clear, and our forecasting said wait, so wait we did.

Seymour is a beautiful small town, but without a tremendous amount to do there. We didn't plan to stay long, so we amused ourselves as best as we could. We found a city park and had a quick lunch, all the while watching the skies. The park also had some outdoor musical instruments such as drums and chimes. We treated the town to an impromptu concert while the clouds rolled in and the skies darkened. I am not sure if the skies darkened because of our show or the approaching storm. The answer will forever remain a mystery. The town residents were probably relieved to see, or more accurately, hear, us take our leave.

We headed generally south while the clouds thickened. As it often happens, we spent the entire morning driving in a vast circle. Most of the time we had nothing to show for it. That day would turn out different.

Radar lit up to indicate a supercell formed near us. Moments after the supercell formed, the tornado warning box appeared in front of the supercell. This was it! It was what every storm chaser looks for, and we were right next to it, but it was not where we had selected as a target. Experience paid off. After a brief but intense discussion we kept on, angling away from the warning box to where we believed a tornado might actually develop. Traffic streamed by us, heading toward the supercell and a hoped-for encounter. We kept heading south, away from the action, on empty roads.

A wall cloud formed a few miles south of Seymour, and a small tornado dropped from it. It was over a ridge, only a mile or so away from us. We stepped out of our vehicle, all by ourselves. We had been watching a supercell different from everyone else. They saw nothing while we saw a tornado. We stayed and watched it for almost ten minutes while it remained on the ground. It gradually grew and drifted closer to us, but we were not in the right position for the best photographs. We got back into our vehicle and headed north, drifting with it. We judged it would cross the road we were on, so we pulled off the roadway and waited.

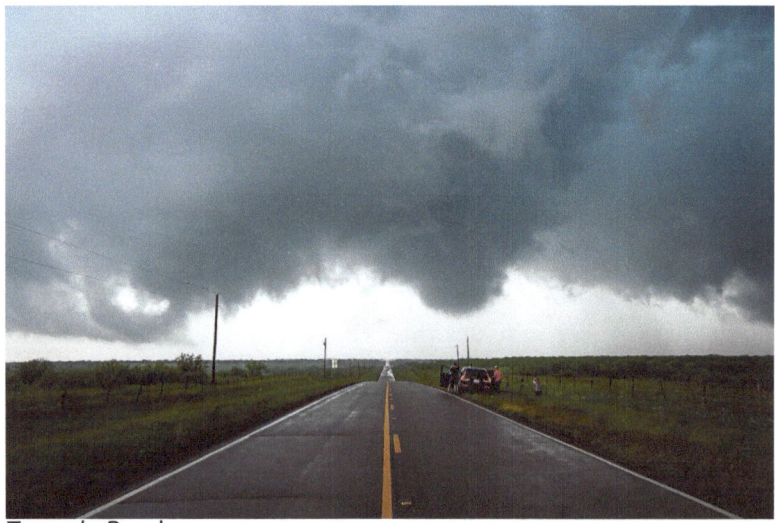
Tornado Road

I made *Tornado Road* as the tornado formed and while a few other storm chasers arrived. Someone stood behind me, watching the road to ensure my safety. The photograph shows the raw power of a forming tornado, when you can feel the intensity in the air. The funnel cloud was above one of the cars pulled off the road and would be a tornado in a few moments.

While we watched the clouds, other storm chasers zipped down from their by-then-gone supercell. Most of them didn't make it to our spot and ended up blocked by the tornado, their view obscured by rain. I was in the absolute perfect position. I had an exceptionally picturesque tornado, almost all to myself, as it swept over a field of verdant grass. In the early afternoon the sun was out, providing the light I needed to make an excellent photograph. Best of all, that tornado caused no damage yet lasted long enough for me to create *Tornado Encounter*, a photograph I am exceptionally proud of for many reasons.

I was enthralled to be standing unprotected so close to one of the most potent forces in nature. In awe at the forces in play a couple of hundred yards in front of me, I also felt safe enough, considering the event, and indeed I was, for I was in an excellent position with an escape route behind me. The tornado cared not what or who it crossed, for it was going

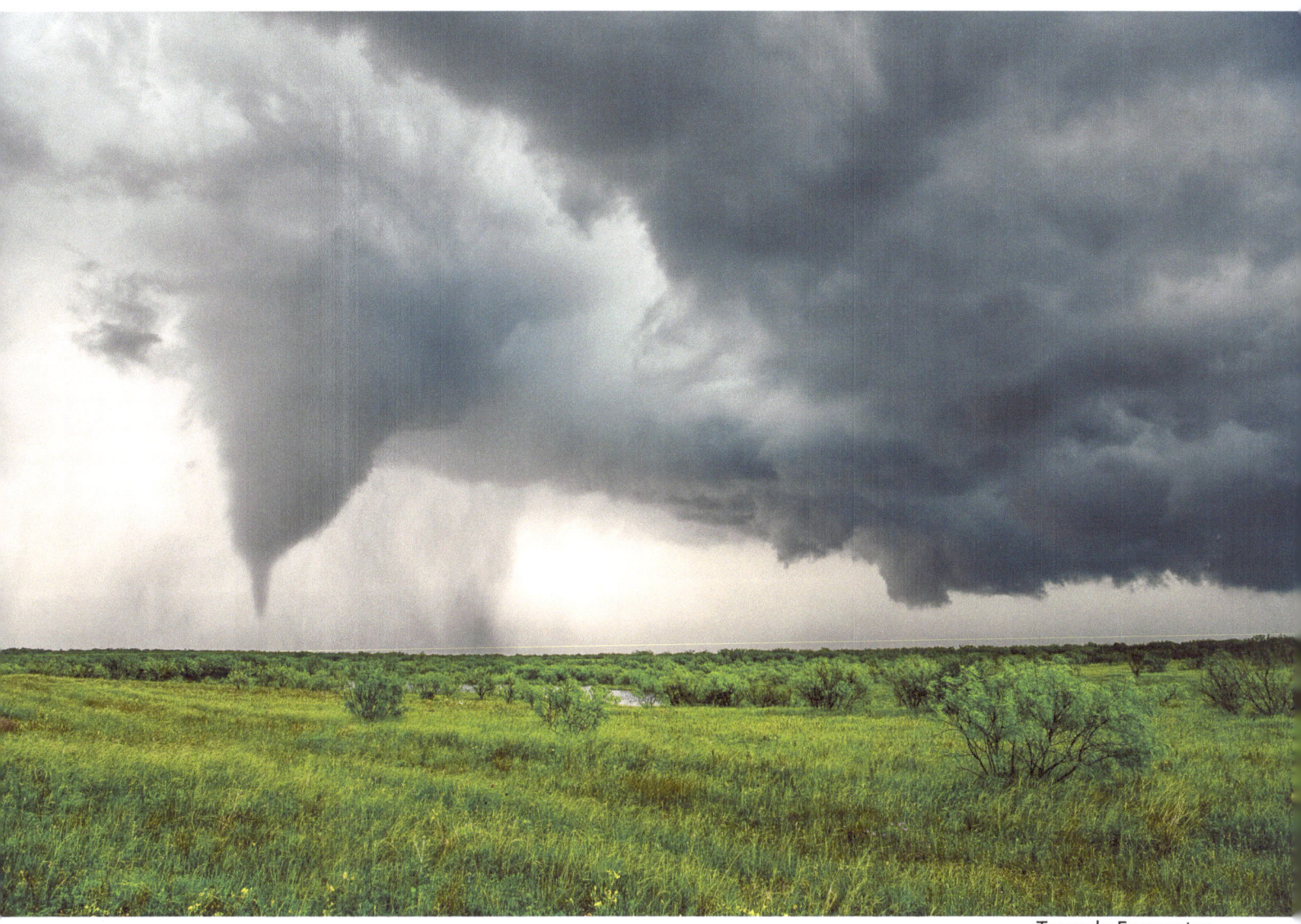

Tornado Encounter

to charge on, regardless. Nothing humans do can stop a tornado, and that thought alone was humbling. I photographed it with these thoughts swirling through my mind at the same speed as the tornadic winds. This photograph changed me in fundamental ways, and today I have a different perspective. Witnessing firsthand the awesome power of nature makes a person reflect on things and ensure their priorities are in correct order. That experience will stay with me forever, and the sense of awe I felt, and still feel, has become a part of me. I'll never look at storms the same way again, and I'll never lose respect for, yet continue to be inspired by, the power and fury they unleash.

The tornado dissipated moments after I made this photograph, and the diminished storm swept onward. It dropped no other twisters that day and did no damage. Later, when I checked the day's results from the National Weather Service, that tornado was one of only three that day in the entire Southwest. The team and I had a good day, and we slept well that night. We had a new story for the next day.

Tornado Encounter wasn't my first tornado. The storm chasers and I had previously encountered several tornados in the time we had been out. The first one is the most memorable by the distinction of being first. That tornado sighting occurred between Wichita Falls and Byers, Texas. Having spent the night in Kansas, we made our way southward toward some potential storms outside of Lubbock, Texas. During our journey the forecast changed, as it often does, and made us point northward. The closer we crept, the better the radar presentation was, and by the time we arrived, the conditions were perfect for a tornado to form.

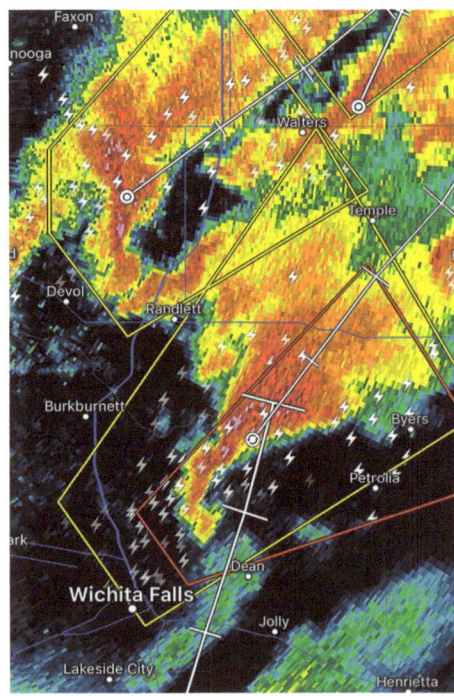

I was eager and nervous; it was the first tornado I had a chance to photograph. That opportunity was the culmination of my years of plotting, planning, and scheming. My plan was coming to fruition, and at long last I would have my photograph. All I had to do was be in the right position.

The road situation leading to the tornado was not ideal, though. We arrived at a fork in the road. Should we take the north-most highway or the south-most one? We paused at the intersection to take a hard look at the radar imagery and give the storm more time to move one way or another. We decided on the northern road, and off we went.

The decision proved problematic, because the storm veered toward the south. Backtracking as expeditiously as possible, we made it back to the intersection and then barreled down the southern route. All the while, the radar presentation improved, and it was clear a tornado was imminent. In the radar image we could see a classic "hook" to the northeast of Wichita Falls, which indicated a tornado had formed or likely would form. We also saw the tornado warning box, outlined in red, which showed where a twister was likely. The rest of the radar indicated that severe storms were all around. We were interested only in the hook and where it might travel next.

Our route had other ideas for us. The highway turned even farther south, leading us away from the tornado. We sped down a series of dirt roads, trying to get as close as possible, but we weren't able to get closer than a mile or so.

I stood to the east of the well-formed tornado staring into the hook while the tornado formed right on cue and roped down to the ground. Like many tornados, it didn't last long and dissipated after a couple minutes. Still, it was a tornado, and it was the first tornado I photographed. My years of planning had come to fruition.

I felt many emotions during those moments: fear, anticipation, excitement, and relief, but mostly awe. To experience one of nature's most potent forces close up brought home my place in this world. That moment wasn't a TV screen showing a distant storm. The tornado was right there in front of me, in person, and the reality of that feat made quite an impression on me.

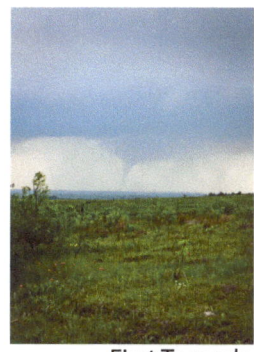
First Tornado

That tornado remains forever etched in my memory, but tornados aren't the only type of stormy weather that provides astonishing photographs. Supercells and lightning contribute their fair share, and I always take advantage of an opportunity when I can.

Not every supercell generates a tornado, and you never know for sure if one will or not. What you do know is that large, dense clouds will form and advance across the helpless landscape. The rains they generate are torrential and often accompanied by hail. Sometimes the hail is large and destructive, making it dangerous to be outside. You don't want to be underneath a supercell.

Being next to a supercell, on the other hand, can pay off photographically. Not every supercell is particularly photogenic, but when the right conditions line up, they are. As a good example, this supercell was drifting across the Kansas prairie late one spring day. Twilight had come and gone, and the sun was drifting peacefully away to the west. The day was finished, and all looked to be in good order. As the sun dove below the horizon, the clouds coalesced into a supercell, which gathered strength and steam. The storm started its inexorable march over the prairie. Ahead of it lightning flared and flashed, with some bolts striking the ground and others dancing a jaunty

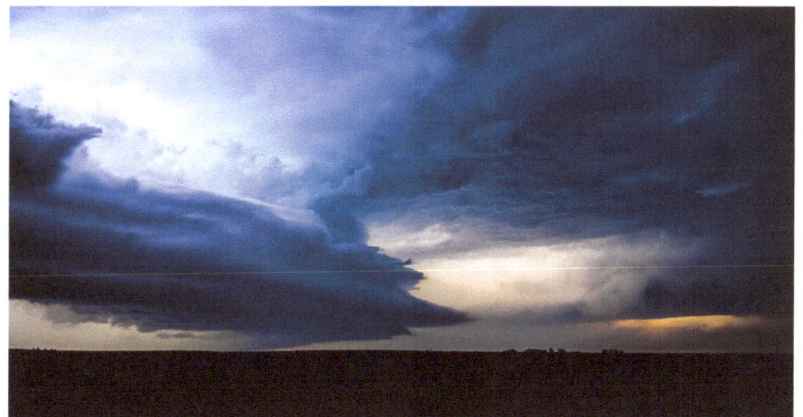
Jetmore's Supercell

jig among the clouds. Everything grew quieter as man and animal alike braced against the oncoming onslaught. The sky became blacker still, inkier than any known color. Thick, ominous clouds blotted out the atmosphere and surrounded everyone with absolute blackness. The silence was complete and everyone waited for the inevitable bombardment.

The rain burst asunder from the clouds, the torrential downpour drenching the grass. At first it drank thirstily, but in the end it struggled to stay above the flooding fields. Hail, some pieces small and some chunks damaging, hurled from the sky, aiming at anyone and everyone unlucky enough to be without shelter. The fury of the heavens tore the air apart, until at long last the storm spent its anger.

The clouds broke apart, letting the stars shine through. Ground dwellers—plants, animals, and man alike—breathed a sigh of relief and began drying themselves off. The stars shone brighter still, perhaps to lend whatever light they could to the recovery. Before long the sun poked above the horizon, gingerly at first, and finally with gusto. The morning dawned clear and bright, the memory of the night long past. Until, that is, the storms came again, when the cycle of fury and atonement would repeat.

Lightning is not constrained to the vast plains of Kansas; it can form anywhere, at any time, and even, although rarely, under clear blue skies. Lightning travels great distances and is a powerful force of nature. Sometimes you don't see the bolt coming, but sometimes you do.

The Desert Southwest is a broad, vast area that includes dazzling terrain and geography. From the proper vantage on a clear day, you can see a hundred miles or more, a staggering distance. You can witness weather change right before your eyes, as in the case of *Needles Strike*.

The day had dawned bright and calm, with no forewarning of what was coming. When I looked out across the Needles District of Canyonlands National Park, Utah, all was peaceful down below. The rugged landscape looked tame, but in reality it was quite treacherous. Few roads dared to carve their way through there, and there was little reason to build one. The land has been left to fend for itself. Rarely some brave soul ventures into the wilderness, but all visitors blaze their own trail and find their way. I was content on a mesa high above it, where my perch afforded me grand vistas in every direction, without having to create my own path.

My goal that morning was to create a panorama of a nearby rock formation. I spent the morning looking at it and pondering the best angle and method to photograph it. In no hurry, I enjoyed myself and the morning. I gave it my best effort to create something I would like, but try as I might, my attempts were fruitless. Not every photograph works out as I hope. With the morning light long gone, I packed my gear and decided to enjoy the view a bit longer. I meandered aimlessly about the mesa and then settled down on a rock facing west. Sometimes even adventurers need a break and time to relax and enjoy the view.

The more I studied the vista, the more interesting rock formations I found off in the distance. A few birds soared high above, perhaps taking in the same scene. I contented myself by soaking in the views, and before I realized it, the day had begun to slip away. I noticed something happening at the edges of the horizon, though.

At first a few wispy clouds breached the far horizon, followed by a few more. The vague clouds gave way to thicker clouds, and with a start, I realized they had moisture in them. It was not out of the question that a summer squall could pop up, and maybe I would get lucky with a photograph of it. My patient waiting gave way to anticipation, and I became determined to see what might develop. Anything can happen in the Southwest desert.

Off in the far distance, an isolated storm cell lazily drifted into view and took direct aim at Canyonlands. I had no way to tell where it might go next, but the fact that it grew larger and larger gave me hope that it might come near me. I had not been able to create a photograph that morning, but that afternoon might be a different story. Time would soon tell. A low roll of thunder punctuated my thoughts.

The closer the storm cell came, the more intense it became. The muted rumbles of thunder became booming, deafening roars, and the storm unleashed torrential rains onto the parched earth below. The sun at my back lit up the wet desert, bringing it to life. The rocks glistened and gleamed in the sun, their colors vivid thanks to the rain. When the rain continued, small rivulets appeared, making a transitory and welcome appearance. The scene transformed before my eyes into iridescent beauty.

Along with the storm came lightning, and with the lightning came *Needles Strike*. Electricity crashed all around the rock formations and all around me. Daring the wrath of nature, I stole a moment to make this photograph and then ducked into cover before the full fury of the storm overtook me.

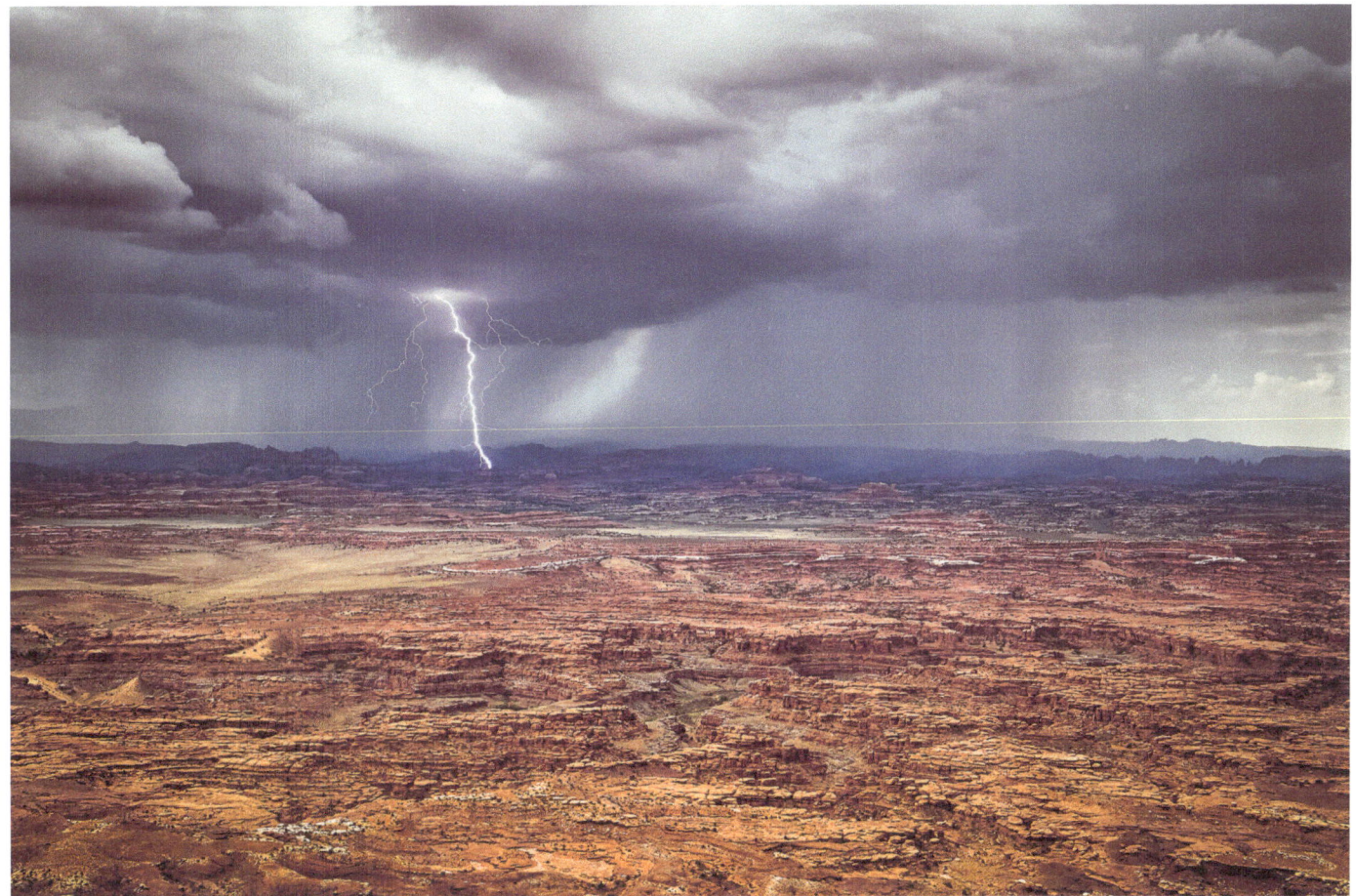

Needles Strike

Soon the cell passed and all grew tranquil again. The clouds broke up, leaving the sky alone and leaving me with the memory of the lightning that came to me.

Earlier I mentioned that as a storm chaser you want to be next to a supercell and not underneath it. You probably smiled, nodded, and thought, "Of course," and then continued reading. That statement was not a passing thought but a statement from experience. You don't want to try to photograph a supercell from within it. I know. I tried. I was lucky it worked out. I alluded to the event earlier, and now is a great time to tell the story.

I was in Grand Teton National Park in Wyoming, photographing the fall colors. The year was an excellent one for the leaves, and I made several stunning photographs, a couple of which appeared earlier. After I finished photographing one morning, I went to Mormon's Row, famous for its old homesteads, especially its barns. Those barns appear in many photographs, and deservedly so, for they are picturesque. I had a passing thought that they would make a dramatic foreground with lightning in the background, but my attention turned to something else before I could think more about it. I continued my adventures in the park.

My photography that day came to an early end. Heavy, thick clouds rolled in, blocking out the sun and any chance for an exciting photograph. The clear skies became overcast, gray, and lifeless. My photographic opportunities vanished. I packed up my gear and headed back to town, grateful for a hot meal at a reasonable hour. While I was eating my dinner, thunder boomed overhead, shaking the plates and silverware. I was as startled as everyone else. Something then niggled at the back of my mind. Thunder. Rain. Storms. Thunder. Thunder! Why did I keep coming back to the word *thunder*? The next boom coincided with the rumble and clatter of me making a beeline out of the restaurant. I had remembered, finally, why thunder was significant. Lightning came with it and the chance to make a photograph with lightning at Mormon's Row. Time to go!

It was pouring rain by the time I made it back to the barns. The path, no longer a dirt road, had become a horizontal mudslide. Not letting the muck deter me, I plowed my 4x4 through the mud, throwing it everywhere. I pushed onward to the barn I thought would look best, hoping I wouldn't become mired down. When I arrived I didn't have to apply my brakes, thanks to the thick, gooey mud, and I jumped out to put on rain gear. Within seconds the rain drenched me to the bone, though, so I didn't bother with the raincoat, which made preparations a tad quicker. A blessing. I set up my tripod and camera in a waterproof shell, taking extra care not to let my equipment get wet during the deluge. Thunder crashed all around me, so I knew I would not have to wait long.

I stood in the pouring rain, shivering and shaking, waiting for the lightning. I found new meanings for the word *wet*. Until that day, I hadn't fully comprehended what it meant to be wet. New words came to me. Drenched. Waterlogged. Saturated. Sopping. It was a miserable experience.

In a barren field outside the barn I continued waiting. The sky was almost dark, so I made long exposures. That technique gave me the best chance to catch the lightning, and best of all rendered the fast-moving raindrops invisible. You cannot tell it was raining by looking at the photographs.

I waited so intently that when the lightning came with a flash brighter than a hundred suns and the thunder roared like a thousand freight trains, it scared me so much I stopped shaking. I then started shaking again, this time not from the

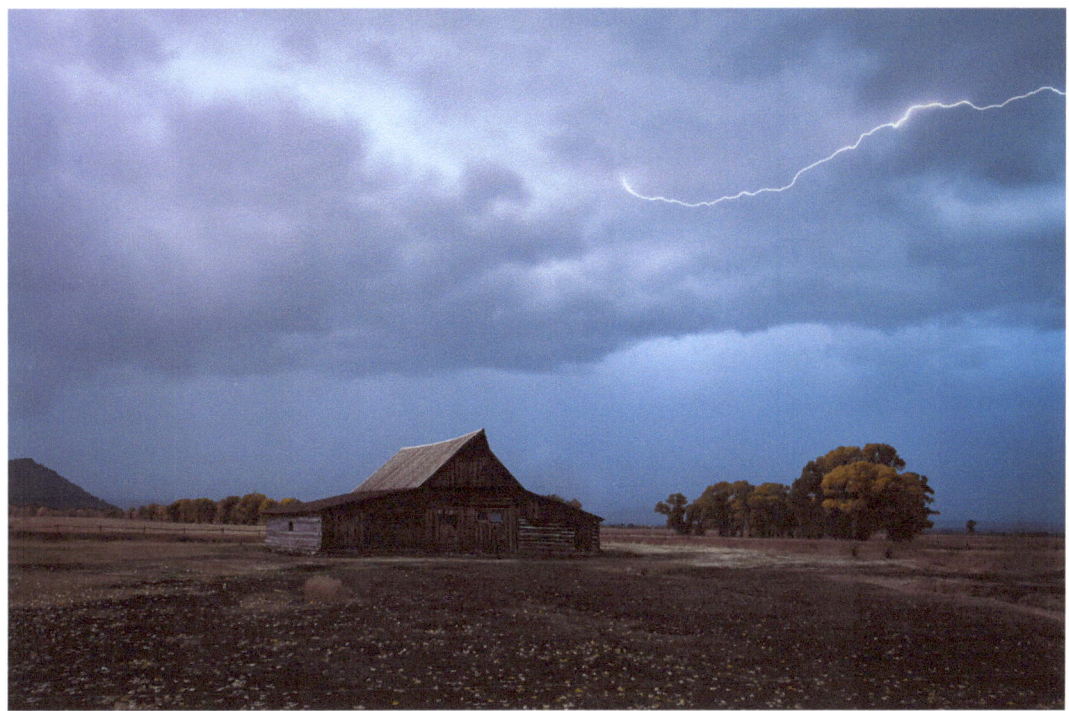
Moulton's Storm

rain. With the lightning bolts above me, I realized the nearly fatal flaw in my plan. I was in the rainstorm. I was part of the landscape. I was standing in an empty field with poles of metal and electric current coursing through my camera. To top it off, I was the most prominent thing in the area. I looked around, looking for cover. Seeing none, I grabbed my gear and made a beeline back to the safety of the 4x4. Whew! I almost became a part of the scene, and not in a good way.

Moulton's Storm turned out well, and I achieved my goal. When I say it is best to be next to, and not under, a supercell while photographing it, I speak with experience.

As a postscript, my 4x4 still isn't completely dry from that storm. I'm told that it should completely dry out within the next few years. Maybe.

All supercells are massive and intense, but not all storms become a supercell. Sometimes a storm cell is small and discrete. A cell outside of Rangely, Colorado, was an excellent example. I was headed home from one of my many Teton excursions by way of Colorado. The drive was pleasant and a relaxing way to wind down the journey. I looked forward to finally being home again and wasn't expecting any weather adventures. The forecast was partly cloudy, which made for perfect traveling conditions. I serenely drove on without a care in the world.

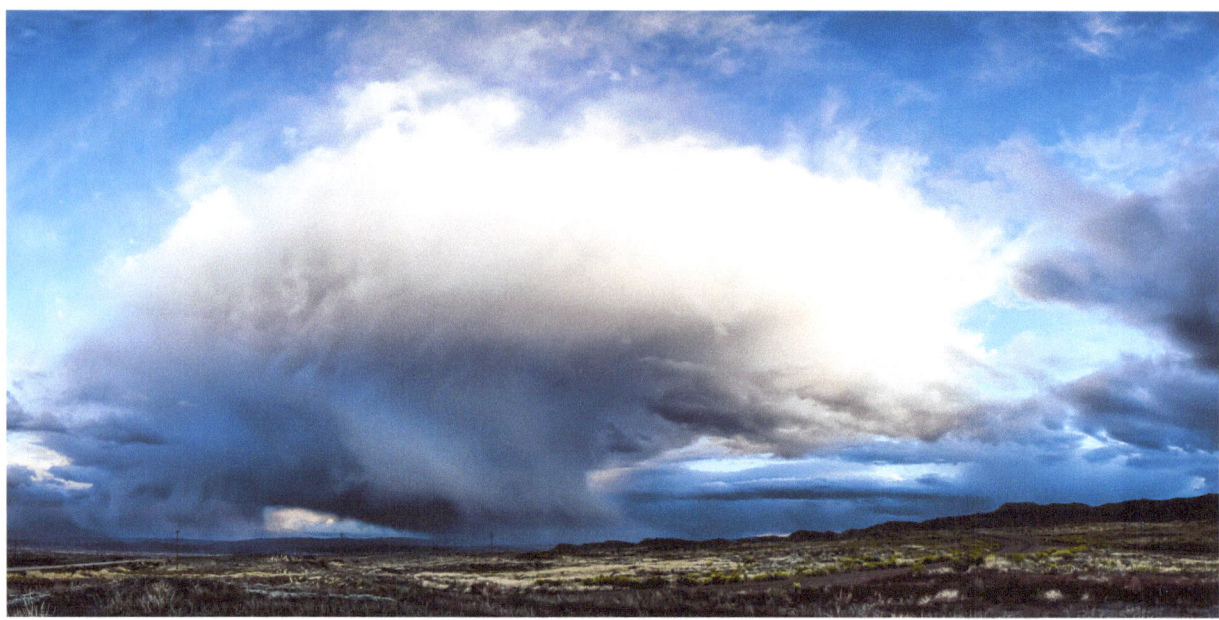

Rangely Cell

A storm cell came roaring out of nowhere. Clearly it had not paid attention to the forecast, because it wasn't supposed to be there. One moment all was quiet under beautiful partly cloudy skies, and the next, thanks to the small storm, I was in the middle of a torrential downpour. "Good grief," I thought. "Here we go again." At least this time I wasn't planning to get out into the rain. I drove through the maelstrom and emerged on the other side. Never one to miss an opportunity, I set up my gear to create *Rangely Cell*. The storm cell was a small one, and I was able to photograph the entire thing while staying dry—a remarkable achievement for me. I adore the structure of the clouds and the shape they take on in this photograph.

Storm cells form because of moisture in the air, instability of the atmosphere, and lift. Without humidity a cell cannot form, as much as it might want to. The terms "unstable air" and "lift" refer to warm air attempting to rise higher into a cooler layer. Although we can't see the interaction, it causes quite a problem for the warm-air and cool-air layers, creating instability. The faster the warm air attempts to rise, the more instability it generates, which gives more potential to the cell. Storm cells can produce significant rain and strong wind gusts but generally are not damaging or violent.

A supercell, by contrast, has a rotating updraft. The rotation makes it a more powerful storm and capable of producing violent and damaging winds. Supercells can spawn tornados too, which, as we've seen, are formidable and potentially destructive. Although not all supercells are destructive, the potential is always there.

Thankful a tornado did not erupt that day, I watched the storm run its course. Before long it dissipated, as if it never happened. I clambered back into my 4x4 and continued home. The rest of that trip was uneventful.

Stormy weather provides marvelous photographic opportunities for any outdoors photographer. Severe weather, which we've focused on in this chapter, has its own set of challenges, including personal safety and being able to photograph in a deluge. When foul weather begins to clear out, though, opportunity rushes in. The mix of the sun pushing away the dark, foreboding clouds is a time of light and magic, moments I specifically seek out. Alas, not every moment works out perfectly, regardless of how much I want it to.

As an example of imperfection, we have this photograph, made early on an autumn morning near the Dallas Divide in the San Juan Mountains of Colorado. The crisp fall eve saw moderate to heavy rain throughout the night, and the forecast indicated the morning would be partly cloudy. The setup was ideal, and I hoped for a dramatic sunrise. The fall colors were at their brightest, and with any luck, broken clouds would complete the scene.

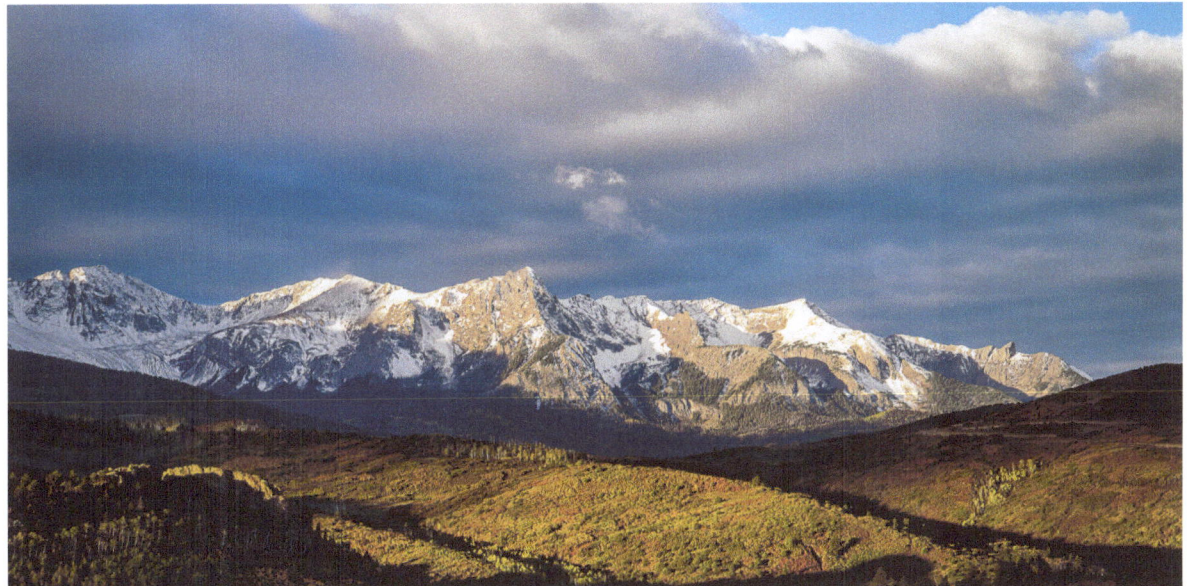

Almost Divine

Sadly such was not the case. I was in position well before dawn, and thick clouds covered the sky. I crossed my fingers and hoped they would move out as the sun rose, but the heavy clouds refused to break up. Instead they continued to hang low and thick over the mountains. The sun ascended and now and then slipped some rays through the clouds. The early morning sun was as beautiful as I had hoped for, but deep shadows engulfed the valley floor, and the scene never fully lit up. I waited all morning, but the conditions never improved.

Sometimes stormy weather doesn't live up to my expectations, but I am accustomed to the photographer's life. I take the gems with the "almost greats," and I always keep trying.

Now it's time to leave stormy weather behind and head north to a new frontier.

Alaskan Frontier

Alaska is truly the last frontier. Untamed and wild, America's penultimate state has wonders that reward explorers for their efforts. From northern lights that can bedazzle a winter night to behemoth whales that breach the deep waters and from soaring eagles to hungry bears that fish for salmon, these stories bring the frontier to you.

Only a few places still provide vast, unexplored areas, and Alaska is undoubtedly one. The simple statement "I'm going to Alaska" evokes an immediate feeling of adventure and wonderment. Alaska was a magnet to me, so how could I not be there? As much fun as it would be to head to Alaska and aimlessly wander about, I set a couple of defined goals, namely, capture the northern lights and explore the Inside Passage. To meet my objectives I needed dedicated expeditions, which, as you can imagine, broke my heart. Who am I kidding? That arrangement delighted me, and I set out to plot my Alaskan adventures.

First up was the northern lights adventure. Deciding on the "what," photographing the Aurora Borealis, was the simple part of my plan. The problematic part was the "where." Alaska is a colossal place of more than 600,000 square miles, and the choices are many. I knew that the farther north I went, the better my odds of success, which created a basic parameter. I also wanted to be on, or near, the road system, to move around easier. Much of Alaska is remote, not easily accessed, and certainly not always accessible by road. I decided that staying on the road system would allow me to scout more areas. Those decisions led me to Fairbanks, from which I could travel in several directions and get far enough away from civilization to make worthy photographs. Perfect! The plan began to come together.

The final part I needed to tackle was then "when," which in theory was straightforward. March is an ideal time, since the nights are still long, the temperatures aren't quite as cold as in deep winter, and moreover, high-pressure systems are frequent. A high-pressure system means clear skies, and clear skies were a critical component of the plan. I was entirely correct on the first two parts of my thinking, but the weather became problematic, as we shall see. Weather is also often a problem, either too clear or too overcast or too hot or too cold, so I've learned to work around it. Or at least accept it. Well, sometimes accept it.

I knew what, when, and where, and I finalized the arrangements. Off to Fairbanks I went. The aurora adventure had officially begun, and I was thrilled to be underway.

Fairbanks turned out to be an ideal location for my operational base. The people were friendly and welcoming, and I enjoyed getting to know and learn about them. Fairbanks has a strong sense of community, which spills over to travelers. Although it was my first time there, it certainly won't be my last.

The daytime temperatures were pleasant enough, but the weather forecast wasn't the best, with a chance for snow every day. Seeing an aurora was going to be hit or miss. It worked out well in the end, but the outcome was not clear until the very end. Regardless, it was time to see what I could create.

The first night I ventured northeast of Fairbanks. With high clouds overhead I stayed hopeful that they would break up as the night wore on. The air was cold and crisp, exactly what I had expected. Still hopeful the clouds would dissipate, I crossed my fingers and I headed deeper into the Alaskan wilderness. The roads were icy and snow packed, which was typical, but I was thankful there was a road in the first place. Driving, while not overly arduous, was also not something I could take for granted in our forty-ninth state. I needed to pay close attention to the road, lest I find myself suddenly not on the road, which would have been a huge problem. My plan of being able to move around at will was working out well. Whew! The northern lights weren't visible, though, and I struggled to stay optimistic. I had several more nights ahead of me, and I was hopeful the weather would cooperate.

Auroras are not consistent or predictable. My initial impression was that they would be easy to photograph, and indeed if you are in the right spot at the right time, all is well. But the "right spot at the right time" is the hard part. My best bet was to select a photogenic location and wait for the northern lights to come to me if I was lucky. I had no other choice, since it was not possible to chase auroras. They either appear or they don't. It is as simple as that. I met several people who had tried for more than a week, and one gentleman two weeks, to see the auroras, but they never did. You never know what each night will bring.

The National Oceanic and Atmospheric Administration publishes the K-Index, known as the Kp number, for the upcoming days. The number, which ranges from zero to nine, is a simple indicator of the forecasted intensity of magnetic storms, which cause auroras. The higher the number, the greater the chance of an aurora, although it is more complicated than that. At high latitudes there are excellent odds an aurora will appear on any given night. The lower the latitude, the higher the Kp Index needs to be to maximize the chances.

Even though higher Kp numbers indicate the possibility of better auroras, nothing can guarantee they will occur. The Kp numbers for my time in Fairbanks were in the low to middle range, but auroras come and go as they wish. They give no warning, and no indicators exist that say for sure that auroras are coming or going. They simply appear and disappear, which meant I would be waiting all night to see what the sky brought me. With the Kp numbers on the lower end, chances were slimmer, but they weren't zero. I just had to hope a little harder. I am good at hoping, so I ended up at the top of a hill a couple hours away from Fairbanks in the middle of an Alaskan night watching the sky.

It was how I saw my first aurora.

I had arrived on my chosen hilltop shortly before midnight. The sky was clear and the temperature bitingly cold. Bundled up in layer upon layer, I stomped my feet and moved around to stay warm, eyes peeled for the faintest hint of anything green in the sky. I waited and stomped and then waited some more. The longer I stood there, the more my eyes adjusted to the pitch darkness, and the more I saw. And the colder I became, but not nearly as cold as I would get in the upcoming nights. Finally, at long last, I spotted a faint glow on the horizon.

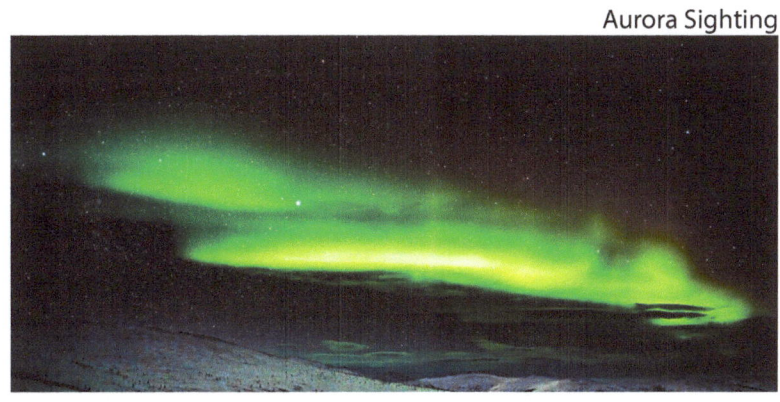
Aurora Sighting

The aurora swept in and gracefully danced across the snow-covered hills, turning and twisting sinuously across the sky. It stretched and contracted, swaying to its own beat with its own rhythm. Far

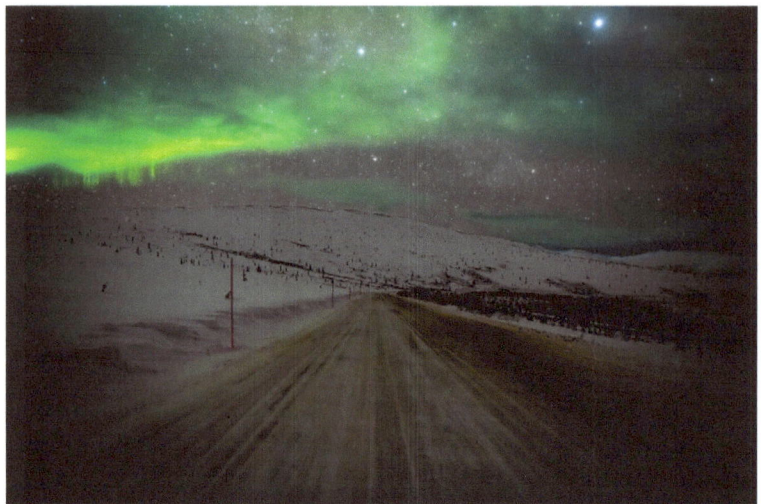
Aurora Road

from being static, the aurora's slow dance was hypnotic, holding me deep in its spell. The bitter cold melted, and my tiredness evaporated, leaving only the swirling aurora and me. I expected the aurora to appear and then disappear and was amazed that it twisted, turned, and swirled across the sky. It was a living entity, lighting the heavens with an otherworldly glow.

That sighting will always be significant, because it was my first time seeing the fabled northern lights. The feeling will stay with me forever. The sense of disappointment I felt when it dissipated as suddenly as it came also stays with me, for it is a feeling of loss and emptiness. As the lights faded, so did my elation. Absolute darkness and the all-encompassing cold surrounded me once again, leaving me alone, cold, and forlorn at the top of the hill. The aurora would not come back for me that night or for several nights that followed.

The next few days and nights were much the same for me: wake up in the middle of the afternoon, find something to eat, and head off into the deepening night hoping to see more auroras, only to be thwarted by clouds or worse, snow. After allowing me my first aurora, the weather seemed determined to make sure it would be my last. Each night I found a beautiful foreground, and each night the sky was overcast. Some nights I could almost see through the clouds, but most nights I waited in total blackness. The process repeated again and again, with no end in sight. Sometimes, just to break up the monotony, it lightly snowed, but usually only the cold accompanied me.

As the days went by, however, I had glimmers of hope. One night I went back to my first spot and was rewarded with this photograph, which tells the story of my time on the roads in the dark.

As the days went by, the moon began to show. It was a new moon when I first arrived, meaning there was no moon at all. The moon came up earlier each night on its journey to becoming a full moon. My time for aurora hunting was rapidly drawing to a close. I had only one or two nights left. During my cloudy night explorations, I had discovered a field that I thought might make a good location, so I went back to it.

Aurora's Moon is the conclusion of that night. The clouds were stubbornly thick and unforgiving, although they almost cleared at one point, allowing me a glimpse of what might be. It was maddening to know the aurora was out and active, but behind clouds. The moon rising behind those clouds gave the billows a purplish glow, however, counterpoint to the aurora's sweeping green, and the overall effect turned out quite lovely. The image wasn't what I was hoping for, but I like how it shows the contrast between the moon and the northern lights.

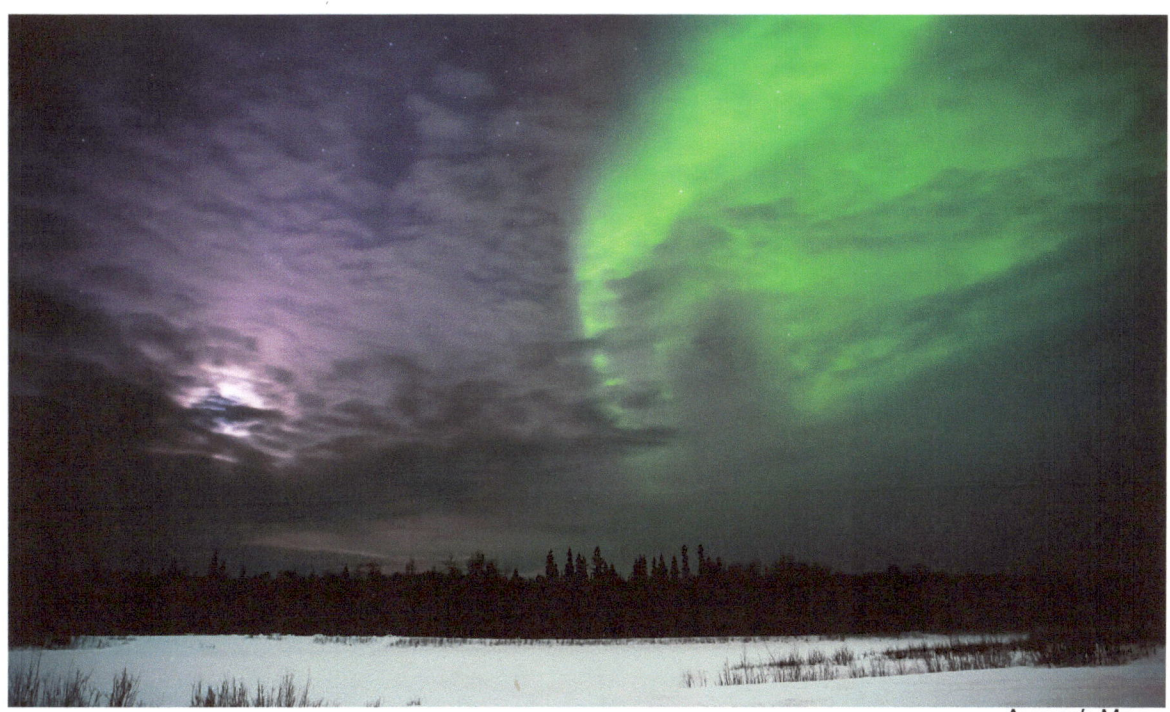
Aurora's Moon

In times like those it is hardest to keep going. I want to give up and pack it in. I want to let despair wash over me and have its way. I want to stay in, sleep, and be warm. As tempting as those thoughts were, I knew I had to keep going. I had to be out in the wilderness to experience what nature had in store for me, for better or worse.

I still didn't have the photograph I had my heart set on, and time was running out. I knew I could eke out one more chance, although based on the Kp index and the weather, the odds were slim. The moon would be in the sky and might well be too bright to photograph the aurora effectively, even if it did appear. I put that worry aside. What choice did I have? I geared up and headed out for one more attempt, trying to stay optimistic. With dogged determination, I headed down the remote, empty roads for one last chance.

Along my earlier travels I had spotted a bend in a frozen river that looked promising. Of all the places, I liked that one the best, so I decided to take my last chance there. I headed out of town and back into the wilderness, and the low clouds that had been my constant friends chose to depart, leaving a crystal-clear sky. The stars greeted me, twinkling their welcome, and were pleasing companions when I reached my destination. The clear skies let the meager warmth of the day escape, and the night became the coldest by far. Alas, although the skies were clear, the aurora was nowhere to be found. If it wasn't one thing, it was another, but such circumstances are far from unusual for me. I thought I was used to the cold, but that night delivered a new low for me, and I experienced how arctic Alaska can be in winter, especially since I was standing still.

When you move around, you have a fighting chance to stay warm. Your muscles generate heat, and moving keeps your attention focused on getting from here to there. You still get cold, but at least your body's energy fights it. Standing still, however, is the worst way to experience cold. Waiting inside a warm vehicle was a short-term option, but the windows fogged up, and I didn't want to miss the aurora. Running the engine also used gas, which I needed to get back to town. However I cut it, sooner or later I was going to be standing still or moving very little in the dead of an Alaskan night, which is when the cold truly settled in, and believe me, it was intense.

River's Aurora

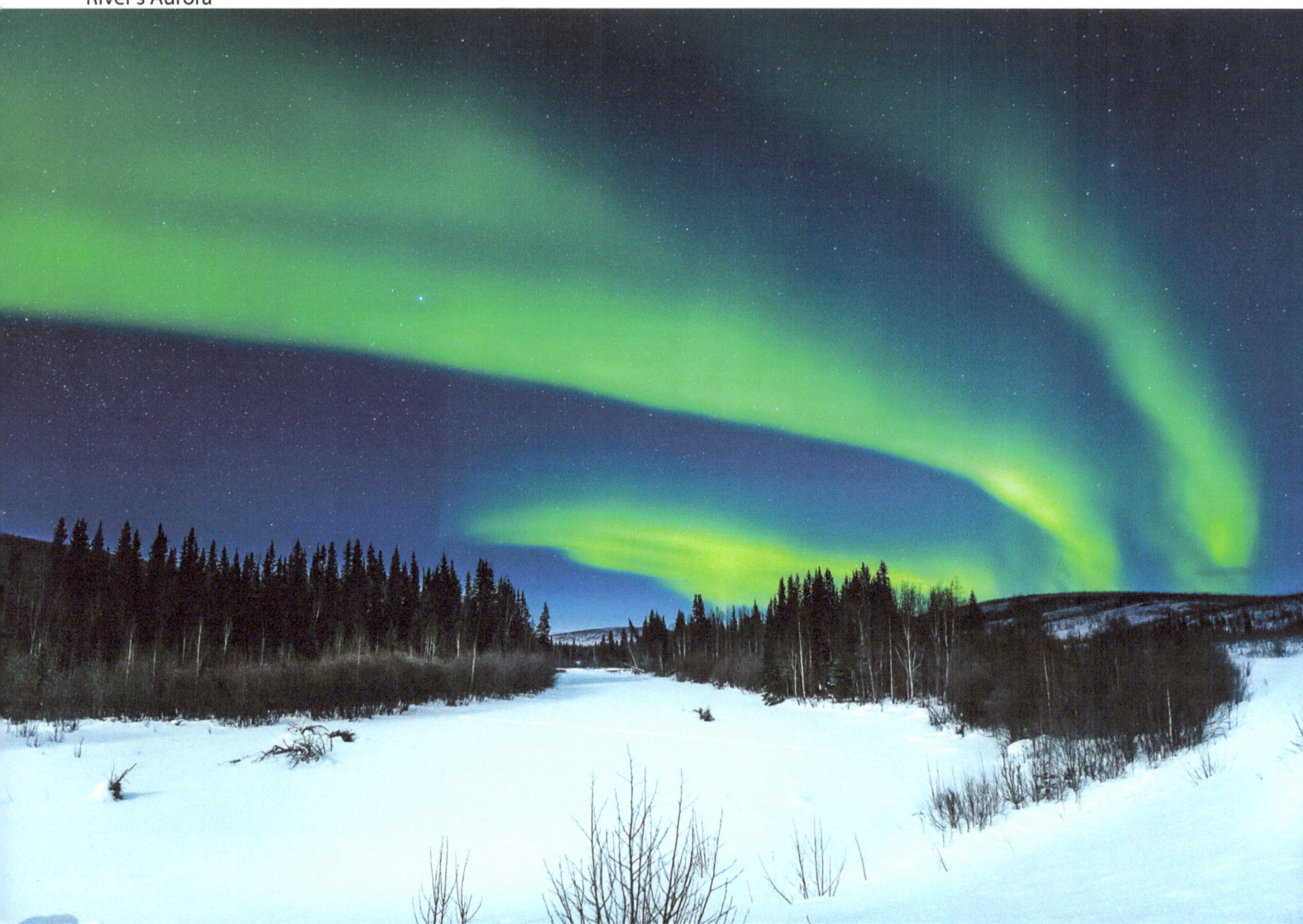

At last the sky lightened, but unfortunately the moon did the job, not the hoped-for northern lights. The rising moon spilled its light onto the landscape. Still low on the horizon, the moon was coming up quickly, and before long the night would be too bright. Hope arrived, though, in the form of a greenish glow that appeared just over the tops of the trees. The race between the two began.

I took up a position in a deep snowbank. As much as I would have preferred otherwise, it was my best bet to give me the best view. The position would work out or it wouldn't, and time would tell. I shivered while I watched the battle of the lights, moon versus aurora. Who would win? My shivers slowly gave way to excitement when the aurora turned into sweeping bands, echoing the bend of the river. The moon provided just enough illumination to light up the foreground. Finally, in the middle of a bitterly cold winter night, I made *River's Aurora,* the photograph I was hoping for. Everything came together for me, and all my planning, traveling, scouting, perseverance, and hard work developed into one photograph. The auroral bands didn't last long and created only this one pattern, but I made the most of my one opportunity.

I shook off the frost that had accumulated on me and headed jubilantly back to town.

Nature rewarded my patience. I realize that making *River's Aurora* was as much luck as anything else, and I know how close I came to not making the photograph. I wish I could say that all you have to do is persevere long enough or try hard enough and everything will come together in the end. It just isn't that way. Sometimes circumstances beyond your control conspire against you, and all you can do is accept the result. Plenty of times, despite my best efforts, my plans do not come to fruition. The failures make moments like *River's Aurora* all the more special for me.

I spent the flight home from Fairbanks thinking about my next Alaskan adventure and how to pull that one off. The problem I faced was how to narrow down my adventure into something manageable. I briefly considered moving to Alaska, which would give me as much time as I needed. I ruled out that thought as impractical, but the more I think about it, the more it is a distinct, albeit distant, possibility. Moving there isn't likely, but it does go to show the pull Alaska has on me.

After a while I decided on the Inside Passage as the next target, and the best way for me to explore it was by boat. The Inside Passage is a coastal route for ships and boats. It weaves among the islands of the Pacific Northwest coast of the North American Fjordland. My decision wasn't completely random, as I knew a captain who owned a boat and sailed those waters. The area had no roads, and flying in bush planes can be logistically challenging, so a ship was my best bet. After several long discussions, the captain eventually agreed to be a part of my journey. The idea turned out to be an excellent decision. I chose to make the expedition in the fall for a solid reason, and we'll see why in a few moments.

I started in Petersburg, Alaska, and sailed to Juneau. As the crow flies and the reasonable boat sails, the trip is a quick one of about a hundred miles. As I went, however, the trip took more than a week. I think it's best not to be in a hurry. That timeframe allowed me to be on my own schedule and itinerary. Before heading out, though, I explored Petersburg and the surrounding Mitkof Island. I made one of my favorite bald eagle photographs there.

The photograph came quite by accident, or perhaps by happenstance. I spent the first part of the day on the western edge of the island on an isolated rocky beach attempting to photograph eagles. Several bald eagles nested there, and they were active. They flew from their tree perches out over the ocean and then back to a different tree. That process repeated throughout the day, but try as I might, I couldn't create my desired photograph. Eventually I conceded that it wouldn't be my day for eagle photographs, and I relaxed and enjoyed being a spectator. I knew I would have more opportunities, and really, being next to the water on an exquisite fall day in Alaska is not a bad thing at all. Alas, it was all too soon time to head back into town, so I packed my gear and took off. Along the way I passed an eagle sitting on an old post in the water with the low sun shedding perfect lighting on it. Talk about timing!

I readied my camera as quickly and carefully as I could. Being cautious and acting like I was not paying attention to the eagle whatsoever, I casually sauntered in the majestic bird's general direction. The idea was to creep a bit closer and drift more to the side, which put the sun at an even better angle, all the while pretending I was doing something else altogether. Wildlife, any wildlife, does not like to be directly approached. Seeming to veer at an angle or appearing to be blissfully unaware of it sometimes helps, which certainly did in this case, as I

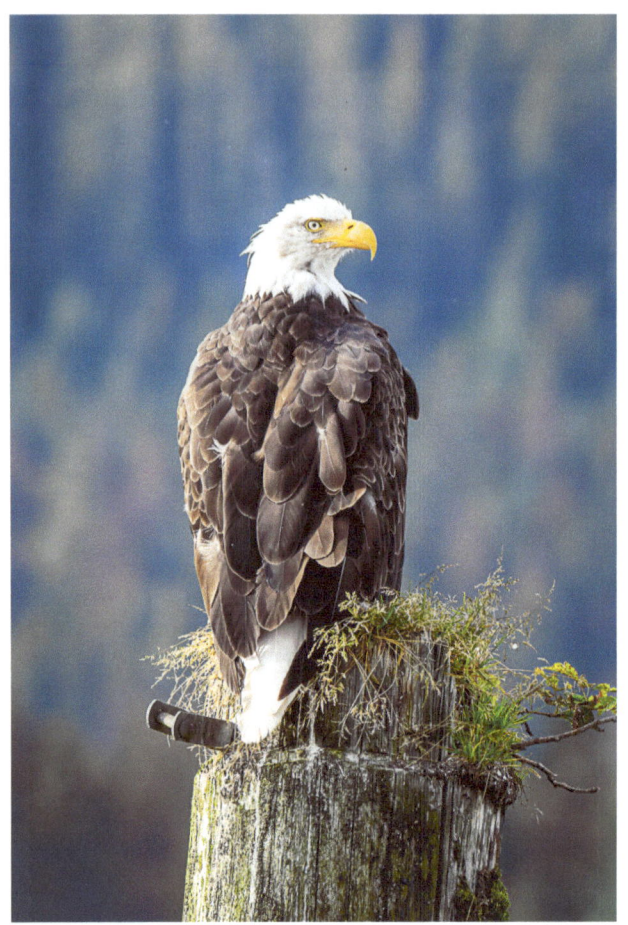

Eagle Post

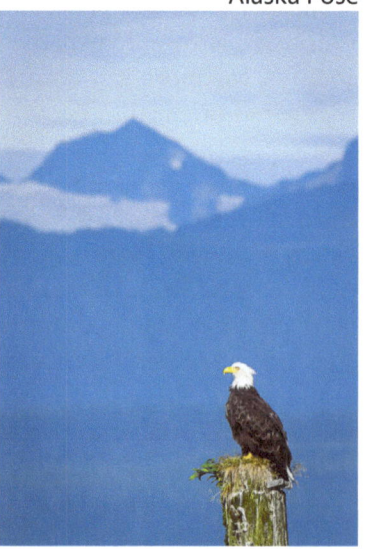

Alaska Pose

achieved an excellent position. After moving deliberately and as casually as I could, I made *Eagle Post*. The eagle knew I was there, of course, but it had relaxed enough that I was able to create the photograph I envisioned. The raptor almost seemed like it enjoyed having its picture taken. In any event, *Eagle Post* remains one of my favorite eagle photographs as well as a reminder that opportunity strikes whenever it wants.

I was also able to make this additional photograph of the eagle, which I also like. The mountain and glacier in the background scream "Made in Alaska," and the eagle adds the perfect counterpoint. The eagle became used to me, leaving me free to experiment and create various views. When I was done, I waved goodbye and thanked the magnificent bird for its time, as I'd completed my day's objective.

Mitkof Island was a pleasure to investigate, and I appreciated my brief time there. Like Fairbanks, people there are good-natured and welcoming. I made two other fun photographs there that I like, *Petersburg Flock* and *Petersburg Harbor*. *Petersburg Flock* was made in the late afternoon on a calm day. The large flock of birds was in a hurry to get from where they were to somewhere else. I like the mountains and glacier in the background and reflection of the birds on the water of the bay.

I created *Petersburg Harbor* in the evening. The winds were calm, and the water in the harbor was completely still, making excellent reflections. I truly enjoy the peacefulness and calm of the boats quietly resting

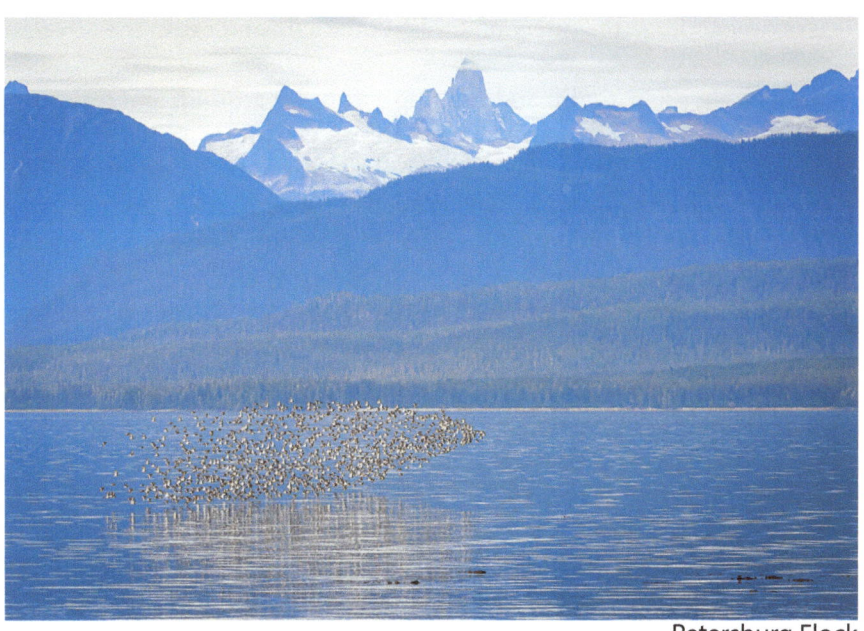

Petersburg Flock

after a long day. The pier lights barely lit the ships, leaving the rest of the scene a mysterious blackness, an effect I especially like. As we know from Oregon, I adore harbors, regardless of whether they are foggy or dark.

Petersburg Harbor

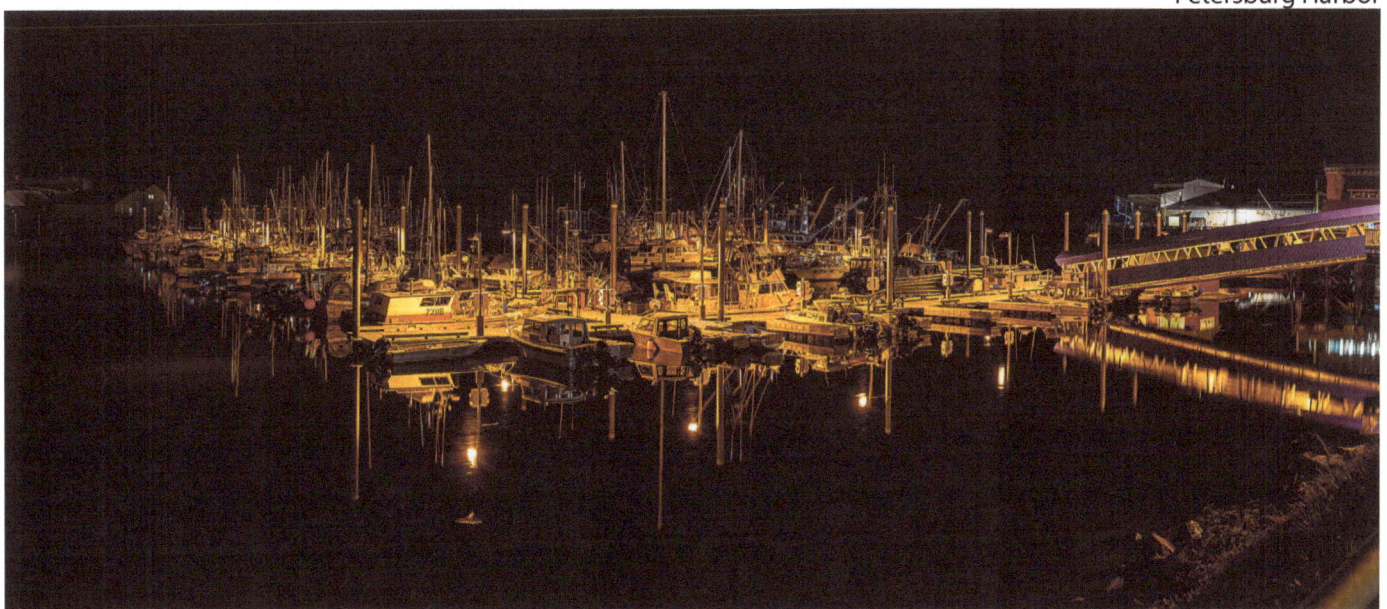

It was time to leave the safety of dry land, though, and begin the adventure proper. The next morning I set sail.

Sailing might seem a calm and relaxing way to get around, and for most people, it is. For me, however, it is something different. For whatever reason, I have always had an irrational fear of boats. I know full well the vessels are perfectly safe and used for as long as people have lived near water. I understand how buoyancy works and why ships float. I know that every day many people travel on boats. I fundamentally understand the concept, yet the irrational part of my mind tells me the ocean is out to get me. The voice is loud. I hear it well and listen to it.

One day I was standing on a beach by the Pacific Ocean. The weather was calm. The waves were, well, there weren't any waves—just a gentle swell. The sky was blue, the day warm, and the day perfect. Feeling completely secure, I went to the edge of the ocean and yelled, "Here I am, ocean! Come get me!" In the next instant a wave rose out of nowhere and soaked me head to toe. The receding surge tried to pull me out to sea. I know, because I felt the strong tug at my feet. When I say the ocean is out to get me, I genuinely mean it. I don't know why. I have no idea what I did to it. I try my level best to give the ocean a healthy amount of respect and keep my distance whenever possible.

All this information is a long way of telling you how nervous I was to be on a ship on the ocean, entirely at its mercy, especially knowing the sea has it out for me. On the plus side, the Inside Passage is almost always calm, and I would constantly be in sight of land. I might not be an Olympic swimmer, but I reasoned that when the ocean grabbed me, I had a fighting chance to make it to shore. I kept a wary eye out for hundred-foot-tall rogue waves and other such dangers the entire voyage. I held on tightly when walking around on the boat, but was ready to let go so I wouldn't be pulled under when it sank suddenly. I sneaked sideways glances at the ocean to see what dirty tricks it might try. I was ready, and it wasn't going to catch me unawares. Not coincidentally, the captain spent the whole trip being much amused by me. It didn't help that he told me from time to time that he wasn't sure the boat would stay afloat. It wouldn't do for me to be completely relaxed.

I'll save you the worry and let you know now that the ocean did not get me. Not that time, anyway. I am still wary of it. It is biding its time and trying to lull me into a false sense of security, but I know better. Oh, I know better.

Before leaving for Alaska, I went to the drugstore and purchased all the Dramamine the store had, including the generic brand. I purchased anti-nausea wristbands and a couple of homeopathic remedies as well, being deathly afraid of being seasick. The look of the person staffing the security scanner at the airport was priceless. He and I exchanged knowing glances, and I wanted to ask him if the ocean was out to get him too, but I refrained. As it turned out, I didn't need any of those precautions and took well to the boat, almost as if I had been born to the sea and was coming home. The movement of the ship felt natural to me, and within moments I had my sea legs. The rhythm of the boat and the waves felt entirely right to me. I gazed across the ocean as if it were the most ordinary thing to do, and I felt a sense of belonging. I need to ponder the revelation, but I'll save it for some other time.

We headed off into the waters of the Inside Passage in search of glaciers. The first stop would be the LeConte Glacier, a short distance away on calm and sheltered waters.

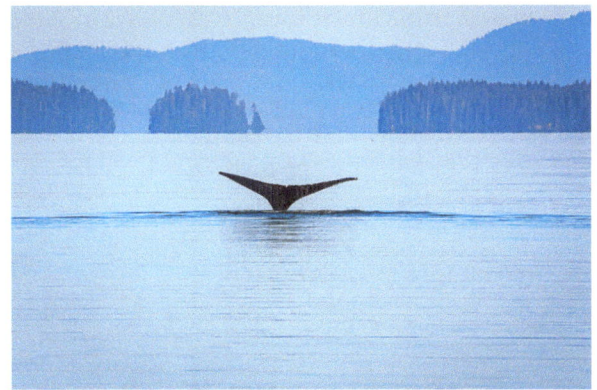

Whale Sighting

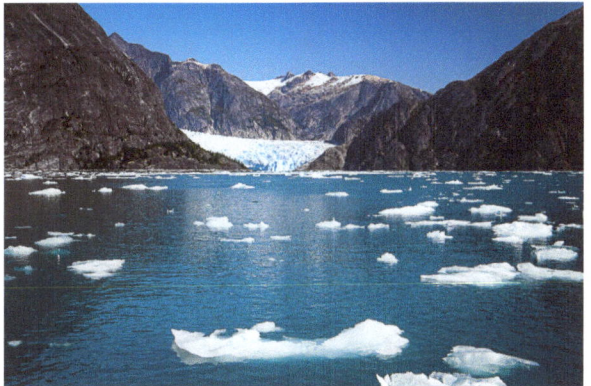

Approaching LeConte

LeConte Closeup

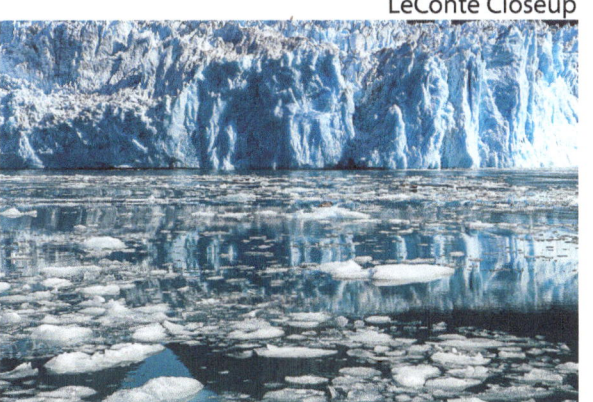

Even before I could get fully settled into the boat, the captain called "Whale!" I rushed to the side, and sure enough, I saw a whale tail slip into the deep. I was awestruck and speechless. Before my eyes a humpback whale paced us. It surfaced, dived, surfaced, and then descended again and again. I am sure the whale's appearance was pure coincidence, but I found it inspiring to share the opening part of the journey with a behemoth of the sea. Watching it move along with us, I knew I was in the right place, even if I was on the water. The whale finally dove and didn't reappear.

It didn't take long to arrive at LeConte Glacier. The closer we came, the more chunks of ice we saw floating. Those icebergs, like all icebergs, have a little bit showing above the water with the bulk below the waterline, and like all icebergs, it is not a good thing to crash into them. The captain carefully and precisely weaved through the ice field until before us the glacier creeped out of the valley and terminated in the water.

We continued our approach, being even more careful. Although the day was calm, the closer we came to the glacier, the colder the air became and the more the wind increased. When we neared the glacier, the winds became steady and significant, a perfect example of highly localized weather. The air remained continuously windy until we retreated from the glacier.

With the glacier before us, we set the anchor and waited, watched, observed, and enjoyed. Sea lions perched on the larger ice pieces, at peace, enjoying the warmth of the sun. Seagulls fluttered about while some landed on the water and on the ice. Impressive and imposing blue ice decorated the glacier edge. What looked small at a distance turned out to be massive when viewed up close, so big it distorted my sense of scale.

LeConte Glacier is the southernmost moving mass of ice that terminates in the ocean on this side of the equator. That's a mouthful, but it is the glacier's claim to fame. About twenty-one miles long and up to a mile wide, it represents an impressive amount of ice, especially when it fills your entire field of view. It definitely provides a sense of your pitiful place in this world.

Even more impressive was the glacier calving. Now and then the glacier calved, or dropped, a piece of ice. Most were relatively small. Some were not. After a loud crack that sounded like a rifle shot, the ice plunged into the sea with a muffled crash, creating a low wave. I could see the wave coming. It bobbed the sea lions lounging on the icebergs ahead of us and then it reached us, rocking the boat.

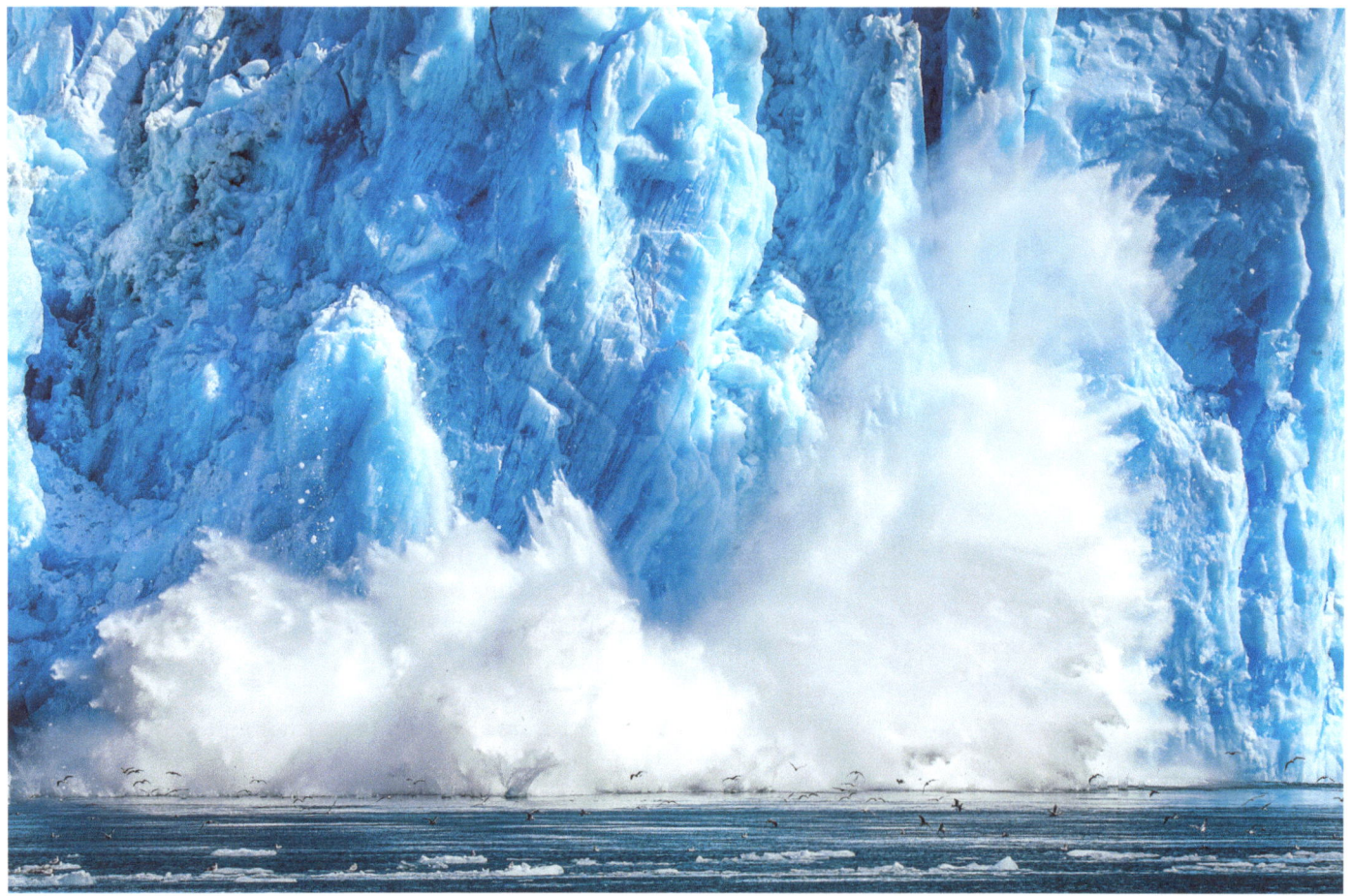

Glacier Crash

When the more significant pieces calved, the splash was quite impressive, as was the resulting wave. The ship tilted and rolled as if we were on an out-of-control roller coaster, but for only a few moments. Once the wave passed, all was calm again. Sometimes the boat rocked so much that I wondered if I would be thrown into the water, but it never happened. Whew!

The entire experience, as impressive as it was, made me more than a bit nervous. Some of the calved pieces were huge, and I was glad we weren't any closer to the edge of the glacier. After a while I became accustomed to the glacier calving, and I settled into the routine. The photograph *Glacier Crash* depicts a significant chunk of ice sloughing off the glacier; the birds at the base of the glacier give the image a sense of scale. Yes, I braced myself when the resulting wave swept toward us, and held on tightly as the boat rocked in the wake.

Unfortunately LeConte Glacier is melting and retreating at an alarming rate, and it is losing more ice than it gains through snowfall. Although it is still an impressive glacier, it is losing its battle and could disappear one day. I'm glad I experienced it.

As we headed away from the glacier and back into the Inside Passage, we cruised past several enormous icebergs. One of the icebergs looked something like a ship plying the waters. We gave it a wide berth, in case it extended farther out below the waterline than we saw. I gained a healthy respect for the icebergs and the trouble they could cause for the unwary sailor.

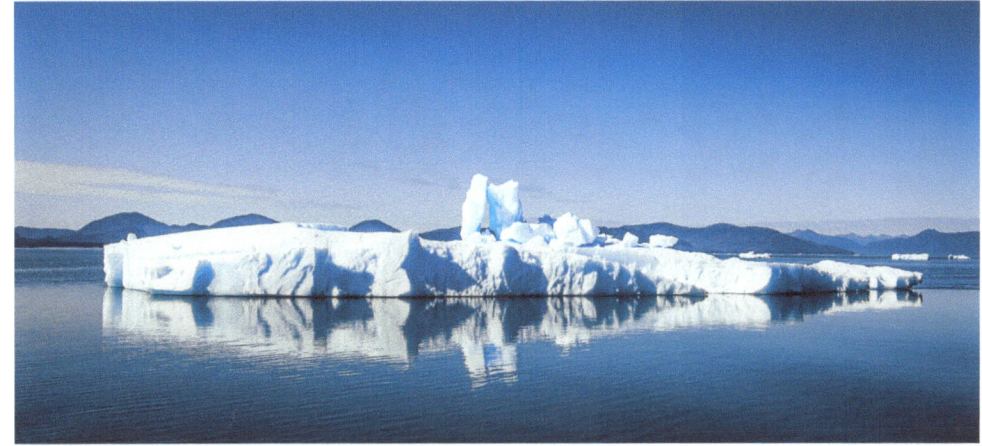

Cruisin' Berg

Most icebergs bobbed serenely in the waters, but one had a vignette I especially adored. The gull watching the two cormorants interacting, kissing, if you will, is priceless. Even among the gigantic glaciers, small moments of nature make me smile, and remind me that priceless vignettes are all around us.

Cormorant Kiss

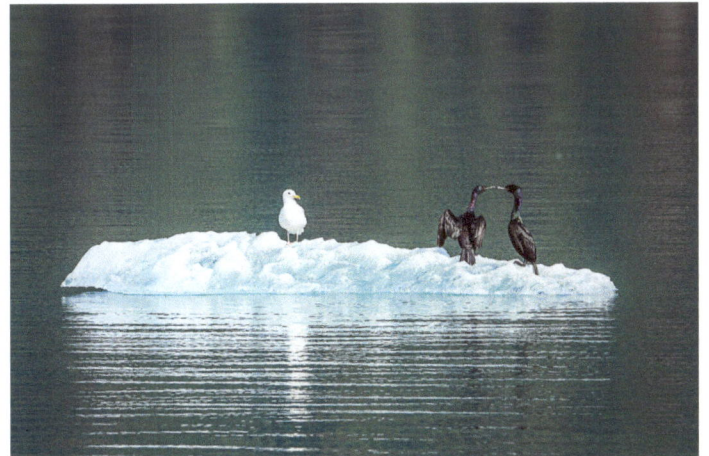

The next destination selected was Five Fingers Lighthouse and the opportunity to visit more humpback whales. We had a perilous voyage ahead of us, full of heavy seas. High waves would put our boat to the test, I felt sure. In actuality the day remained calm and the sailing uneventful. In any event, we were going to spend some time around Five Fingers, and I hoped the whales would be there as well.

Five Fingers Lighthouse is a crewless light station on a small island more or less in the middle of Frederick Sound, one of the main waterways of the Inside Passage. Not far from Juneau, the passage has a fair amount of traffic, including small fishing vessels, Alaska Marine Highway ferries, and even enormous cruise ships. The

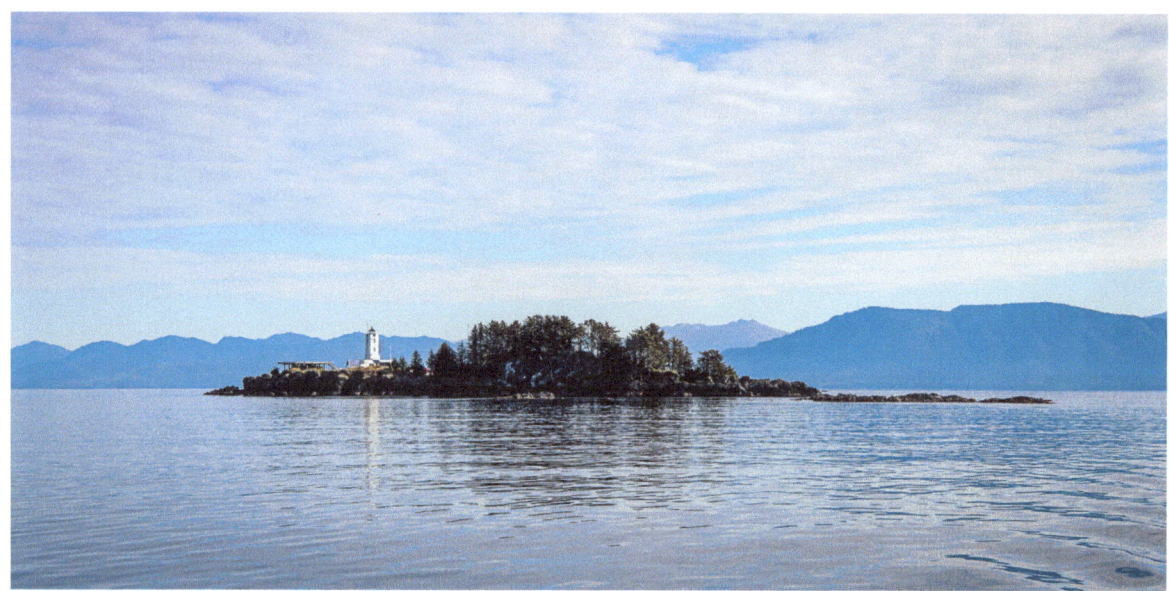

Five Fingers

light station is an essential navigational aid and keeps larger boats in deeper waters, plus it is a light station, so I was naturally attracted to it.

Five Fingers Lighthouse has a few small rooms where, in recent years, researchers stay from time to time. The accommodations could best be called sparse, but at least the building offers a roof overhead. The island was empty of humans when I was there, although some smaller ships occasionally landed with tourists. The island isn't precisely empty, but then again, neither did it have anything on it other than the lighthouse.

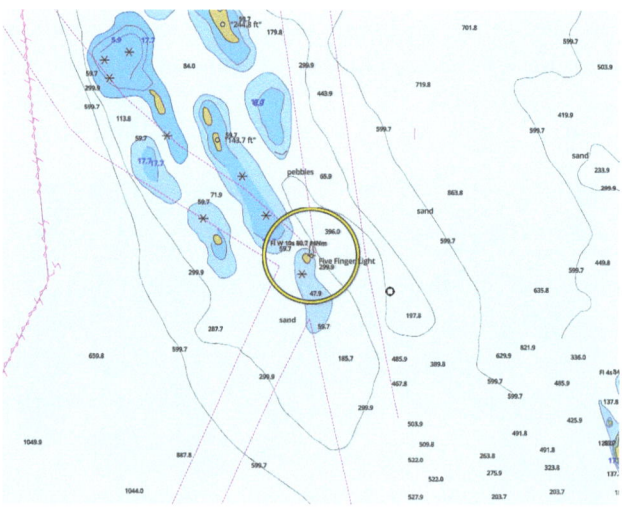

We anchored a little offshore and made our way onto the island. The landing was problematic, because the island lacks a proper dock, so we took a Zodiac inflatable boat over to the island and pulled alongside a jetty of sorts. We timed the waves just right and jumped out when the wave was at its highest point. If all went well we would be left standing on a concrete block. Our other option was to land on the rocky side of the island, seen in the photograph to the right of the island, but we would have had to scramble up the rocks. Either way, getting to and from the island became a mini-adventure in itself, yet each time, I made it without mishap. I felt a profound sense of relief when I set foot on solid land, even if it was a small island. Still, dry land is dry land.

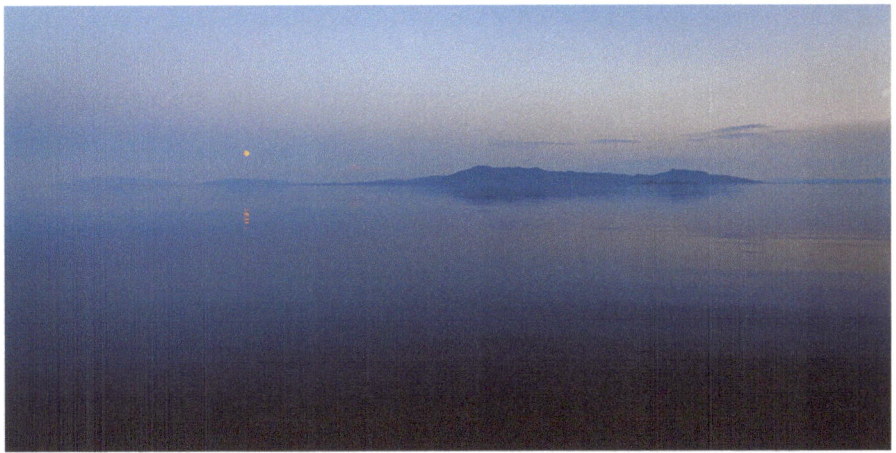

Frederick Moon

The island and my experiences there were marvelous. I spent the days whale watching, both from the boat and on land, or photographing a pair of nesting eagles that made the island their home. Evenings were quiet and tranquil. At that latitude the sunset lasted longer than I was used to, giving me more time to enjoy each one. The full moon rising over the sound made for an ethereal photograph, *Frederick Moon*, full of deep blues, perfectly capturing the moment. The moon reflecting over the calm waters reminds me to continue to reflect on the day, and every time I look at this photograph, I do. Even today, I can still feel the intensity, yet tranquility, of that moment.

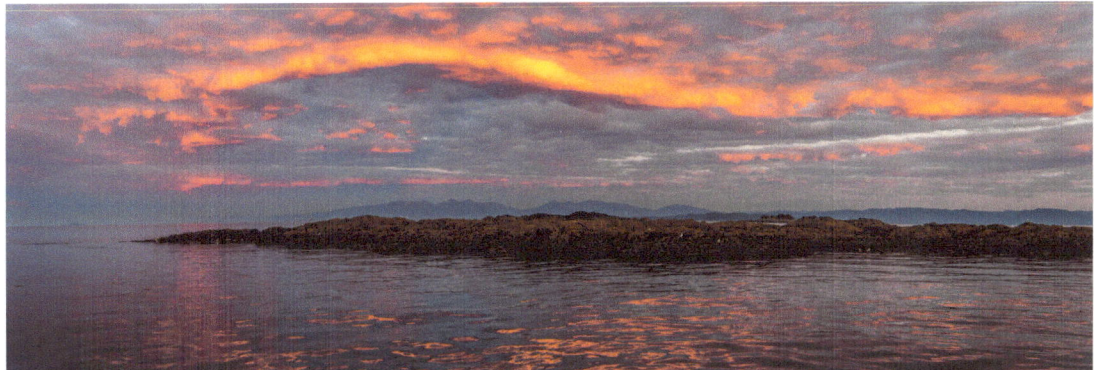

Passage Sunset

In stark contrast to the peacefulness of *Frederick Moon*, however, was the next night when I made *Passage Sunset*. A storm was brewing, and a roaring sunset and roiling clouds replaced the clear skies of the previous days. Still, even that evening had an absolute peace to it, although stormy weather was coming. The clouds reflected the last of the evening sun, which was not about to slip quietly and unnoticed below the horizon. The water reflected the turmoil of the clouds, and it was hard to tell where the clouds ended and the sea began. Eventually all faded to black when the evening won.

The highlights of the Five Fingers time, though, were the humpback whales and bald eagles. The waters there are deep, reaching down almost six hundred feet right off the island. The deep waters provide an excellent feeding range for the whales, and they come back year after year. And whales, well, the whales are worthy of a book to themselves.

I would wake up well before dawn, feeling the boat's rhythm and marveling that the ocean left me alone long enough to rest. The gentle slip-slap of the waves, accompanied by a small rocking motion, was the first thing I was aware of when I woke. The second thing I was aware of was the breathing of the whales in the pre-dawn darkness. I was hoping for the first thing. The second, I was not expecting.

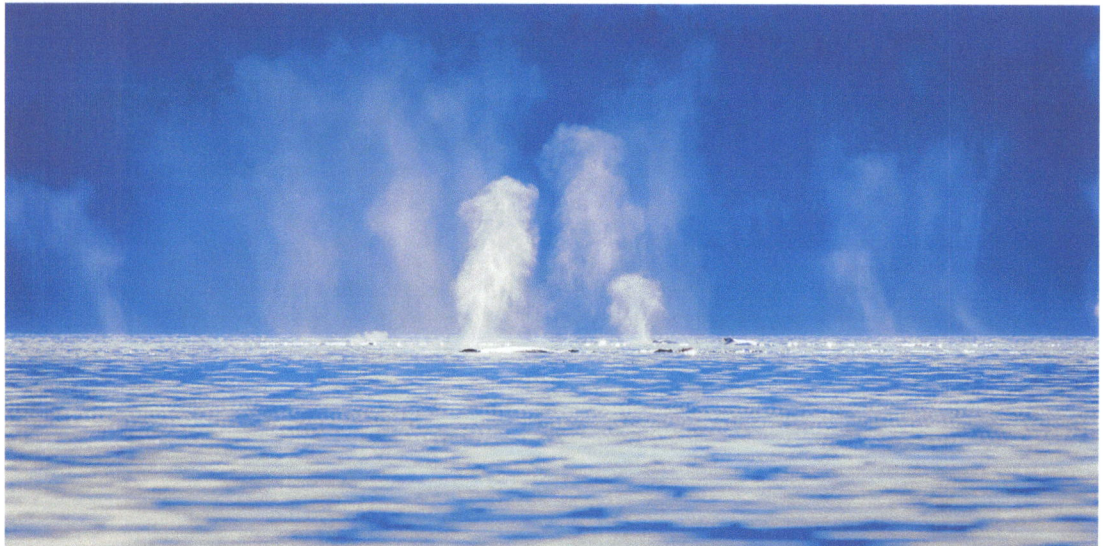

Vaporous Whales

I crept out onto the deck and sat quietly, the sole awake human for miles. From out in the darkness I could hear the deep breaths of the whales, an eerie and surreal sound. They sounded almost human, except much louder. I listened to one far away and then another behind me, and later, more left and right and then far out in front. Near me and far away and on and on, they breathed, in and out, slow and steady, deep and sure. Now and then I heard one slip beneath the waves, and later I listened to one come back to the surface, not as a crash, but as a graceful animal piercing the morning dawn. The sun rose slowly, giving light to the scene, and all around me I could see their breath plumes in the crisp morning air, the sun glinting off the resting whales' backs. I made *Vaporous Whales* in celebration of that morning. After a while I stirred and got up quietly, lest I add a human sound to a scene that did not belong to me, and stretched to shake off the morning stiffness and dew that had accumulated on me.

Later I was able to make *Whale's Morning*, thanks to a humpback whale's well-timed dive. The sun was having trouble clearing the low clouds of the morning, although it was able to cast a beautiful yellow light. As the sun rose above the mountains, the yellows reached their peak and reflected all around me. As I marveled at the scene, a whale dove, its tail

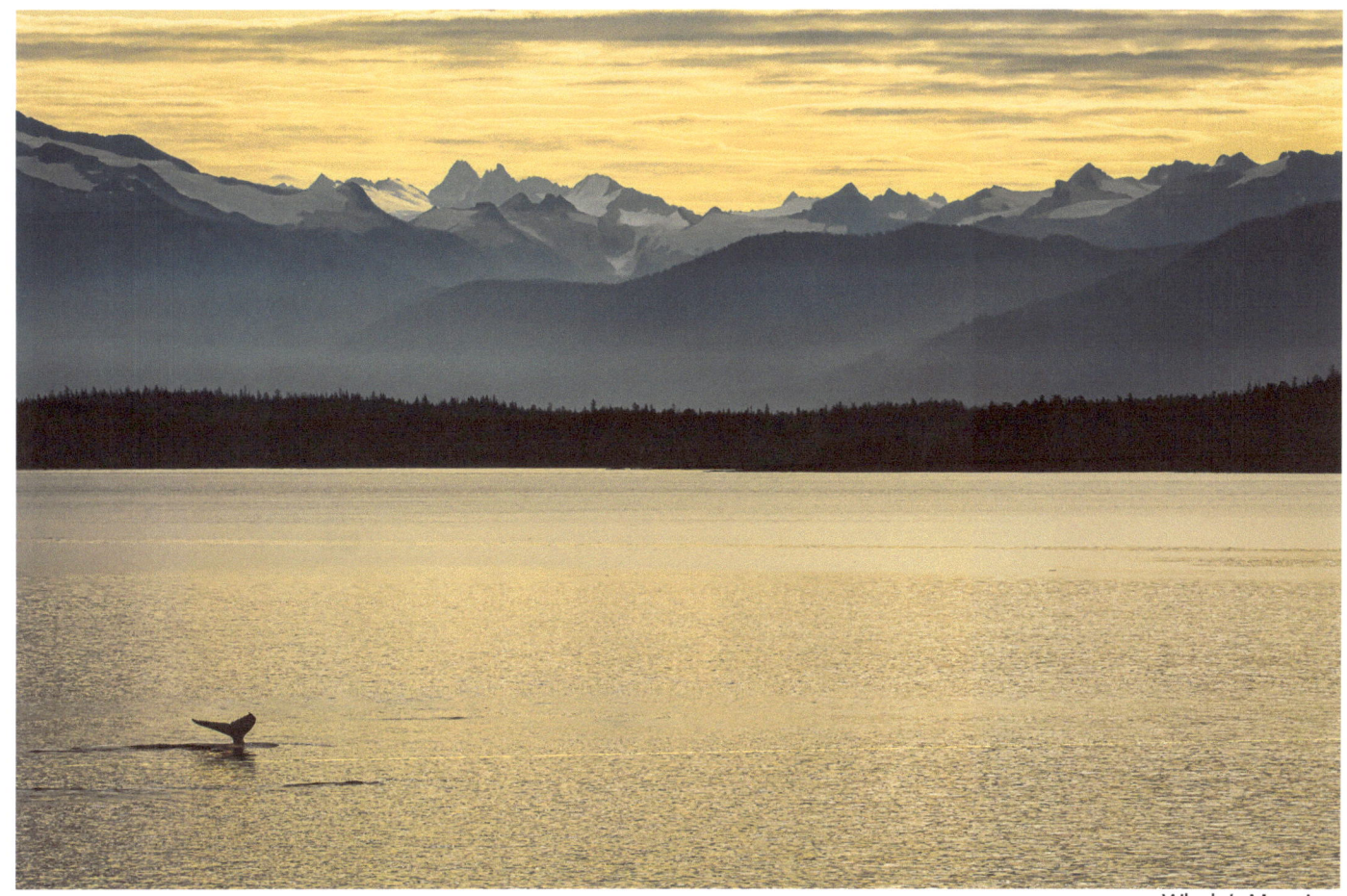
Whale's Morning

suspended just long enough for me to make the photograph. The image captures the majesty of the morning. This one photograph represents the Alaska experience the best among all I made.

The whales have been here forever, diving deep to forage and then surfacing again to catch their breath. That knowledge gives me a sense of wonder. To think of the endless cycles that have gone on here, some witnessed and most not, humbles me and helps me recognize our place in this astonishing world. It truly is my privilege and honor to preserve and present some of these moments. I was not there the next morning, but I take comfort in knowing the whales were. I can still hear their breathing.

Watching the whales on the surface and diving for food is fascinating, but watching them breach the surface on their return is exhilarating. One moment the water is unbroken, and the next it roils as a fifty-foot whale reaches for the sky.

Sometimes almost all of the whale is out of the water, with just its tail remaining in the ocean. The venerable adage of what goes up must come down holds true, and the whales return to the water with a thundering crash and deafening boom. The crashes startled me until I became used to the sound. Watching the graceful whales twist and turn while in the air belies the sheer power of their breaches, although the resulting clamor quickly reminded me.

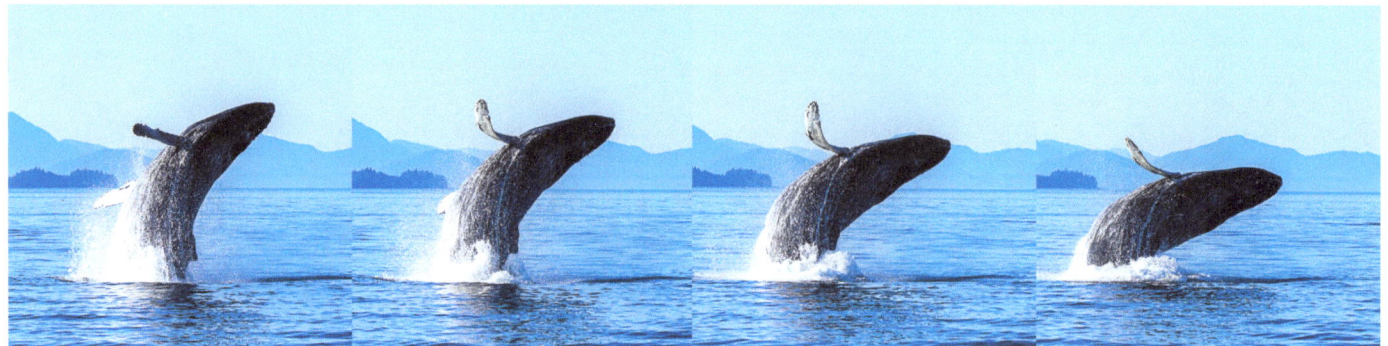

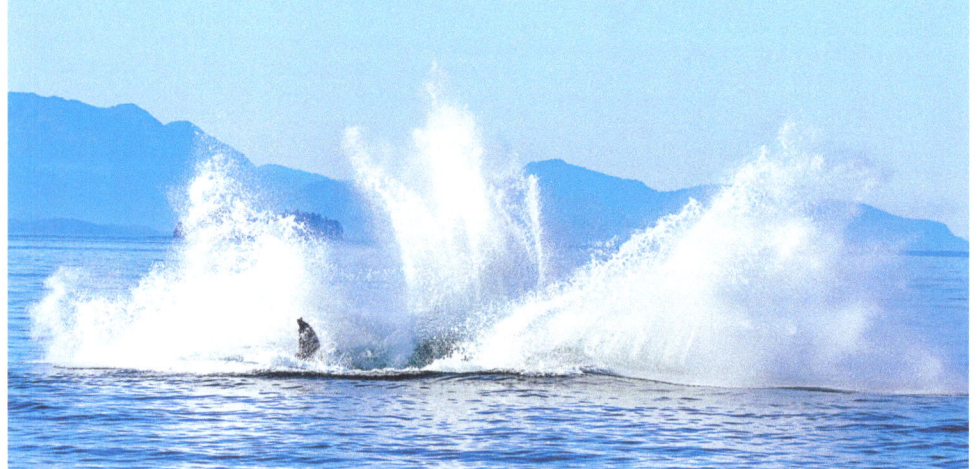

Humpback Splashdown

Headed Down

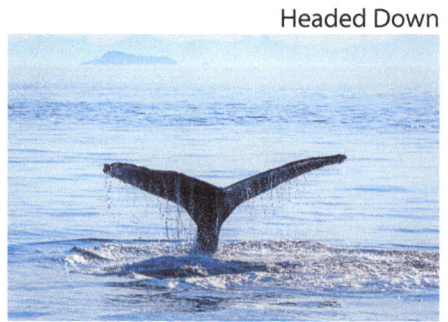

Most of the time the whales slide quietly below the waves, showing their tail for but a moment before disappearing. Sometimes the whales seem to show off, though, or perhaps just have fun. They splash their tails loudly on the water and sometimes repeat the gesture. After a while they settle down and simply loiter at the surface. I spent hour upon hour watching the whales and could have spent hours upon hours more. Luckily the whales accompanied me the entire time I was on the water, although I never got tired of seeing them. I'd look for whales first thing in the morning, and I'd look for them last thing in the evening, and always found their presence and companionship comforting.

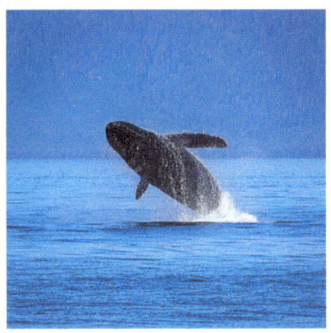
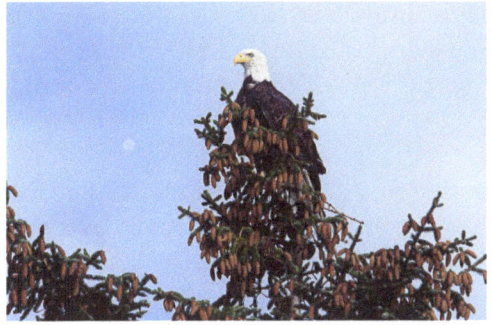
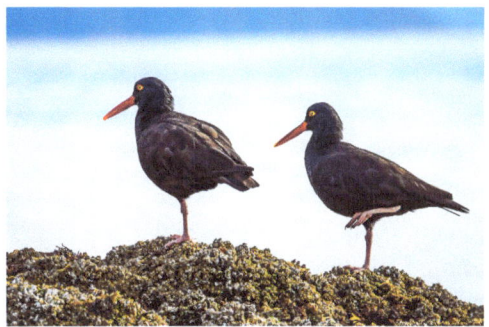

Joyous Humpback   Finger's Eagle   Finger's Oystercatchers

Whales were not the only thing to watch at Five Fingers. Eagles and other birds call it home too, and I had an excellent vantage point to photograph them. These photographs of an eagle and black oystercatchers are among my favorites. The eagle perched at the top of a tree and waited for me to make this photograph before flying away. Oystercatchers are colorful birds that are fun to watch. Their eyes are something else too.

It was time to depart Five Fingers and begin the next part of my adventure looking for bears on Admiralty Island.

Fingers Morning

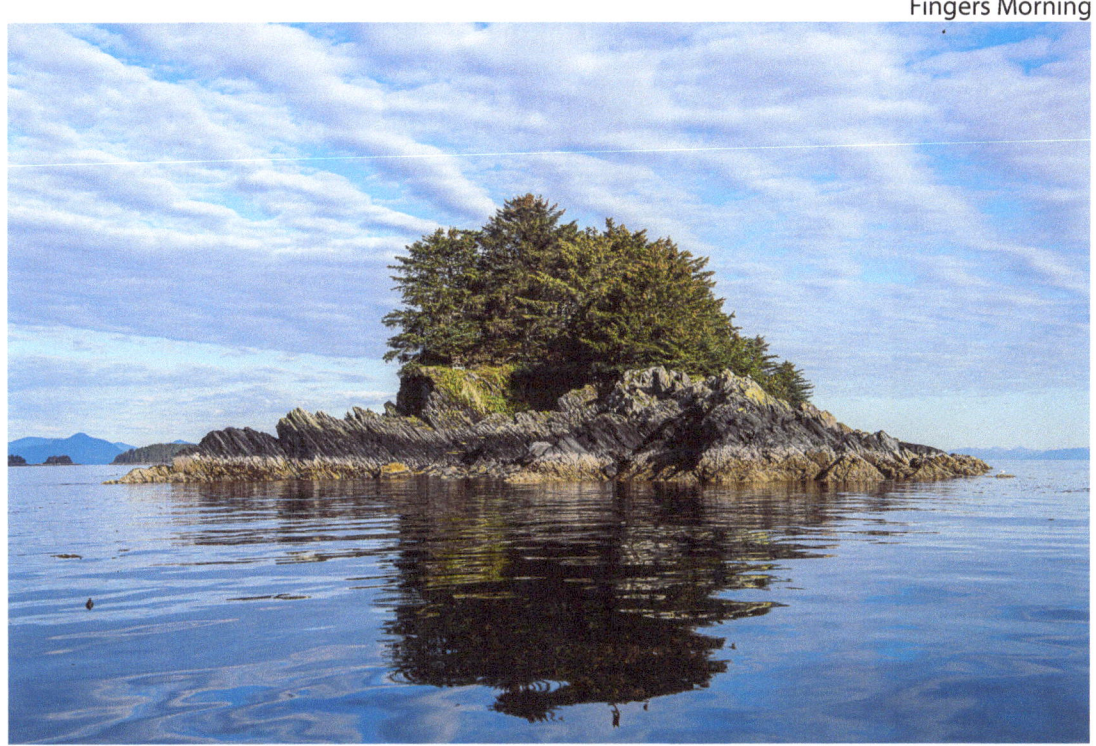

Admiralty Island has one of the densest bear populations anywhere, and since I wanted to photograph bears, it became a prime destination. An estimated one bear per square mile might not sound like much, but bears are abundant on the large island. It is not like you will encounter a bear every time you set foot on the island, but you have outstanding odds of finding one or more when you go looking for them.

Admiralty Island is the seventh-largest island in the United States, with a little more than sixteen hundred square miles. It has a small full-time population at the southern end of the island, although I would not go anywhere near there. Most of the island is a National Monument, and the vast majority is undeveloped. The wilderness is pristine and untouched by man. It has no trails, no docks, no infrastructure such as cell phone towers, no developments, or anything else that we have come to expect. Once you step off the boat, you are on your own. I was seeking isolation and remoteness, and that is exactly what I found.

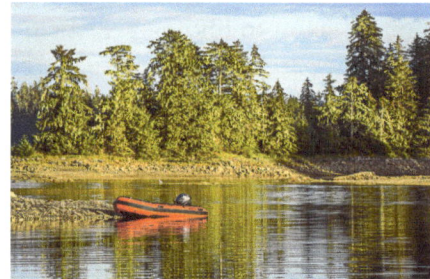

I timed my trip with the running salmon, knowing that the salmon would attract bears. The timing would make it easier for me, in theory, to find the bears, the entire reason I chose fall. My plan worked perfectly. How often does that happen? We sailed along the island coastline looking for protected bays that had one or more good-sized streams emptying into it. Such a location would provide protected anchorage and a place to explore for bears. We settled on a small cove that looked promising and set the anchor. The next morning, bright and early, I launched the Zodiac and headed to shore.

Waiting Zodiac

Once at the shoreline, I jumped out of the Zodiac and waded to dry land. Usually I find a rock or tree to which I tie the Zodiac securely, and then I have a small celebration for being off the water. Paying attention to the tide was essential, since it was either going out or coming in. Either way, the Zodiac would not be where it was left, and I needed to be careful to make sure it would still float when I got back. The last thing I wanted was to drag a heavy dinghy over a mudflat to refloat it because the tide went out, so I paid attention and stayed careful when disembarking.

Swimming Salmon

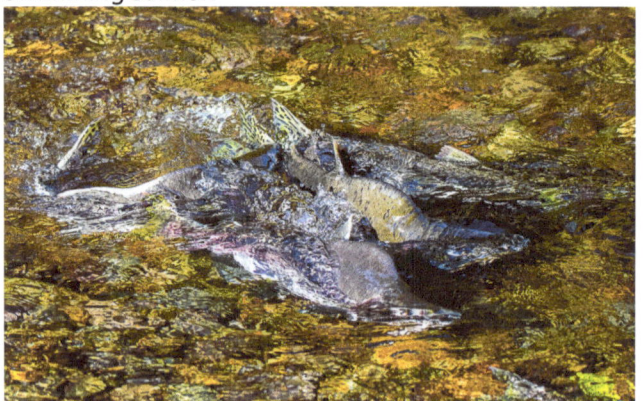

I found the stream terminus and took a hard look to see if salmon were in it. If salmon weren't at the creek mouth, I saw little point in proceeding, because bears were not likely to be fishing in those waters. On the other hand, if I saw salmon, I had a chance to see bears. By luck the first stream had a reasonable number of salmon, so I headed upstream to explore. Walking through a brook full of salmon is a wild experience. I assumed the fish would avoid me, thinking I was a predator. Quite the opposite was the case. The fish routinely ran headlong into me and got my attention when they bumped into my boots. It didn't take long to see that a bear would have little trouble catching a salmon.

Walking up that creek was a lot harder than it sounds, just like walking up Left Fork North Creek in Zion National Park was harder than it sounds. "Let's head upstream!" makes it seem like you can quickly and easily do it. The reality is far, far different. As in Zion, I could traverse the first few yards without any issue, taking care to avoid any large, slippery rocks. The farther I went, though, the more difficult it became. Downed trees blocked my path. I could sometimes go under them and sometimes go over, but I usually went around them. Going around an obstacle required bushwhacking, which is slow and tedious. High banks and deep water also slowed me down. When I encountered both downed trees and steep banks, I often ended up going way out of my way to get around that section. Once I was out of the stream, I had to clear the brush to make my way. Unlike Zion, if I was lucky I could find a game trail that made it substantially easier to move, but the game trail, which might or might not have been going to where I wanted, meant that I had to be extra careful that something else was not on the path with me. By definition, I was on a wild-animal superhighway, and I had to respect that fact.

I was alone on an island with rescue far away, if getting help was even possible, and I was explicitly looking for bears that could harm me if the situation went sideways. And the bears had far better senses than I do. I could not relax in that environment, not even for a moment.

Was it impossible to make my way upstream? No, not at all. Some sections were slow going, but in others, I made my way pretty quickly. All the while, I needed to stop and listen and be constantly aware of my surroundings. If all went according to plan, sooner or later, I would not be alone. The idea was to figure out the situation before the bear did.

I was looking for a place in the stream where bears caught salmon. Initially I thought the furry beasts would wade into the stream at any old spot and catch a fish. The reality was that they use the same ideal place time and again. They look for spacious areas with large banks that provide easy access. The dead giveaway was nearby salmon carcasses, which I smelled before I saw them.

While watching National Geographic TV at home, I'd seen bears fishing. The cinematography was terrific, and I felt as if I was right there with the bears. They caught and ate the fish and then sauntered off. What I didn't realize was that catching a fish is a violent process. The bears don't consume one hundred percent of the fish, and they don't clean up after themselves. Rotting carcasses litter the area, and it smells horrific. I won't dwell on this topic, but suffice it to say that I knew when I found a spot the bears used for fishing.

After a while I found precisely such a location. Bears obviously used it for fishing, and the dappled sunlight streamed through the trees. I found several sight lines I could use. All that remained was to find a suitable hiding place and wait.

Finding that ideal location was all I managed to accomplish the first day, which didn't seem overly productive. It was, though, excellent progress. I headed back out to the bay, relaunched the Zodiac, and spent the night on the boat. I knew exactly where to go, so the next day would be all about the wait. I tossed and turned that night, eager for the next day to begin. Even the eternal rocking of the boat couldn't lull me into sleep, but at last, somehow, I managed to slumber for a few fitful hours. I went over the plan again and again, and as long as the bears appeared, all would be well.

The day dawned clear and bright. The first portion of the trek was a repeat of the previous day's scouting mission, but it went much faster, since I had a specific destination. I even found an overland shortcut that saved a lot of time. Crouching behind a large fallen log, I began the long wait. I would wait all day if need be and the next day as well. Beyond that, I'd see when I got there.

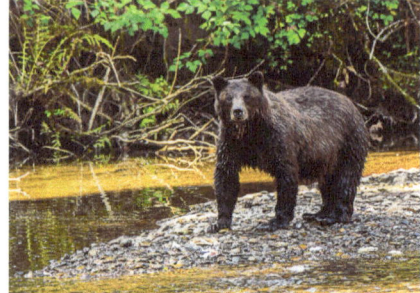

Inquisitive Momma

As it turns out I didn't wait long at all—perhaps thirty minutes. The bushes began rustling, and the leaves shook as a large brown bear ambled out of the woods and into the stream. Perfect! I started photographing her, when much to my surprise, a cub tumbled out of the brush behind her. What a stroke of luck! As I was recovering from that surprise, another cub popped out. Two cubs are far better than one, any day of the week. As if it couldn't get any better, a third cub slowly appeared. The last cub was smaller than the first two and more shy, but there it was, all the same. Momma bear didn't waste any time and waded into the stream. Not thirty seconds later, she had her first salmon, which she promptly delivered to the first cub. She repeated the process twice more and then retrieved a fish for herself. In under two minutes, all the bears had eaten and disappeared back into the forest.

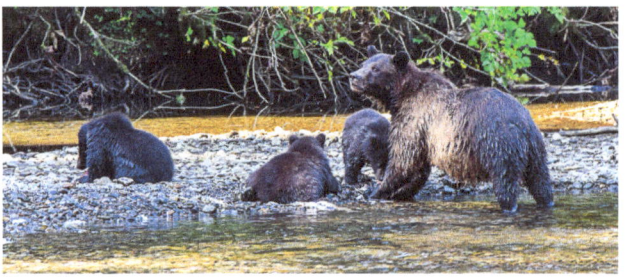

Bear Family

The four bears reappeared a short while later, and the process repeated throughout the day, all the while either oblivious to me or paying me no attention. Either way, I felt safe in my hiding place and was able to create several photographs. Momma Bear was excellent at catching fish, and her cubs were magnificent at devouring them.

Despite my good fortune, there was a classic "bear fishing" photograph I had yet to make. I watched and waited, yet the opportunity did not come. I continued my wait and eventually realized I would have to be a bit more daring to get what I truly wanted. I waited until the bears were finished feasting and wandered farther upstream instead of going back into the woods. Quietly and carefully, as cautious as I have ever been, I broke cover

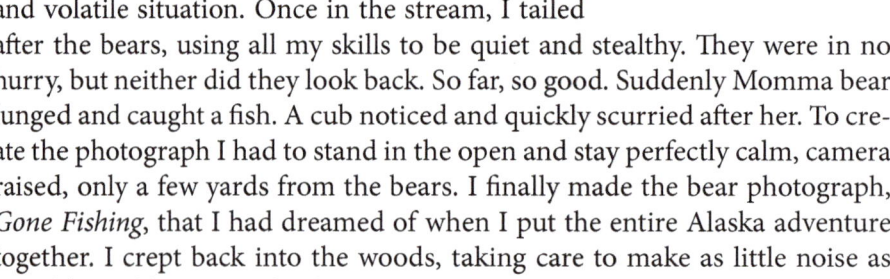

Fishing Momma

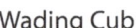

Wading Cub

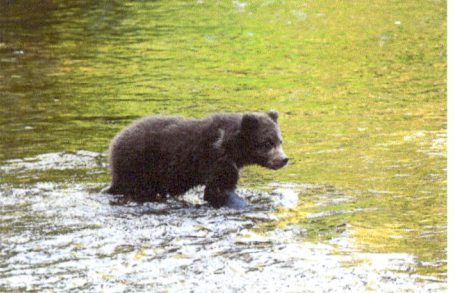

and went down to the stream. I was in a dangerous and volatile situation. Once in the stream, I tailed after the bears, using all my skills to be quiet and stealthy. They were in no hurry, but neither did they look back. So far, so good. Suddenly Momma bear lunged and caught a fish. A cub noticed and quickly scurried after her. To create the photograph I had to stand in the open and stay perfectly calm, camera raised, only a few yards from the bears. I finally made the bear photograph, *Gone Fishing*, that I had dreamed of when I put the entire Alaska adventure together. I crept back into the woods, taking care to make as little noise as possible, and kept out of sight.

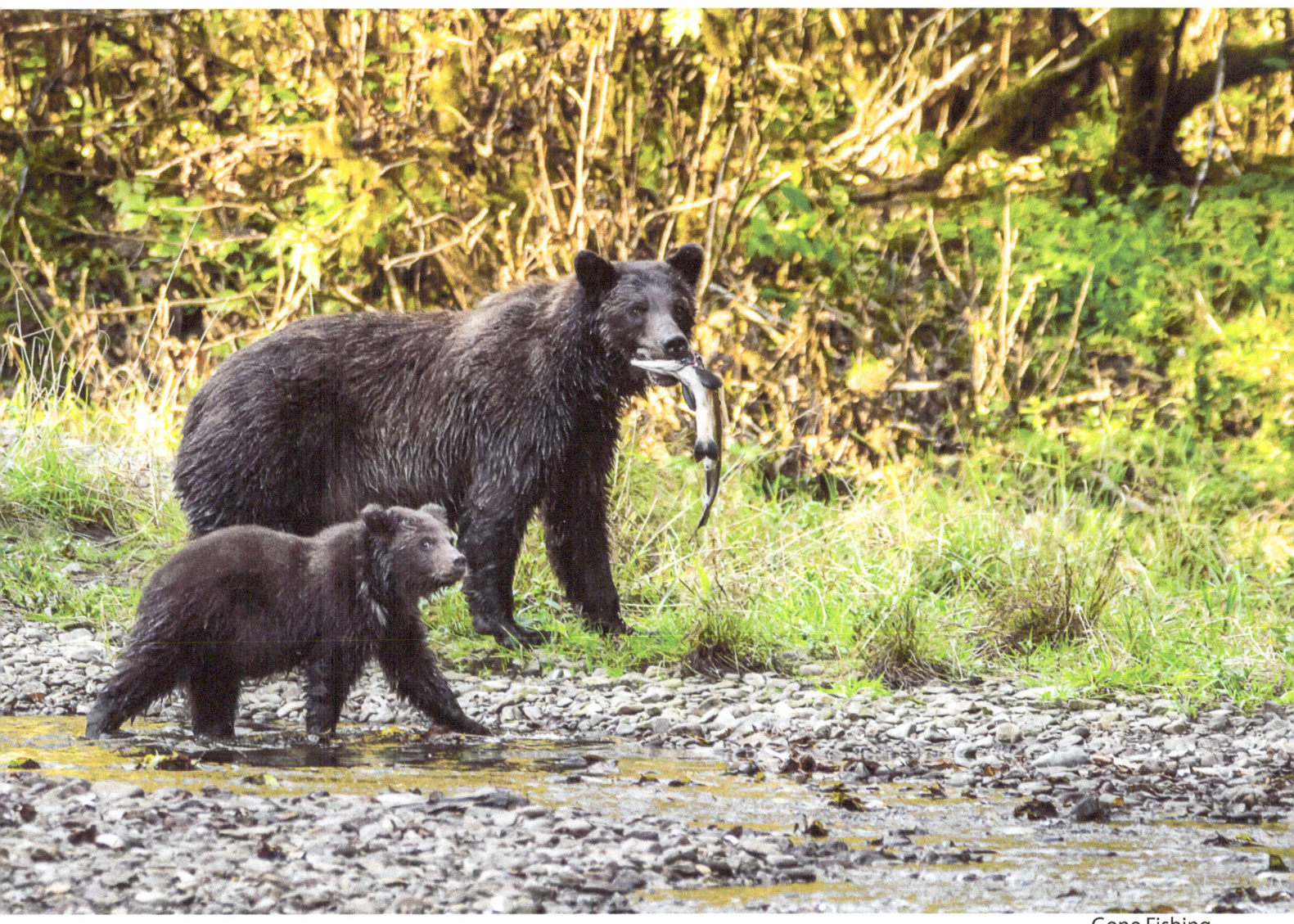

Gone Fishing

The photograph of Momma Bear and her fish was what I had dreamed of making when I first starting thinking about Alaska—the cub was icing on the cake. I was in the pure Alaskan wilderness, and those bears were not tame. They had likely never seen a human, and there were no rangers or protection for me. I wasn't on a platform or behind a fence. Locating the bears was up to me, and success, or failure, was mine alone. I was standing right there with the bears, and it was entirely up to me to make or not make the photograph I desperately wanted. It was a powerful experience and one that defines me as a photographer.

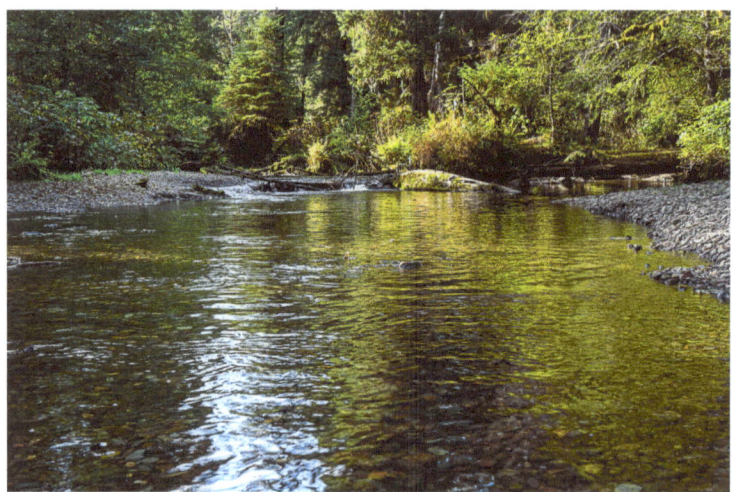
Admiralty's Stream

Admiralty Island is a gorgeous wilderness. This photograph, made just around the corner from where I made *Gone Fishing*, illustrates how tranquil the stream is during the late afternoon. Not all the streams look like this one, but it is possible to find intimate, picturesque scenes, and it reflects the feeling of the untamed and pristine wilderness.

I continued to explore other streams on Admiralty Island; however, none were as productive for me as the first one. Oddly, the streams I most expected salmon to be in were empty of them, and none of the other ones had any signs of bear. The lack of more opportunity meant that I needed to explore more, but alas, it was time to head toward Juneau. I am grateful for my time on the island, thankful that I was able to make the photograph I hoped I would, and grateful that I was able to do it safely and without incident. My time on the island reached its end, and it was time to complete the adventure. The fact that I had to sail for my final destination, Juneau, didn't mean I had to be quick about it, though. I wanted to stop and explore a couple of places first.

One of those locations was Taku Harbor and the old fishing cannery ruins there. More precisely, pilings left from the San Juan Fishing and Packing Company processing plant, which was built in 1901 and dismantled in 1947. Preceding the plant, the harbor was home to Fort Durham, a trading post from the mid-1800s. More importantly, the port has always been home to native Alaskans. Harbor communities have come and gone over time; it is currently used for fishing and as an overnight anchorage for boaters. For me, though, it provided photographic opportunities.

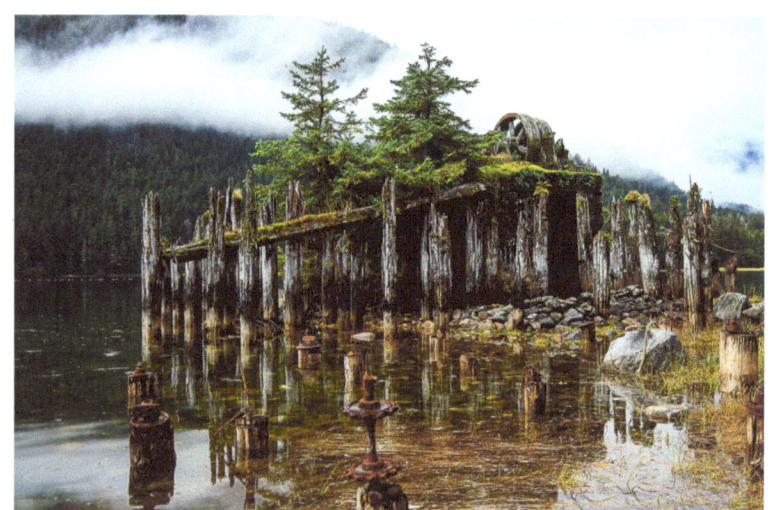
Taku Cannery

Although the plant is long gone, the pilings remain. The rotting logs hold up a rickety platform with old machinery on it. It makes for a compelling and dramatic image, almost abstract, of days long gone. Over the years people have collected odd bits and pieces and arranged them on some of the low posts. The low-lying clouds add a touch of moodiness to the image. The entire result is *Taku Cannery*. I spent hours exploring this area, hearing the echoes of the past. I also heard echoes of bald eagles.

The harbor is home to a pair of bald eagles. They wheeled overhead, at times landing so I could get a good look at them. Tall trees surround the harbor, providing an ideal resting place for eagles and an exemplary backdrop for me. I made full use of it, especially in *Eagle Perch*.

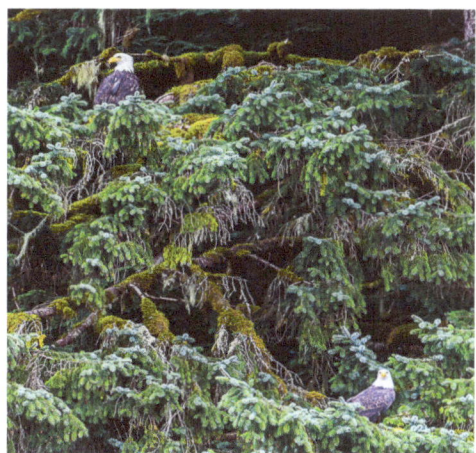
Eagle Perch

The intermittent rain also allowed me to photograph a very soggy bald eagle. I watched one of the eagles endure a rainstorm that unexpectedly developed. One moment the day was dry, and the next moment found us in a torrential downpour. The eagle didn't flinch, but it didn't look happy about

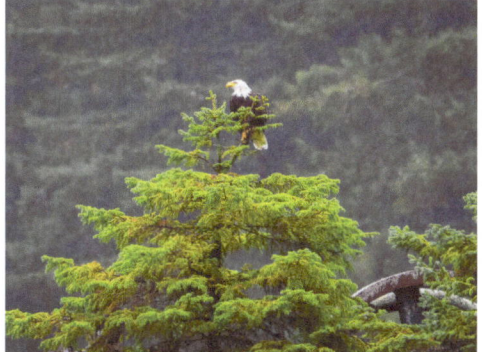
Soggy Eagle

being rained on, either. In Alaska rainy days are par for the course, and occasionally the eagle shook out its feathers and went back to watching for its next meal while trying to ignore the rain.

I don't know which I enjoyed more, photographing the cannery ruins or the eagles. Luckily I don't have to choose a favorite.

Back on the boat later that evening, I made *Passage Moon* with the rising moon. I was treated once again to a dramatic Alaskan sunset.

Passage Moon

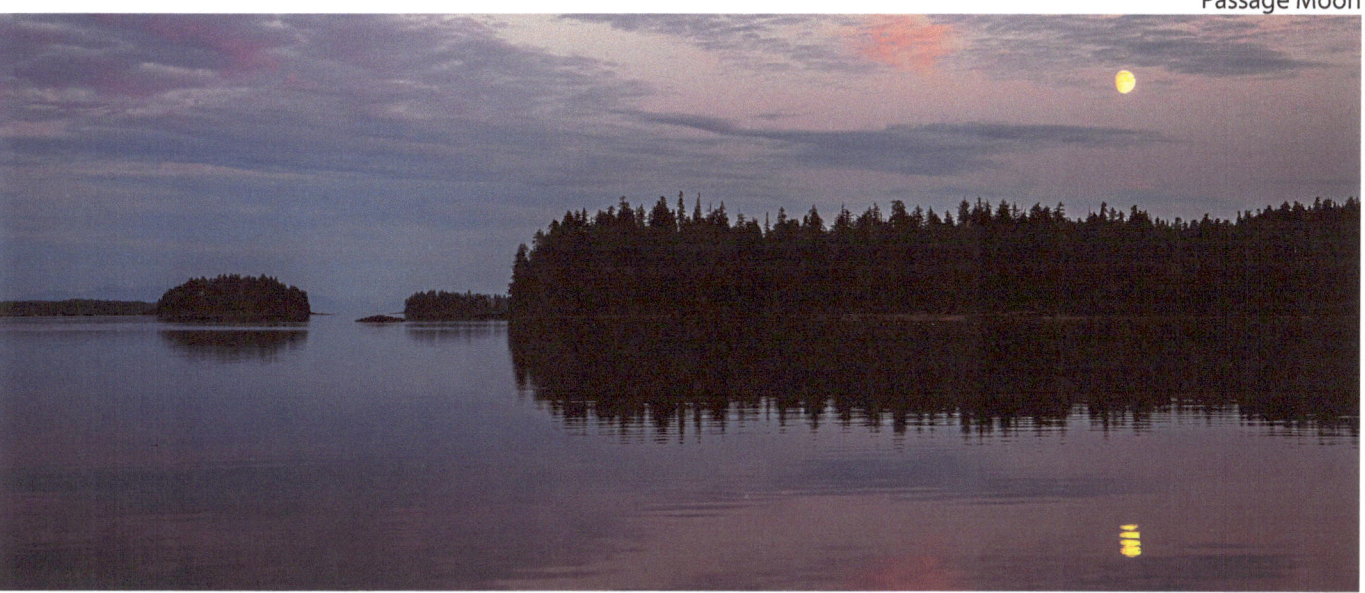

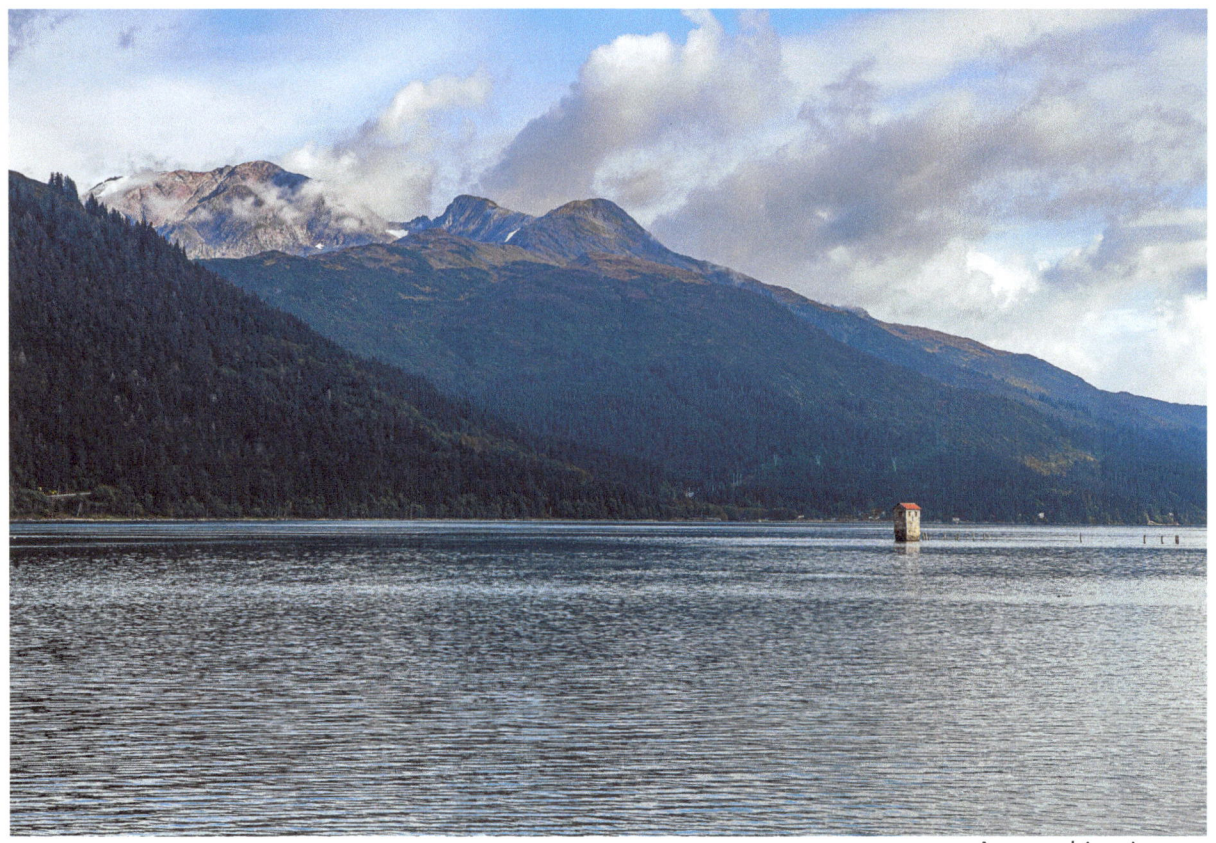
Approaching Juneau

Alas, it was time to sail straight for Juneau, which was a short distance away. The waterway coming into Juneau was as picturesque as I could ever want. An old mining building makes an interesting subject, so I took full advantage of it.

As soon as I stepped off the boat for the last time I missed the water. Dry land felt still and unmoving, and the sea beckoned. Regardless, I said goodbye to the captain. He was surprised as I was that I made the trip without falling prey to the sea. The ocean had its chance at me, and it passed, this time. There was no way I was letting my guard down, though, not even for a moment.

The sailing portion of my adventure worked exceptionally well, and I was grateful for the rare opportunity. Did I ever completely relax while I was on the boat? No, not really. I might make light of it, but I always had an underlying sense that I was in the ocean's grasp, even if the waters were mostly sheltered. Sheltered waters or not, they were deep waters. The sea and I came to a truce, however. Although I know deep in my heart that the ocean has it out for me, I also sensed it was willing to let me explore its waters. I found it interesting how quickly my sea legs developed, along with the feeling of belonging. Perhaps the ocean isn't out to get me as much as it is trying to pull me home.

As much as I wanted to ponder those feelings, there were still more photographs to make. I had learned about an eagle hot spot outside of Juneau that I wanted to explore, and it was readily accessible to me. I needed to make the most of the possibility. I found the area readily enough, and sure enough, the eagles were there.

I set up my equipment and began my vigil. Bald eagles are interesting to watch, but they are not in constant motion. Their flight is concise and to the point, and then they find a suitable perch and patiently wait. They will sit on a branch, rock, or whatever they find to rest on, looking in all directions, sometimes for more than an hour before deciding to move on. Photographing eagles is an exercise in patience, as I must remain ever alert and ready to spring into action. Then again, spending a couple days watching eagles is marvelous in itself.

It was in Juneau that I made *Intense Eagle* and *Eagle Call*. I watched this particular eagle for an entire morning and into the afternoon. During that time I had worked out the perfect vantage point as the bird moved among the trees, and I took full advantage for these photographs. The raptor certainly knew I was there but largely ignored me. I stood still and didn't call any attention to myself, and we each settled into our routines. Making these photographs was an excellent way to finish my exhilarating Alaskan adventures.

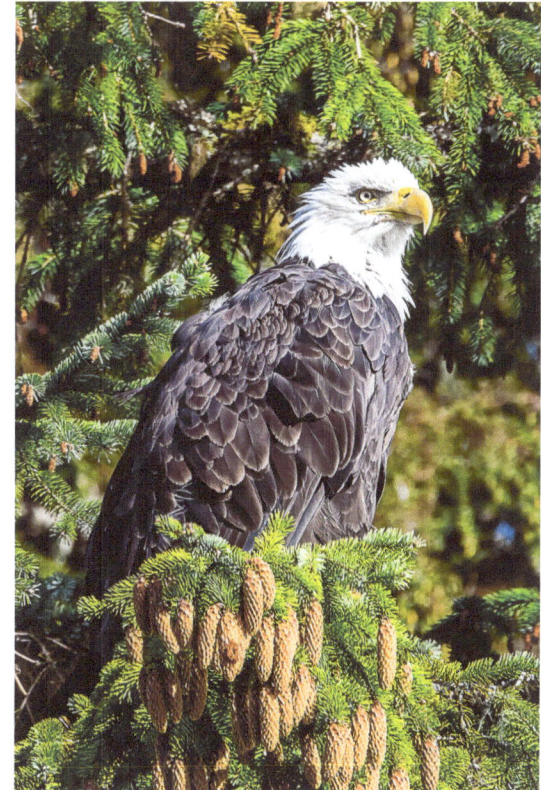
Intense Eagle

Eagle Call

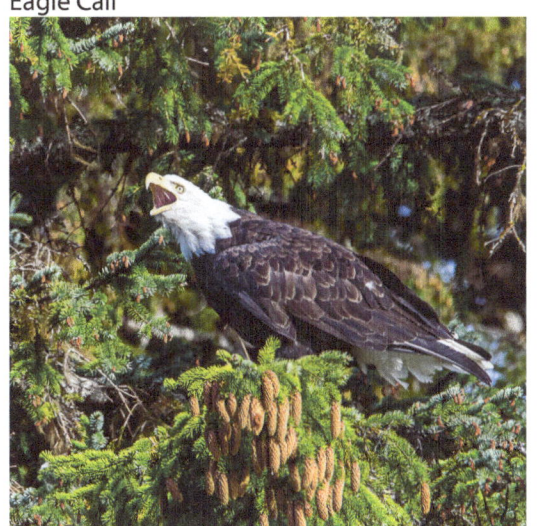

I often think about Alaska, and it has become a part of me. It is still a wild frontier with wild places, and exploring it, even a small portion of it, made me hunger to keep exploring and keep expanding my personal boundaries.

Alaska is truly an adventurer's paradise, but let's turn away from today's frontier to yesterday's frontier and venture into the ancient past of the Desert Southwest. As much as I adore Alaska's here and now, exploring and understanding the past has a special place in my heart as well.

Southwest Expeditions

The Desert Southwest is wide, vast, arid, and mostly empty. Echoes of the past are everywhere, though, a silent testament to the ancient people who called it home. The past's stories paint a tapestry of a rich and vibrant time. These photographs document some of my expeditions in the Southwest.

I've long been fascinated with the ancient inhabitants of the Southwest. The culture and traditions they created have endured for centuries and continue through today. They will continue, I am sure, for a long time to come. The structures they made also remain, although time has taken its toll on most of them. Even at that, it is remarkable how seemingly simple stone-block structures can survive through the ages to tell their stories. Luckily many of these buildings are preserved in places such as Mesa Verde National Park in Colorado, where we study, learn from, and experience them.

Not every building has been fortunate to survive, and untold numbers are lost to the ages because the land swallowed them, their bricks and blocks were repurposed, or people senselessly destroyed them. Such decay makes our national lands, the wilderness areas, forests, monuments, and parks all the more special, for without protection, our past fades away. Allowing it to happen is a tragedy of epic proportions and removes the past from our future. Thankfully our National Lands actively prevent complete erosion.

The principal ancient sites and pueblos of the Southwest, such as Chaco, Canyon de Chelly, Canyons of the Ancients, Hovenweep, Bandelier, and Mesa Verde have protected status as a national monument or national park. Each of these units is open to the public, so we can learn, explore, and tour them, all while protecting them. Protecting the sites is the best possible outcome; we are free to see the sites ourselves while ensuring our children and their children can do it as well. To prevent history from being lost, restrictions are enforced, such as no climbing on the walls and no taking anything as a souvenir. I've been to these locations multiple times, have photographed them more than once, and extensively researched all of them. I've also pored over ancient diaries and expedition notes from the modern-day people who "discovered" them. Much of my research has involved talking to experts in the field. I have enjoyed all of it, and I am always eager to learn something new about our history.

I am also eager to photograph these places in ways many do not. My challenge has been that the public, which sometimes means me, can be in only certain spots and only at certain times. For example, because a pueblo is protected, I cannot wander freely within it to create the perfect photograph. I am, understandably, confined to the same places as everyone else. Most of these sites even regulate the "when," and after-hours access is forbidden. Making an excellent photograph is about the "when" as much as the "where." Sunrises and sunsets are often the best time to make the photograph, yet these very times are when the sites are closed. Those necessary restrictions take away a powerful tool and prime opportunities, and are challenging to overcome.

Over the years, however, I've received special permission to be alone in a few of these places and created some exceptional photographs. An excellent example is *Abo Night*, which I made in the Salinas Pueblo Missions National Monument in New Mexico. I was alone at the ruins in the middle of the night, with the monument manager's permission. I wanted to create a photograph of the mission and remaining pueblo walls against a starry night sky and was able to accomplish that goal with this photograph.

The Salinas Pueblo Missions contain three units, each of which protects its pueblo and attendant Spanish mission. The site is a favorite haunt of mine because of the stark beauty and proximity. It's close enough to where I live that I can and do frequently visit. If I am thinking through an issue or just need to get away for a while, I head there. I ask the empty

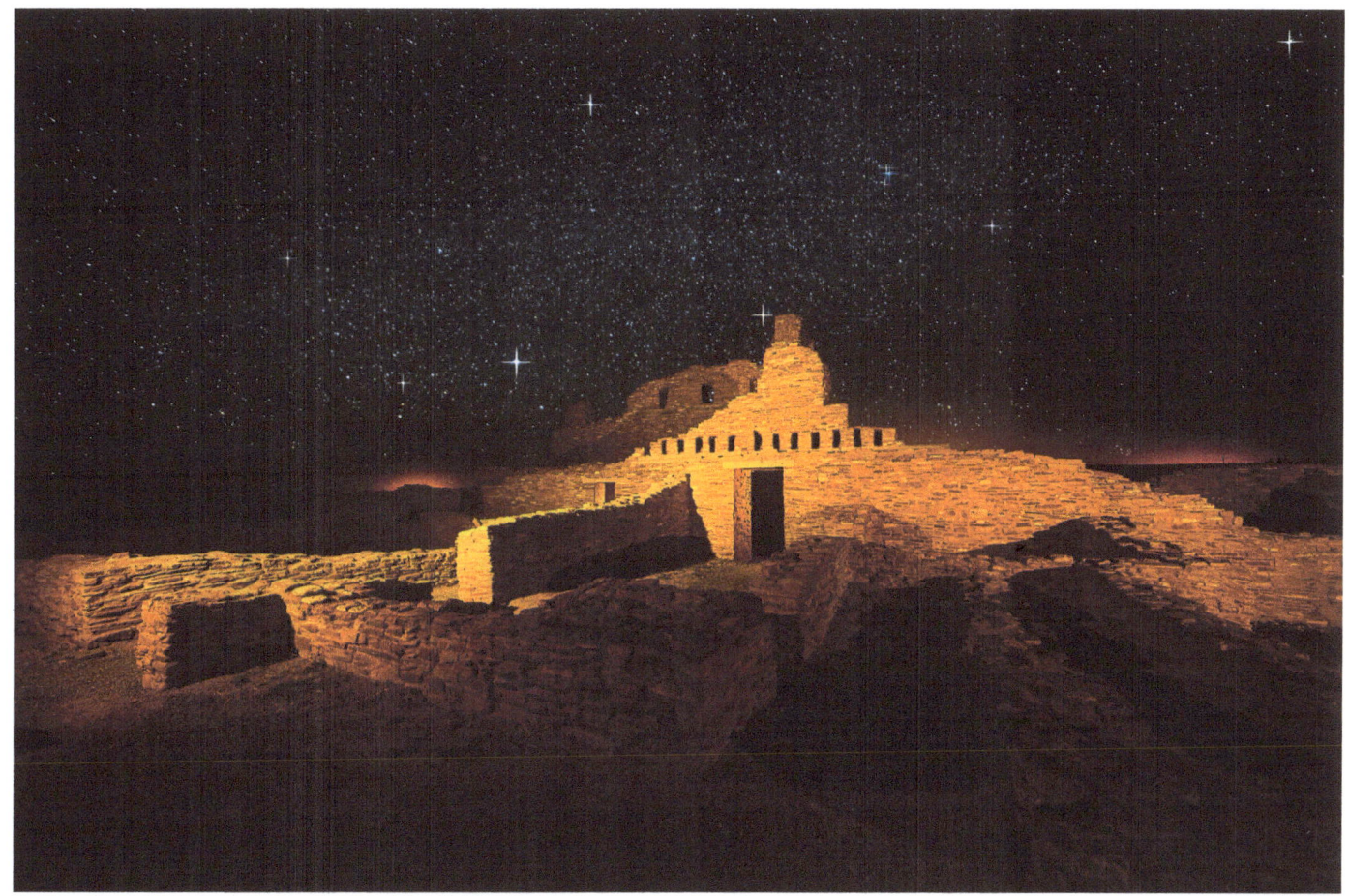
Abo Night

walls the questions I am pondering, and sometimes I receive an answer. What better place to photograph at night? I set off on a clear night to make the photograph happen at the Abo unit.

Getting there was as easy as driving up the paved road and parking. I could, and did, bring everything necessary to light up the mission and pueblo. Because the parking lot was at the pueblo, I could take all the time I needed without having to carry everything in and then back out of the location. If I wanted a different light, switching it with another was quick and easy. If I wanted to make the light higher, I replaced it with a higher stand. I fiddled and fussed, moved a light mere inches, moved it back, and then moved it yet again. I looked, and I considered. I adjusted and aligned. The pueblo kept me company, perhaps being thrilled at once again having nighttime visitors. The silence enveloped me, for I was the only human there. I could feel, as well as see, the night deepening. It was a powerful, guttural feeling, yet I was not alone, in ways I could not explain. The sense of belonging and purpose was strong, and my thoughts drifted.

Long after the day's visitors depart, Abo comes alive, and its ghosts of the past live in the here and now. The shadows dance and play under the starlight, and whispers of the wind power them in their merry gambols. Facing the night alone, I found it easy to slip between eras and feel the pueblo and mission as they once were. Making *Abo Night* brought me to a time long ago when people called this place home, and the photograph is a reflection of then as well as now. Could I hear a conversation, and were people preparing to settle in for the evening? Or was it my imagination? The stars knew, but they said nothing as they continued to wink and twinkle knowingly.

Like in all places when I am alone, my imagination sometimes gets the best of me. When I was making *Abo Night*, I heard coyotes howling in the far distance and then in the near distance. The canines sounded mournful at first, but as I listened, I found their calls remarkably comforting. Perhaps they were keeping guard for me, or maybe they were on guard because of me. I focused on making the photograph I envisioned, and with the encouragement of the past, it turned out beautifully. After the midnight hour came and went, I packed my gear, checked to make sure I had it all, and then stood alone in starlight with the pueblo. I don't know how long I remained there. It was a timeless moment for me. I eventually broke the spell and made my way back home and to the here and now.

This photograph doesn't change the case that most of the time, photographing a pueblo or ancient ruins differently from anyone else is a challenging proposition. Now and then, though, an opportunity presents itself. Such is the case in Colorado's Mesa Verde National Park. Twice, in fact.

Mesa Verde hosts an after-dark open house every December. As part of the celebration volunteers place luminarias, thousands of them, around the park pathways and then turn off all modern lights. The effect is enchanting, and while visitors stroll through the park, they step back in time to bygone days. Until recently the park set up lights outside and inside Spruce Tree House, one of the most easily accessible pueblos in the park. To see the pueblo lit up surrounded by luminarias is an impressive sight. The best views are on a ledge above the pueblo. When you look down and into it, lit only by lanterns, it's easy to imagine it fully occupied and full of life as its residents go about their daily life.

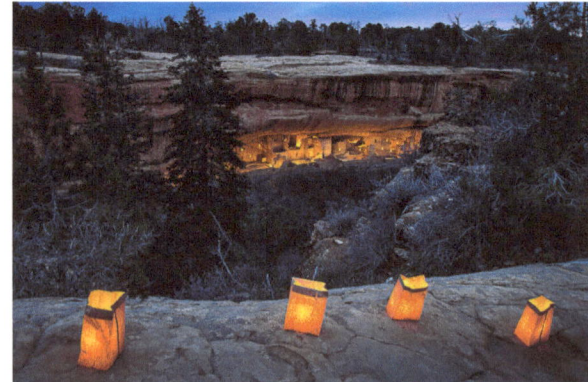

Spruce's Luminarias

Sadly, because of a structural fault in the rocks above the pueblo, the Park Service has restricted entry for safety reasons, and Spruce Tree House remains dark in recent years.

One year was different, though. The Park Service was one hundred years old, and every unit in the system wanted to acknowledge and celebrate the momentous event. Each unit celebrated in a way that made sense to it, and Mesa Verde was no different. In addition to the usual luminarias and lighting of Spruce Tree House, it also chose to light up Cliff Palace, one of the largest, if not the largest, pueblos in the Southwest. The effort was a labor of love for the park, not something the staff had to do. A large team of rangers and skilled volunteers took three days to carry in and set up propane and battery-powered lanterns. They had to carry them down the narrow, steep trail to the pueblo, which is not overly difficult when empty-handed, but was not easy when carrying a heavy propane tank. Each carefully placed light provided the illusion that the pueblo was occupied. The staff took their time, constantly mindful of the overall effect. They created the tableau for themselves as well as for anyone who viewed the final result. They were fussy too, which I deeply appreciated. They moved each lantern the slightest amount to remove or create a shadow. The rangers, experienced in lighting Spruce Tree House, wanted to outdo themselves with Cliff Palace. The event was a once-in-a-lifetime opportunity, and everyone involved wanted to make the most of it. The results were stunning.

I was like a moth to a flame for the event and made sure I was in position well ahead of time. I spent a day scouting for the best location, which turned out to be far away, across an arroyo. Bundled up against the cold, because it was December in Colorado, I waited for darkness to fall. Eventually it did, although it was hard for me to tell, when I was already shivering. Several thermoses of coffee and hot chocolate kept the cold away for a while, but not as long as I would have liked. A small crowd slowly congregated alongside me.

Darkness crept over the park, and the few of us who were there stopped talking. The silence didn't happen by any signal; we just slowly ceased chatting and stared at the sight. There, across the way, was the lit-up pueblo, as it must have looked a thousand years earlier.

Palace Light

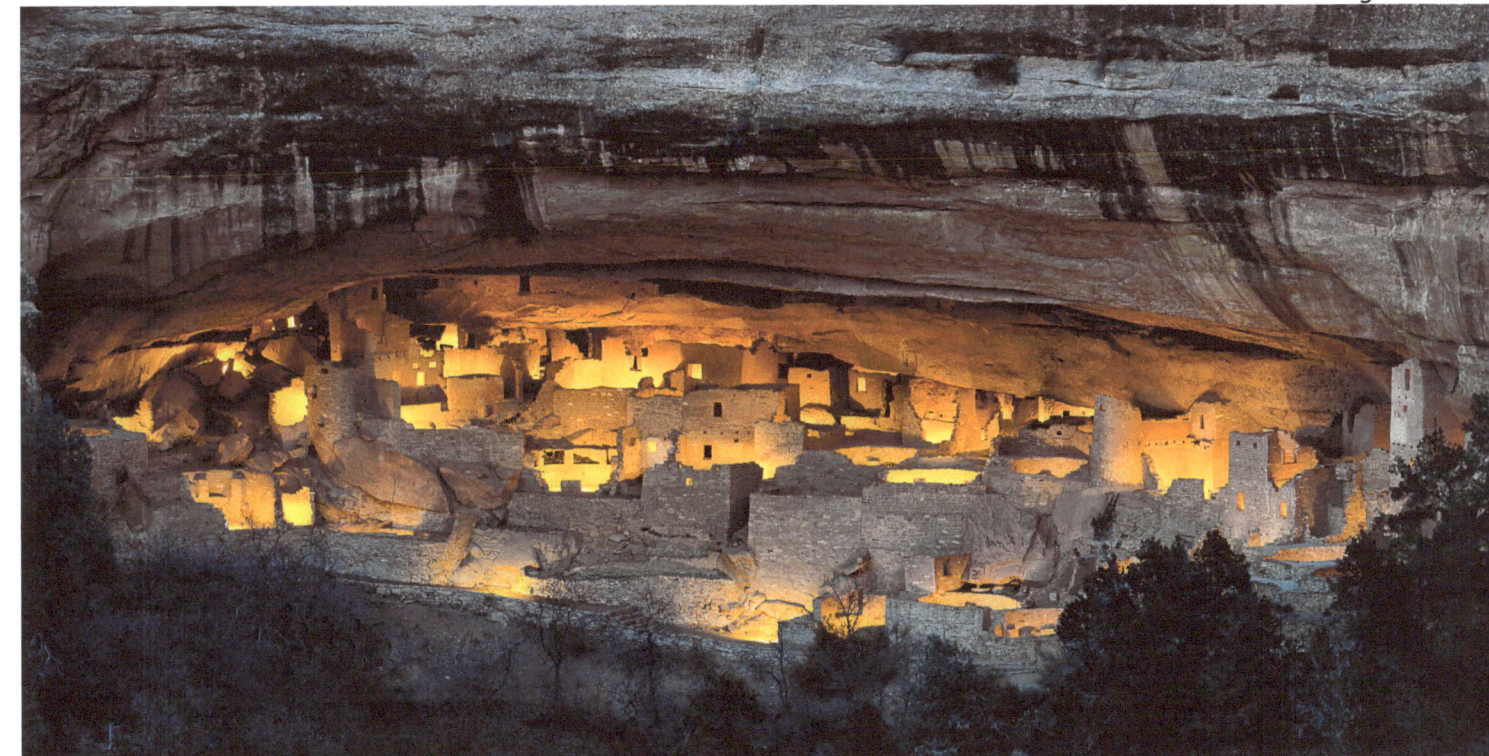

A photograph, if we are skilled enough, captures a precise moment in time. I had the chance to create one that captured a moment from a thousand years ago, though, and that day the illusion was complete. Each light had a complimentary color temperature to make the cliff dwelling seem lit by campfires and torches. Every light contributed to the overall effect and brought the pueblo to life. The completed effort was breathtaking. None of us found it possible to talk, merely observe, when the darkness came and the pueblo lights glowed and were transported back in time. The earlier cold was gone, and the shivers became ones of awe, not chill.

For that all-too-brief moment, I became part of that earlier era. I saw myself having been out all day hunting and gathering on a distant mesa, finally on my way home. The day had felt long, and I was tired. I looked forward to getting back to the warmth of home, for that night would be chilly. As I trudged along, eager to get home, I looked up and across the arroyo. There before me was the welcoming sight of the pueblo. Fires were burning brightly, and the faint sounds of daily life reached my ears. Was that one of my children waving to me from my window? Wondering what we would have for dinner, I picked up my pace, excited to be back home with the day's bounty. With a song in my heart and spring in my step, I made my way back home. This photograph, *Palace Light*, takes me back to then. For that moment when Cliff Palace came alive, the past met my reality of today.

There are no further plans to light Cliff Palace, making *Palace Light* even more special. I'm sure the Park Service eventually will, though, and I hope to be able to witness its transformation again.

Another opportunity came to me when *Notre Dame Magazine* was preparing an article for its monthly magazine. The feature would focus on archeology in the Southwest and Mesa Verde in particular. The editors had seen *Palace Light* and called me for permission to use it in the article. I said they could and asked if they wanted a photographer to go along with the photograph. The person laughed. We chatted a bit more and then ended the call. A little while later, the phone rang. It was an editor from *Notre Dame Magazine* again. The editor asked if I was serious about my quip, which is how I found myself attached to a writer and small team of archeologists in the back county of Mesa Verde.

The goal was simple: document the multi-day expedition for the magazine article. The editors had specific photographs they needed and trusted my eye to provide whatever else I thought would work. Also attached to the team was a park archeologist who would be our guide. She would take us to various locations in the park and then take us into the backcountry. The arrangement was right up my alley and turned out to be an epic experience. I had a rare opportunity to photograph the park from an entirely different point of view.

As a brief introduction to the park, a guide took our group into a couple of the cliff dwellings, including Cliff Palace and Long House. I'd been to Cliff Palace as part of a public tour, but this visit was something special. On a typical public tour, a guide takes a group to the front of the pueblo where you and fifty of your new best friends crowd around a small area. Creating a unique photograph in such a situation is challenging, but it is all you have, so you make the best of it. The Notre Dame expedition was different. We were able to explore the entire pueblo, alone and by ourselves. The back part of the structure is considered backcountry and off-limits, but our group had the appropriate permissions to venture there, and we were able to examine the normally off-limits nooks and crannies.

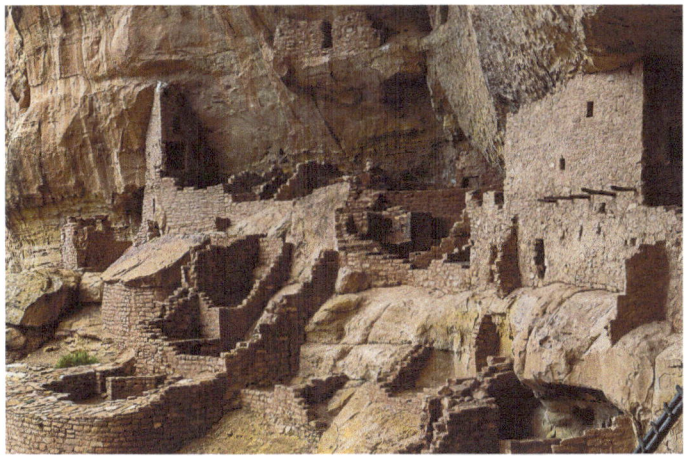
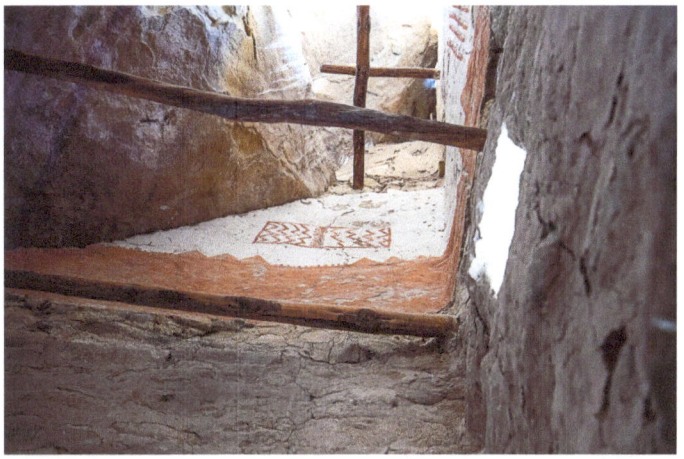
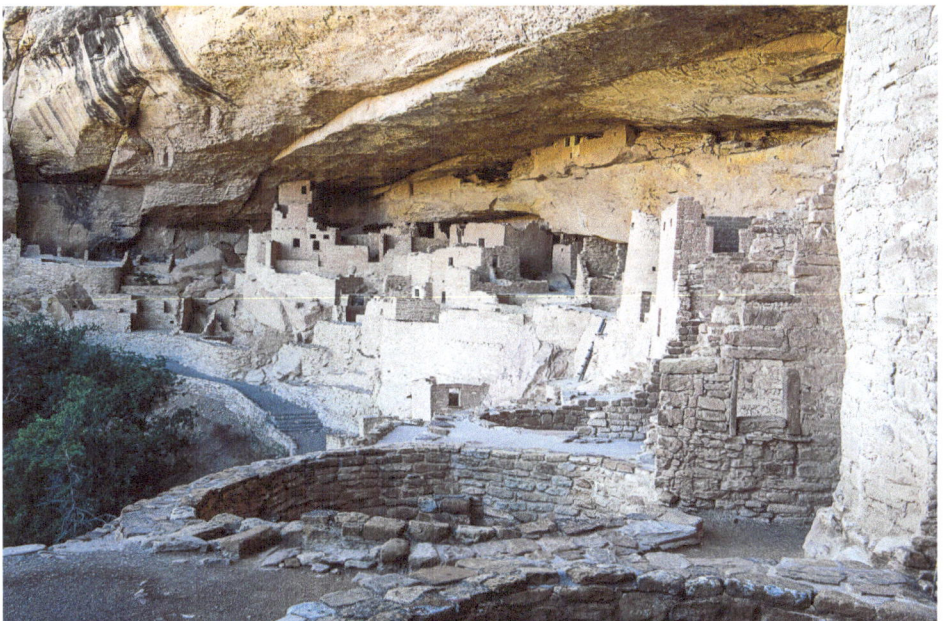
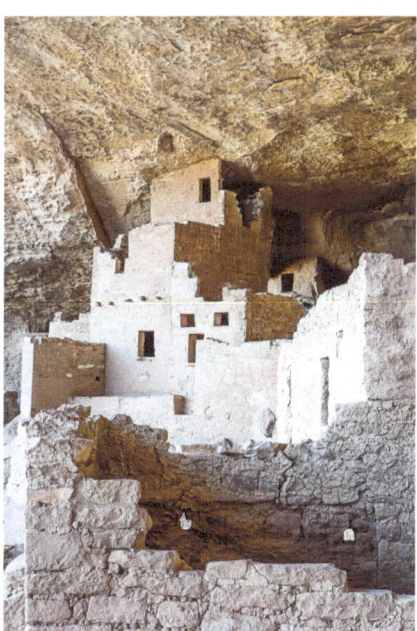

These rarely seen views are photographs I made in the Cliff Palace backcountry. Cliff Palace is far more extensive than I suspected when I looked at it from the front. From that view it appears to have only a few rooms, but once I was inside, the rooms became endless. I realized how many levels the dwelling contains, making it more significant still.

Years earlier the public tours went back almost as far as we were, but because people did not respect boundaries, the practice stopped long ago. Today the public is restricted to the front of the structure and carefully watched by the rangers. To be back where few people now go was a treat, and I made the most of the opportunity.

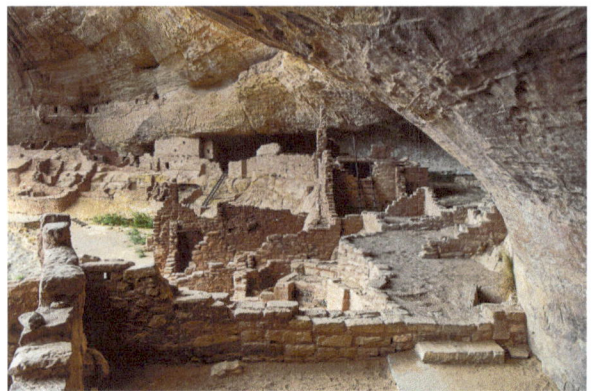

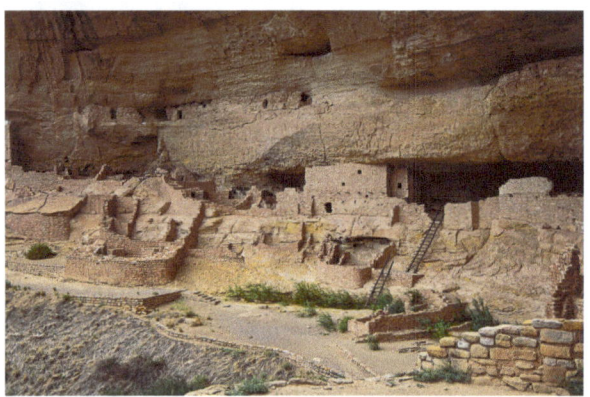

We toured Long House in the same fashion. It was just as impressive as Cliff Palace. We had the pueblo to ourselves and could go anywhere, and as before, I was treated to views seldom seen. The ladders are more than decoration; they are functional and integral to moving everywhere in the structure. The small rooms above the pueblo proper, shown in the upper left of the lower photograph, are intriguing. There's no easy or direct way to access them. Access was by way of rope or ladder and not for the faint of heart. The pueblo builders used every square inch of space in the cliff alcove, and when there wasn't enough space, they made it. The engineering is impressive even by today's standards.

One of the biggest takeaways for me wasn't the stunning views, but rather the silence. I was struck by how utterly quiet it was in the cliff dwelling and what it must have been like when occupied. The archeologist explained that I had it backward. It would have been far from quiet. Upon reflection, I can tell she made sense. Several hundred people lived in the pueblo. Think of the everyday sounds that would amplify and echo throughout the canyon—people talking, children shouting and playing and all the day-to-day sounds, some soft, some boisterous, that punctuate everyday life. The place would have been noisy, and finding a quiet moment among the cacophony must have been blessing to those who lived there. I have a new appreciation for what daily life was like in a pueblo. It's a good lesson too, not to view the past through the lens of the present.

After we had our introduction to the cliff dwellings, it was time to head into the backcountry for some archeological research. "Archeological research" sounds lofty, doesn't it? We'd be doing actual research and discovering new—well, whatever we found. Perhaps it would be a previously unknown pueblo. Maybe it would be something even more significant. Maybe it would be a discovery that altered the understanding of the area. All was possible, but in reality archeology involves a lot of arduous work that takes a long time to perform, and sometimes it produces nothing.

We made our way into the backcountry of the park to a location I've been asked not to disclose. I found myself far

Mesa Backcountry

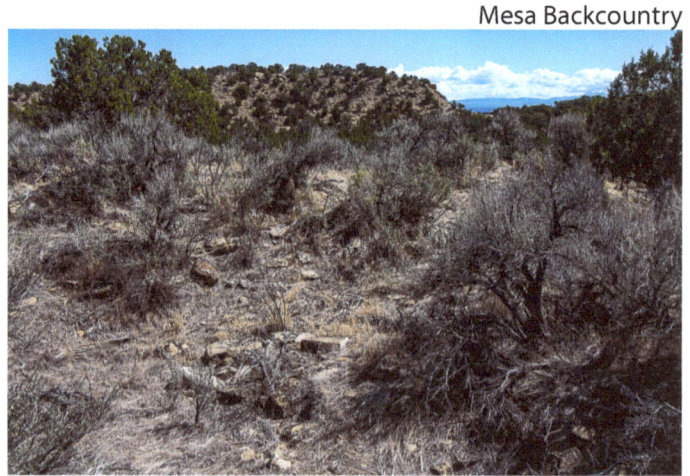

away from the roads, far away from the people, and far away from everything. We walked several miles to get there. These protected areas are not open to the public and require special permission and permits to visit. A large number of pueblos were there, although they were not photogenic. For example, this scene shows a room block, or maybe a pueblo, of an unknown number of rooms. It was unexcavated, and because of the time required and the cost of excavation, it never will be. It is preserved in-situ for whatever, if anything, the future holds. The plan is vital, for it protects the artifacts of this pueblo so they can rest in peace. Our national lands protect these sites, ensuring they have a future.

Today we look at the pueblos after they have been excavated, restored, and prepped for tourists. The view is sanitized and doesn't tell the story of finding them. To walk through a landscape like this one and realize a pueblo is lurking just under the surface takes a well-trained eye, and sometimes luck. I can't imagine what it was like to make the discovery. What did the ranchers who found some of the pueblos of Mesa Verde first think when they came across them? Imagine the wonder of seeing the remains of an alcove dwelling for the first time.

The process of excavating and researching a pueblo is not quick or easy. It can take years to unearth one fully and even more time to prepare it for modern-day visitors. Inch by inch, layer by layer, room by room, the dirt has to be removed, preserving the artifacts and any remains. The work is painstaking, and the archeologist has to sustain rapt attention to the details. Standing at the very beginning of the pueblo's modern-day story gave me an appreciation for how much effort goes into bringing history to life, which is often the primary factor in leaving discoveries alone.

Even though the structure is unexcavated, I learned plenty from studying what we can see. By examining the style and methods used in construction, the trained eye can determine with reasonable accuracy the period the structure was built and occupied. The structure, coupled with the artifacts such as potsherds—pottery fragments—found on the ground, tell us who lived here and when. The occupation period doesn't always have a single stopping point, as different groups might have used the space over time. Structure modifications and differing artifacts decipher the clues of various prior tenants. Multiple occupancies of a site are common, sometimes making it more challenging to determine the site's original builders. Simply examining a site as it is allows researchers to glean a huge amount of information. Still, it is essential to realize the knowledge comes from researchers' experience and prior research. Researchers and archaeologists determine a portrayal of the site, and piece by piece they build a view of the entire region, with each site fitting into the extended puzzle. Only by considering all the sites in an area can researchers make an accurate assessment.

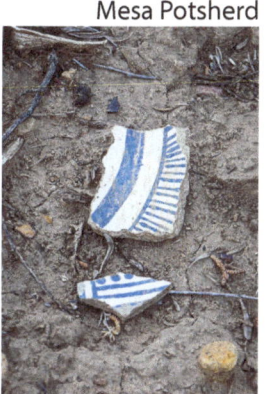
Mesa Potsherd

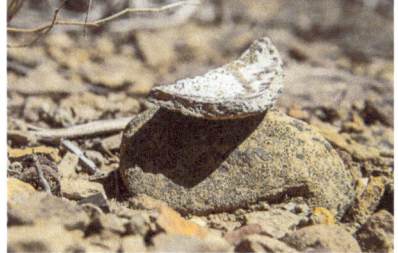

Archeologists show respect and are careful at the sites they examine. They catalog found artifacts, study them, and then leave them as they were. Leaving objects helps future archeologists too, because where an artifact rests is critical information. Moving it, even a short distance, can distort the historical record. Workers take care when walking; their footsteps are light and gentle. The site stays as undisturbed as possible, left for the future.

Thousands upon thousands of these sites exist in the Mesa Verde region; however, the casual observer wouldn't see anything out of the ordinary at first glance. Some sites are tiny, while others are more significant structures that housed multiple families. Finding and counting them is a major, time-consuming challenge, and the team I was with was transversing a search area. *Transversing* means walking the entire zone in a grid and recording anything of note. If an area warrants further examination, it is prioritized, and a future team might come back to it. Given the sheer number of sites, though, most go untouched, and the goal is to record the sites and move on.

After gathering the photographs the team needed, I put down the camera and helped as best I could. I found and counted potsherds, made measurements, and did whatever else the researchers needed. I was happy to lend a hand and lighten their load. Back and forth we walked, all in a spread-out line. Eyes focused on the ground, we looked left, looked right, and then took a step. We were careful to stay in line, at least as much as practical. If we found something, we called out, and the archeologist came to check on it. Once the item was recorded, we moved forward. Grid searching is not a quick process, and after a while my eyes began to play tricks on me. Still, I had to keep a sharp eye to the ground.

I'll admit that I was hoping we would stumble across a temple with a stone statue that we could grab. I had my best running shoes on and was ready for any boulders that rolled toward us. Prepared to dodge poison darts and find a room full of snakes, I had my adventure hat on to make me look good. Alas, the reality is not as Indiana Jones portrays it, but it is fascinating nonetheless, just at a slower pace than the movies would have you believe. I didn't find any lost temples or pueblos, but I did find plenty of potsherds.

As it turns out, potsherds are fascinating. I never thought about it before, perhaps figuring someone would pick up a potsherd and instantly know that someone made it in August 1098 or something like that. Or maybe there would be a stamp on the bottom: "Made in Mesa Verde." As usual, reality differs from imagination. The researchers indeed examine the potsherds, and not merely at a glance. They were the subject of much discussion and debate. Lines, patterns, thickness, material, color, and whatever else possible to glean from a one-inch pottery fragment all entered the discourse. Eventually the group formed a consensus concerning a probable date. We looked around the immediate area for more potsherds in hopes of confirming the assumption. The more sherds we found, the more confident we were of the dating, and eventually we achieved certainty. One potsherd alone is interesting; many together tell a story.

The research at Mesa Verde is invaluable in the quest for understanding the locale. It takes years upon years of fieldwork to document even a small section fully. Only once the broad outlines are known can any significant interpretation be made, and everything takes time and effort. We don't see the people doing this work when we are in the parks. They are far away, toiling in silence and providing the hard data necessary to tell the story accurately. Thank you to everyone out in the field doing this important work.

Evenings were my own to do with as I would, which for me meant exploring the park until the rangers eventually chased me out when the park closed. I was on a summer expedition, and summer means the possibilities of thunderstorms. And a storm might mean lightning. I was rewarded with a couple of summer thunderstorms and made one of my favorite lightning photographs.

I scouted around and settled on a high overlook that gave me commanding views of the park. Summer storms are likely that time of year, and I had good odds of seeing one. I didn't think I needed to chase after one, though, and decided to see if I would get lucky and one would materialize near me. If nothing else I'd spend a pleasant evening looking over the park. Either way, I would enjoy the time. I got out of my 4x4, stretched, and began my vigil. I'm used to waiting for things to happen and have learned they will or won't, and I'll know the outcome soon enough. I might as well be patient and enjoy. Who am I kidding? I was excited and antsy, and I wanted a storm right now!

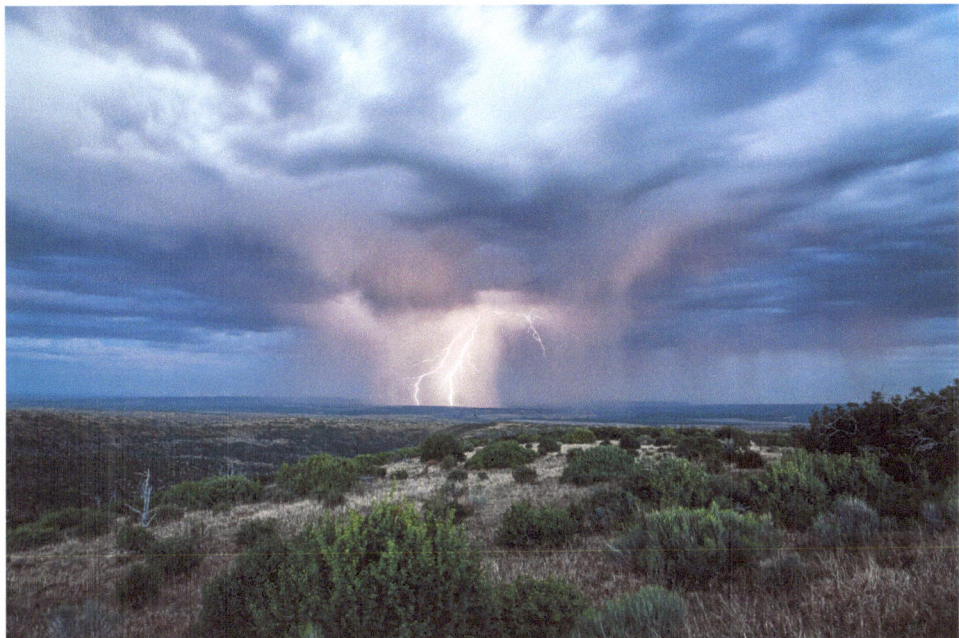

Mesa Lightning

Amazingly enough, as if on cue, a storm flared up in the distance and headed toward me. I made full use of my vantage as the storm rolled in. It swept across the landscape rapidly, intensifying along the way. Just before twilight and before the driving rain reached me, the thunderstorm let loose with lightning bolts. Crashing and roaring, Zeus threw thick bolts of lighting into the ground with the force of ten thousand suns, lighting up the low clouds. The result, Mesa Lightning, was impressive and more than a little nerve-racking.

I had learned my lesson about lightning when making *Moulton's Storm*, so during this storm, I was extra conscious about my safety. I made sure I was away from the thunderstorm and not in it and made sure I had a safe place to duck into, if needed. I was very aware that I was, once again, standing exposed with metal and electronics and well within reach of an errant bolt. I held my ground and waited for the perfect moment.

Mesa Verde National Park is near and dear to me, both the public and backcountry areas. Whenever I return I look to the far hills and quietly thank the researchers who are working to bring our past back to us.

Death Valley

Death Valley is a timeless land of extremes, from the lowest point on the continent to soaring vistas to rocks that sail across a lake. Let's explore the valley, examine its challenges and wonders, and hear a tale about a plane, which may or may not be accurate.

Some places on this planet are hot. Some places have scorching heat. There are even places that are below sea level. And then there is Death Valley National Park, which is all these things and more. Along with the harsh environment, however, the park holds wonders.

California's Death Valley National Park is isolated and remote. Perhaps because of its remoteness, the valley has a timelessness to it, and it is easy to forget the modern world while you are there. The valley endures today as it always has and always will. The landscape is arid and barren, because life takes effort in one of the harshest environments anywhere on the planet. Its early history is one of struggle and perseverance, as the early settlers and 49ers found out when they traveled through here in the mid-1800s.

Vegetation is sparse, at best, leaving a landscape composed essentially of sand and rocks. Winds howl through the valley, further drying it out, and the searing summer heat parches the unwary. The desolation is endless, even as you climb out of the valley and into the surrounding mountains. Although some low bushes and shrubs survive in the hills and even some trees at the higher elevations, it is still a desert environment. Water remains precious and not easily found, and the summer heat is formidable.

As much as I shudder at the thought of being cold, I dread high temperatures even more. Like almost everyone else, I enjoy moderate temperatures. It's funny how I end up in the extremes, though, and when I am shivering I think of the desert, and when I am roasting I ponder sub-zero temperatures.

Death Valley possesses the lowest spot in North America, Badwater Basin, at 282 feet below sea level. Being in Badwater Basin doesn't feel any different than being at sea level, except in the summer when the temperature routinely holds the county's record high temperature at 130 degrees. That's hot! The heat hits you like a blast oven and can easily overwhelm you before you realize what is happening. Aside from the heat, though, the experience of being in the lowest place on the continent is a powerful and moving one.

Despite the lack of vegetation, beauty is everywhere. Even this inhospitable environment yields soaring landscapes and breathtaking scenes. From sweeping panoramas to intimate moments, Death Valley is a photographer's wonderland. Looking up at the surrounding mountains while you are in the valley is spectacular. The mountains meet the valley floor in a sharp line, making a dramatic transition. Although without any sheer cliffs, the mountainsides are steep, unforgiving, and imposing. Looking down at the valley from up above is equally inspiring, and I'll show that view in detail at Zabriskie Point in a little while. Although the name implies the landscapes may be stark and barren, nothing could be further from the truth, and Death Valley contains powerful and moving vignettes.

First let's stop at Artist's Palette. The area is renowned for its uniquely colored slopes. The jagged hillside features unusual and unexpected colors jumbled together. Turquoises, purples, oranges, greens, and blues are everywhere, and the area does indeed resemble a large palette. Metals have oxidized the soil, creating hues very different from the usual landscape colors. Instead of the mounds being a jumble of pigments as you might expect, each pile has a unique color, creating the palette effect when seen from afar.

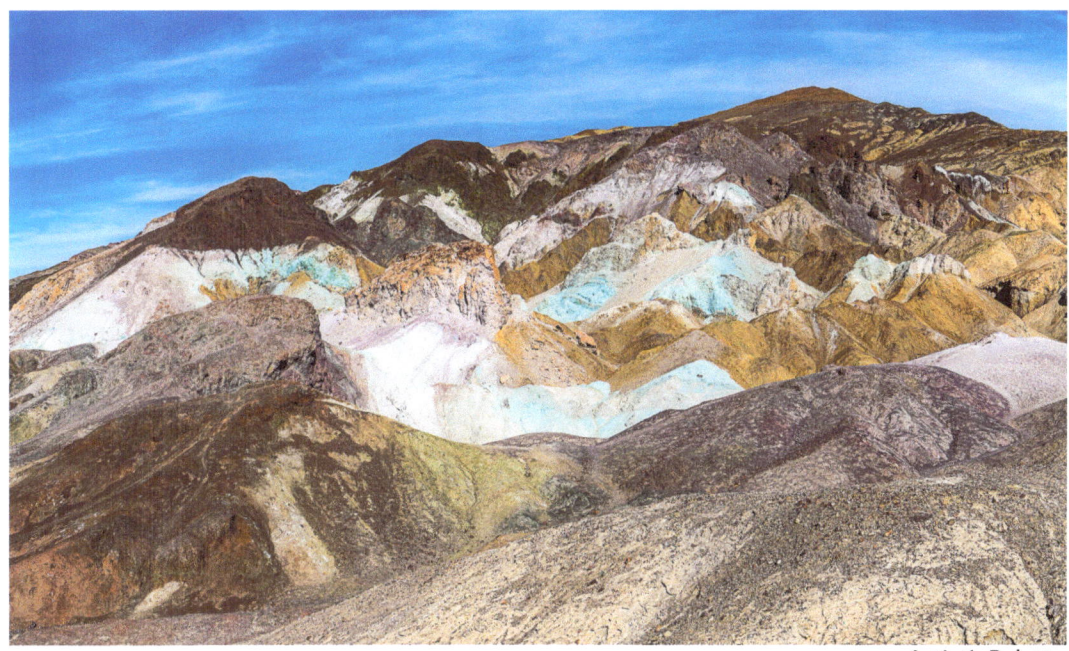
Artist's Palette

It was surreal to make my way through the purple sand to the top of a low hill to make this photograph. Every step I took, I kept looking down, wondering if I would see brown beneath my feet. I never did. On the other side of the purple hill was a green one, which I also dutifully scaled. All around me, colors assailed my senses, and Artist's Palette left a long-lasting impression on me. I've never seen such colorful hills anywhere else. The longer I lingered there, the more the colors struck me, and as I write this, I am still thinking about climbing a hill of purple sand. If I had told people I would be doing that, most would consider me a raving lunatic, yet the purple dune remains. Purple. Green. The area is most unusual, and that's putting it mildly.

Badwater Basin is another must-visit section of Death Valley. Amazingly, water is here, but it isn't drinkable. It is salty and bitter and unpalatable, even to the most desperate. An old story says the name comes from the first explorer. He happened upon this basin, desperate and thirsty, and couldn't believe his luck for finding water. He ran toward the salvation of the water, but alas, he couldn't drink it, and neither could his horse, because of the salts. He named it Badwater Basin, and the name has stuck. I also found water when I was there, but mindful of the stories and the water's reputation, I decided not to try it. This decision is not one I regret.

What makes the area even more novel is the massive salt flat, miles upon miles across, unbroken almost as far as the eye can see. I made this photograph after walking a mile out on the salt flat. Even at that, it felt as if the far side was no closer than when I started, and the distances began to fool my eye. The more I walked, the farther away the mountains became, and my sense of scale was off-kilter the entire time I was out there. I can't imagine what it felt like to

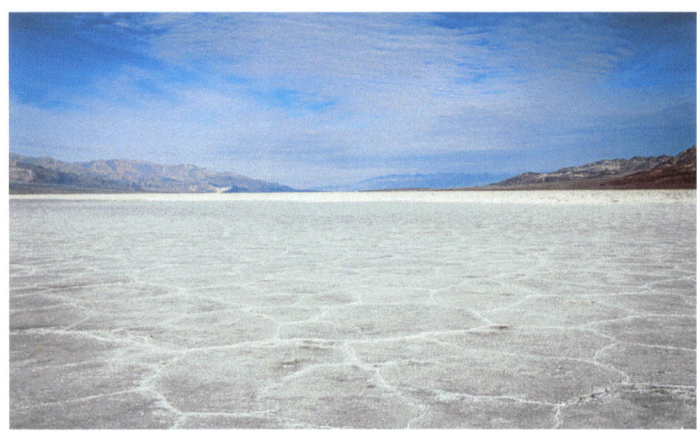
Badwater Basin

travel through the area in the mid-1800s, pulling loaded wagons and being hot, tired, and thirsty. To have water around you that is undrinkable while in the hottest place in North America had to be difficult and heart-wrenching. The early settlers would have crossed miles of water while thirsty, yet drinking the refreshing-looking liquid under their feet was not an option. I am thankful I could return to my 4x4 and take a cold, refreshing drink from my water bottle and enjoy the air conditioning.

I often think about what the "early days" must have been like, and how they compare to our modern times. I'm always up for new experiences, but today, mine is called an adventure. Back in the mid-1800s, people called it "making it through today." I further wonder what it would have been like to be a photographer in those days. All the wildernesses would have been pristine and unspoiled. Throngs of tourists wouldn't create crowds and congestion. There wouldn't be any pesky lines or required permits. I would have been fortunate to make it through each day, though. With those thoughts, we'll leave Badwater Basin and continue exploring Death Valley.

Next we need to visit Zabriskie Point, where I spent quite some time, including at sunrise and sunset. Zabriskie Point is easy to get to, but far harder to leave. It is close to the main road and even has a short paved trail to the top of an overlook. When you crest the top of the overlook, an astonishing sight greets you. The colors and sinewy structure of the tortured rock weave and twist together, and as the sun moves, the entire scene gambols with it. I didn't see a straight line anywhere, and erosion had created a stone fairyland. The colors, while not as colorful as Artist's Palette, are vibrant, especially in the warm glow of the early morning and late afternoon. You will want to linger for a moment

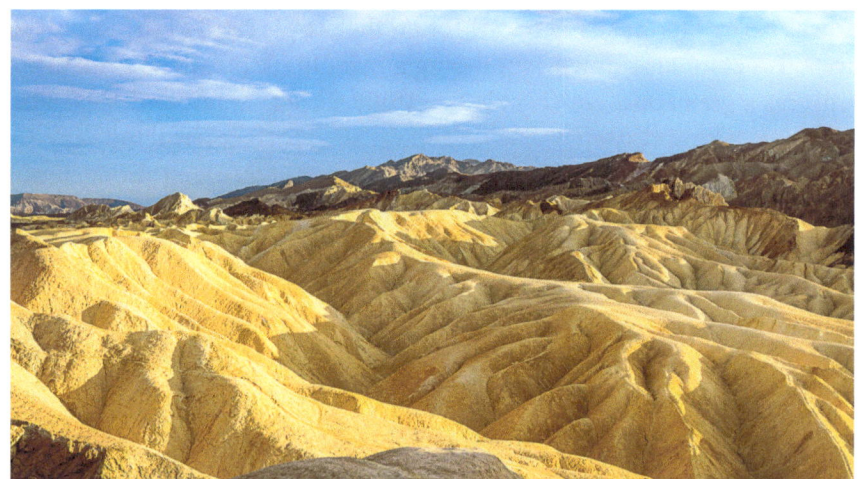
Zabriskie Afternoon

longer to witness how the display changes. When I got ready to depart, I couldn't help waiting a little more to see what might happen next. The timelessness of Death Valley is strong there, and knowing how many people had beheld the scene before me was a powerful reminder. Some of the most iconic Death Valley photographs and posters feature this area, and it was thrilling to be able to create my own iconic photograph here.

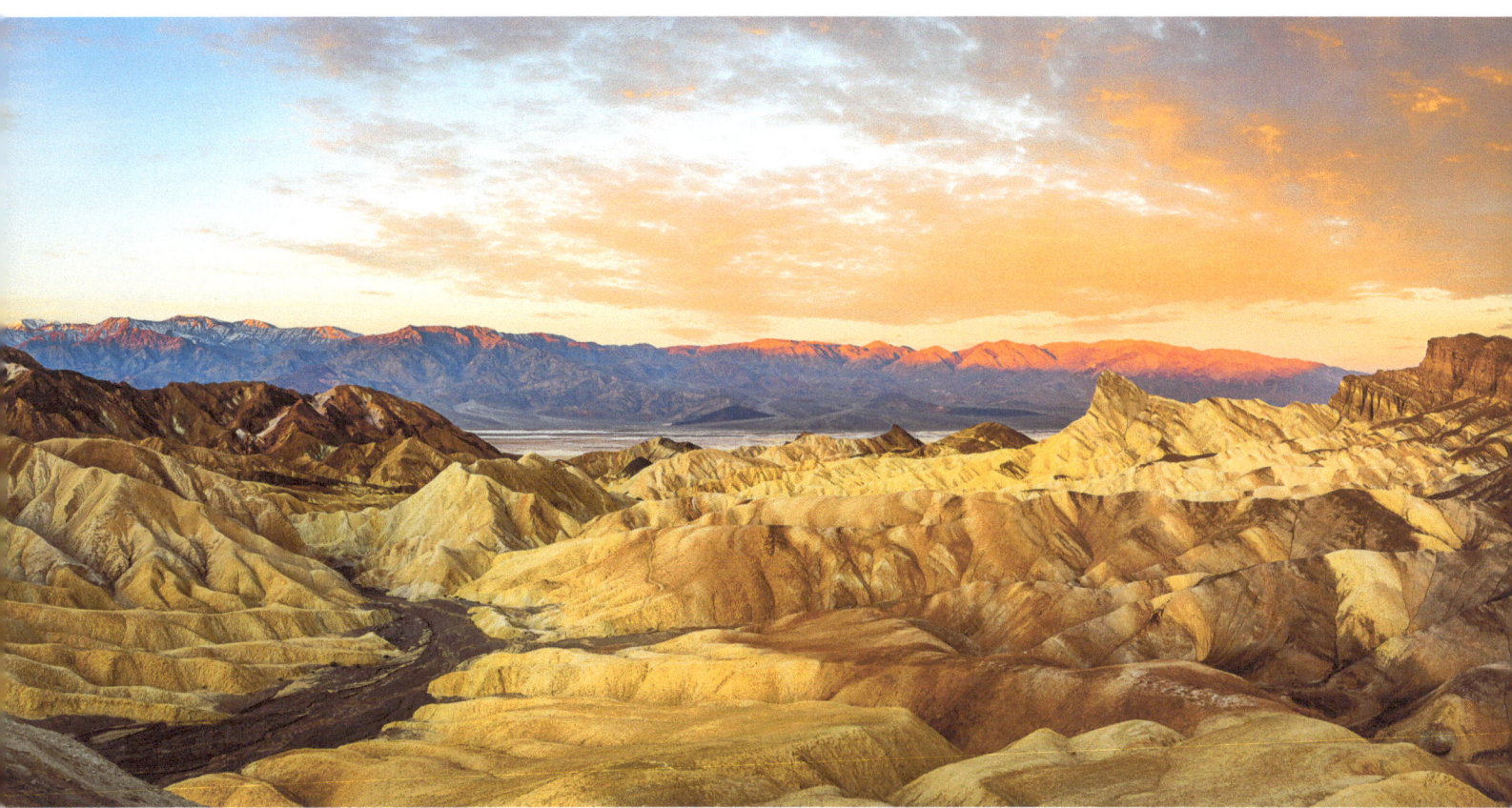

Zabriskie Point

Each morning in Death Valley tells a different story, and each morning presents unique imagery. It isn't until the sun breaks the horizon that you know how each morning will play out, and the anticipation builds as the sun rises. This photograph, *Zabriskie Point*, is my favorite of all the ones I made in the park. Some mornings were full of reds, but this morning the clouds briefly glowed an ethereal orange. Coupled with the oranges and deep yellows of the rocks below and contrasted by darker ridges and the faraway mountains lighting up, *Zabriskie Point* is a classic Southwest desert photograph. Within it I feel the drama of the sunrise yet the tranquility of the desert. It shows tension, but a counterpoint of calmness. Each day I was disappointed when the sun raced higher into the sky, washing out the colors, but I was thankful I witnessed the early-morning spectacles.

Death Valley National Park covers a vast area and, despite the word *valley* in the name, a wide range of topologies. It has mountains, hills, plains, valleys, and even sand dunes within its borders. One area particularly stands out to me, the Playa. The Playa is commonly known as The Racetrack, notably because of its ultra-flat surface and sailing rocks. The Playa is a lake bed, almost always dry, but now and then rains turn it back into a shallow lake, at least for a few hours. The lake bed isn't the most notable thing, however, as we shall soon see.

Before we can explore The Racetrack, we first need to get there. On the surface it is as simple as driving out twenty-six miles on a rocky road. The road is flat, has minimal elevation gain, and doesn't require any problematic navigation, except going straight at a well-marked intersection. Simple, right? Appearances are deceiving, as is often the case.

The road looks easy enough at first blush, but its rocks are not round, nor are they easily driven over. Although relatively small, the stones are exceptionally sharp and quite fond of puncturing tires. You may think, "How bad can it be?" The answer is, "Beyond your imagination." Traveling on the route is an exercise in careful, precise driving, choosing what looks to be the least worrisome section to traverse, and hoping to miss the worst of it. Hint: you won't. In addition to worrying about routine punctures, you also have to worry about tearing your sidewalls out, should you venture too close to the edges. Some people severely underestimate those rocks. Because the stones are small and unassuming, drivers may think they can drive fast and make a quick trip of it. Sometimes that strategy works, but all too often, it does not. The tire repair shops surrounding Death Valley do a robust business. I know firsthand. I've talked to the owners of both the tire shops and the people who needed new tires.

If the rocks don't do in your tires, the constant vibration of twenty-six miles of washboards and bone-jarring bumps will shake something important loose or cause an engine component to fail. Your suspension is unlikely to be the same after the experience. Far too many people have decided the laws of physics do not apply to them, making their vehicles immune to the road, and far too many people have learned the hard way that retrieving a broken-down vehicle is not immediate, inexpensive, or uncomplicated. I don't want to give you the impression that the road is entirely impassable; it is eminently drivable. It is possible to take an ordinary passenger car on it and drive back in the same car. It is just not advisable, and you must make preparations for a breakdown well beyond cell phone service. In short, travelers must be well-prepared.

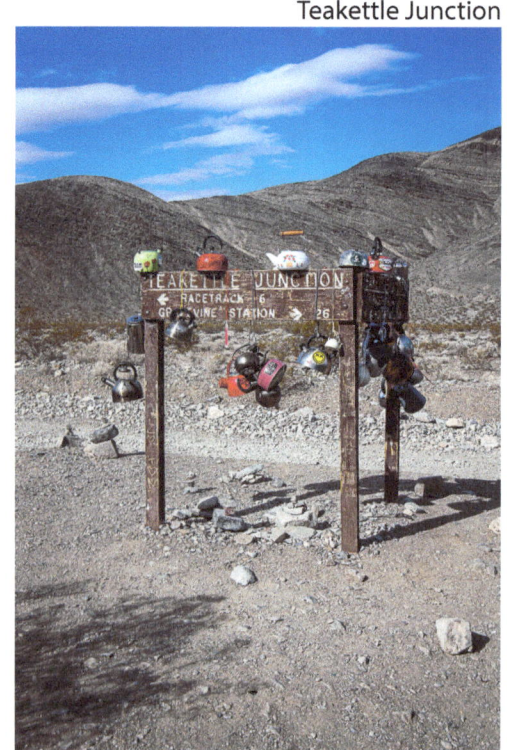

Teakettle Junction

In any event, I safely made it to The Playa in a few hours. I did not find a lot to see, and even less to photograph along the way, except for Teakettle Junction, which is the only possible turn on the entire route. Right behind the sign, you can see what passes for a road. Legend has it that teakettles were left at this location by early settlers to indicate water was nearby. Although it may indeed be true, I suspect it is more of a myth than fact. Another story has it that teakettles pointed the way the last person traveled. That story makes more sense to me, but as with many legends, the actual truth remains lost to the ages. Today some consider it good luck to leave a teapot, sometimes inscribed with a message, at the junction. The Park Service occasionally clears out most of them, and the collection slowly begins again. Water or not, myth or reality, Tea Kettle Junction is a welcome waypoint and a good place to stop and stretch after enduring a bumpy ride. We'll come back and examine the origin story in a moment.

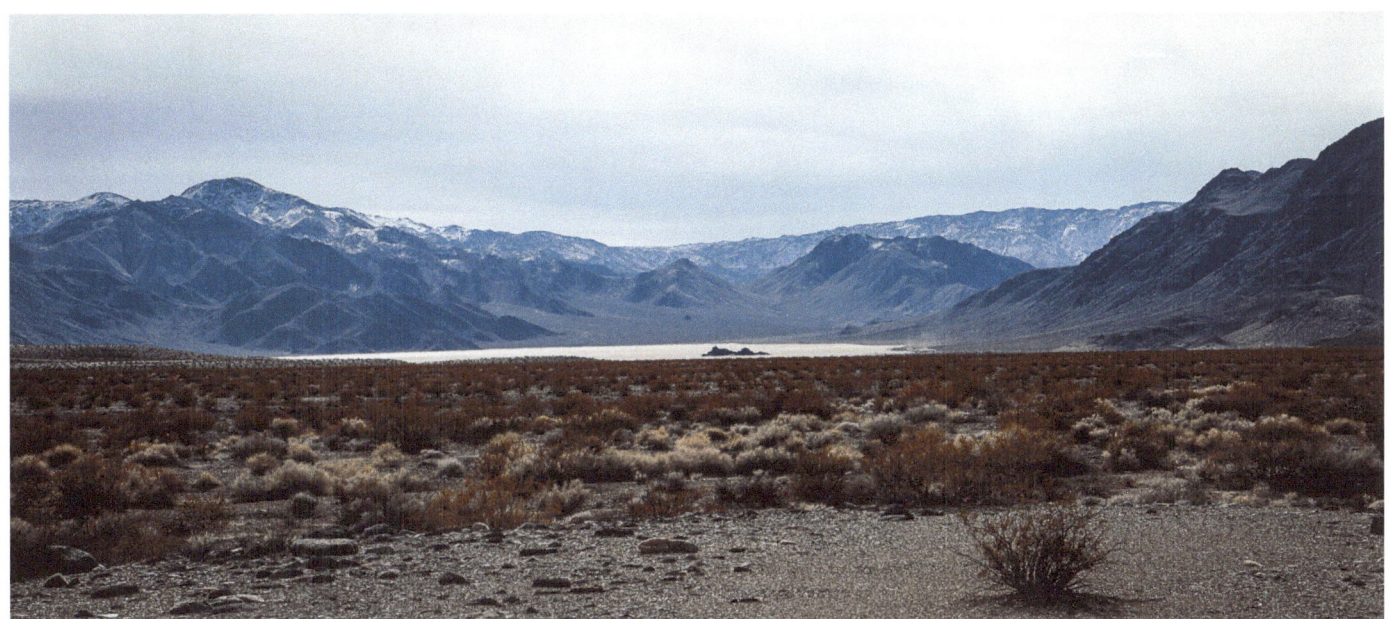
Distant Playa

Near the end of the track I caught a glimpse of the entire Playa sprawling in the distance. It looked small, but it is almost a mile wide and nearly three miles long. Distance and size are not always easy to gauge in the desert. I liked how the Playa sprawled in the distance, also a welcome waypoint.

Finally I got to the Playa itself, and it certainly was worth the effort. The ancient lake bed is flat as a pancake across its entire surface with no ripples or small swells worth mentioning. It is perfectly flat everywhere from edge to edge. It is featureless too, except for its sailing stones.

The sailing stones are the main attraction and what I came to see. Scattered across the lake bed are numerous rocks of all shapes and sizes, some of which are quite large, and behind them lie their trails, indicating that the stones moved across the lake bed. Some tracks are small, others long, some straight, and some curved. Until recently how those nuggets moved had been a mystery. The Playa and its sailing rocks in the middle of the Death Valley make an interesting juxtaposition. The more you think about the rocks, the more you think of how wrong their movement is. At some point you simply accept that they move and realize you are looking at a natural wonder.

Low hills surround the lake, and the stones appear to originate from the hillside to the east. That section of the lake has, by far, the most extensive collection of rocks, and their numbers dwindle the farther you go from that edge. By the time you get out to the middle, fewer rocks can be found. Interestingly, some rocks still make their way to the far end, meaning they potentially traveled a couple of miles. A large outcropping in the lake bed, the only outcropping or feature, is called the Grandstand, and a couple of sailing stones surround it. Somehow or other, the rocks get around.

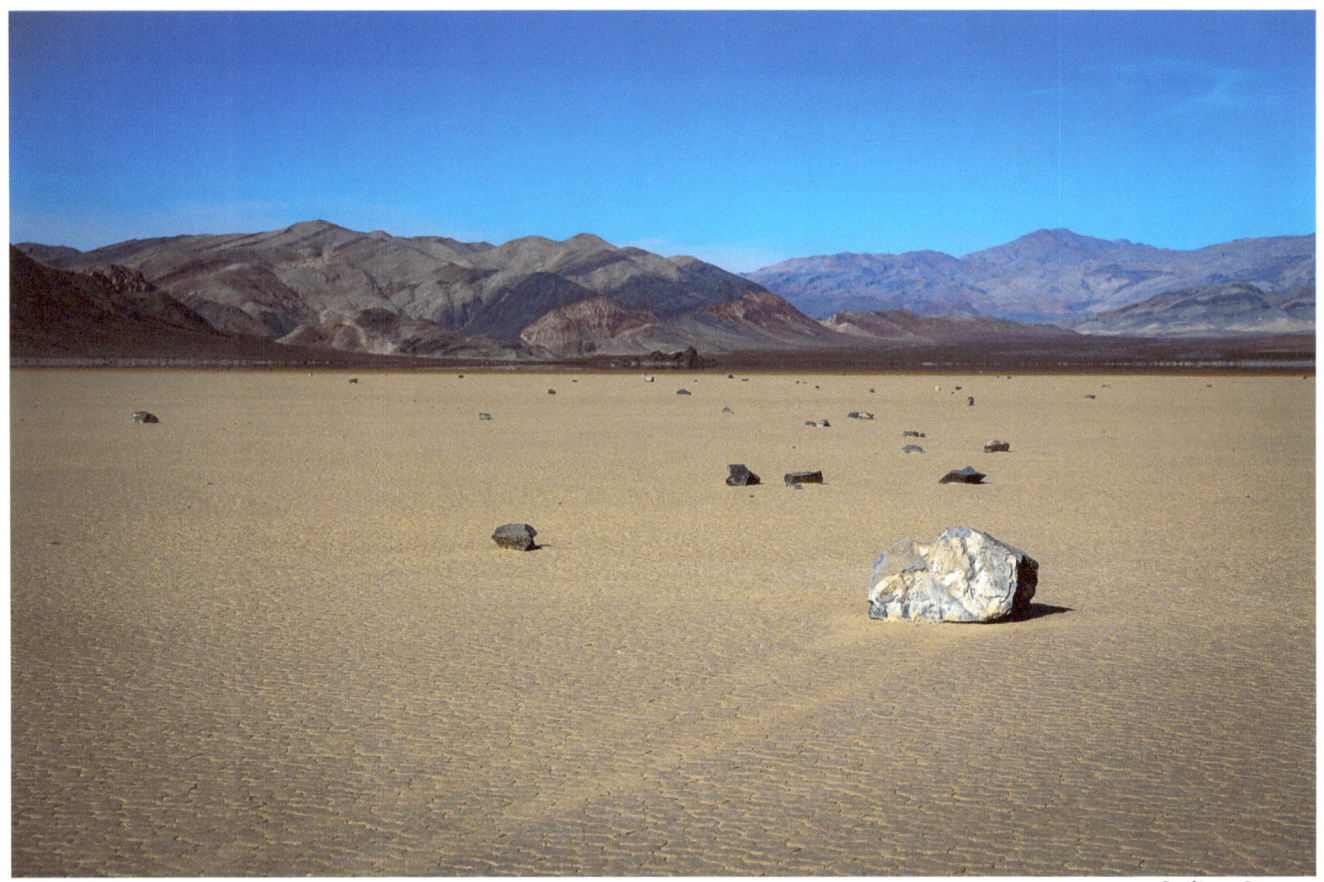

Sailing Stones

Because the lake bed was bone dry, I spent hours wandering about, examining every rock and every trail I came across. I bent down and looked from their point of view to see where they might be going. Peering around them, I wondered if they would move, but they remained stubbornly in place for me. I looked at small rocks and I looked at the largest ones. I examined every stone I could find. Mostly I found, and photographed, wonderment.

Visiting The Playa is a unique and unexpected experience. If it weren't for the sailing stones, you'd be wandering around on an unremarkable, usually dry, lake bed. The rocks make all the difference, making the area a marvel to behold.

The Playa and its rocks are not the only stories I learned. I met many interesting people in my travels in Death Valley, but one individual told me a fascinating tale I cannot verify, and I tried. The person has been in and around the valley for an entire lifetime, and the person's father has too. If anyone knows of its comings and goings, it would be that person, who told me that The Playa was "discovered" during a military training mission gone wrong. Since I love a good story, here it is. Make of it what you will.

Shortly after World War II, the United States Air Force conducted a routine training mission which flew over Death Valley. Unfortunately the plane experienced engine trouble, and the pilots were unable to continue the exercise. The plane was going down, and it would crash unless the pilot could find a place in the desert to try a landing. Luckily he spied a lake bed that looked like an ideal, and the only, possible landing spot. After some tense flying, he managed to land the plane on the lake bed and the crew hiked out to safety. The Air Force wanted its aircraft back, though, and since it was in one piece, getting it made sense. There was no road, trail, or track to the lake bed, but the military created a roadway in a matter of days, because it could, and the military is efficient. Bulldozers made short work of the desert and created a track to the lake bed. The military removed the plane, and that was that.

Here's where things get interesting, though. Today we call the dry lake bed The Playa, and it is also known as The Racetrack. In truth the road itself is known as The Racetrack, nicknamed by the people who built and then later drove over it to retrieve the plane. Over time the two names have merged. In support of this fact, you can still find people who call the road The Racetrack, and you can find written references to the roadway as The Racetrack, but they are few and far between. The Park Service itself calls The Playa "The Racetrack," as evidenced by the Teakettle Junction sign.

Finally, let's return to Teakettle Junction. If the military built the road to retrieve the downed plane, then every story about Teakettle Junction is a myth, because the road didn't exist before the plane incident. If the road didn't exist, there wasn't a junction. You can hypothesize that the military merely extended the road, but if that was the case, then why name a simple turn a junction?

I believe the story of the plane and the military building the road. My source was credible. There is little water to be had in this area, so the idea of teakettles pointing toward water doesn't make sense. The story of the teapots being used to indicate which way the last person traveled does make sense, but it doesn't mean the story is all that old. And finally, other planes have gone down in Death Valley. You can still hike to the remains of a significant crash, so I believe it, but then again, I want to believe in a lot of things, so take this entire explanation as you wish.

Oh! You wanted to know how the sailing stones move? Several things have to happen all at the same time: rain has to fill up the lake bed with water, just enough to cover the bottom, but not too much, plus ice has to form just right at night. The next day has to be sunny, and finally, there have to be light winds. If everything lines up correctly, the ice is capable of moving the rocks little by little. Over the years they sometimes leave trails in the mud, and startlingly, over long years, the rocks can "sail" an impressive distance. They take their time getting from the hillside to wherever they end up. Let's take a cue from them and also take our time getting from there to here by exploring meandering byways.

Meandering Byways

Where does that road lead? That's a question I must answer every time I pass one. Many times it goes nowhere except to a locked gate. Now and then, though, my inquisitiveness is rewarded with something unexpected. These stories take us down small byways, even if some of the byways aren't on land.

I actively seek adventures and new places to explore. I spend hours upon countless hours of research before undertaking any journey, as I like to have at least a vague sense of what I am attempting to accomplish. Once on-site, I spend my time getting to know the area, because what someone told me or what I read doesn't always match with what actually is.

Sometimes, when I have the time, I simply drive aimlessly around an area, open to whatever I might find. Far more often than not I have an enjoyable day, seeing alluring sights I have never seen. I have traveled hundreds of dirt roads exploring what was there, only to turn around at the end because the answer turned out to be absolutely nothing. Every single side road I pass by, I wonder, "What's down there?" What a blessing that I can find out!

Now and then, though, something unexpected comes as a result of taking one of those unassuming roads, which was precisely the case in Ballarat, California.

According to a rusty sign on the outskirts of the town, Ballarat was founded in 1897 when the nearby Radcliff Mine opened up. The town served as a mining resupply and recreation area, although it became a boom town. The sign concludes that the colorful town died out in 1917 when the post office closed. Today in a couple of minutes I can walk from one end to the other of what remains, and it is, remarkably, still occupied. I met the residents, all three of them, and they told me a most incredible story. I've even got the photograph as proof positive, but we're getting ahead of ourselves. Let's back up to the beginning.

While photographing Death Valley National Park, I took the time to wander over every paved road of the park and even some of its dirt roads, such as The Racetrack. I also explored many of the roads outside the park. Most people come in by a highway and make a beeline from wherever they are to the park, because everything interesting must be inside the park boundaries, right? I can't tell you how many cars pass me, or how many times I pull over because inevitably the people behind me want to cruise far faster than I do. One morning, not being in a hurry at all, I spied

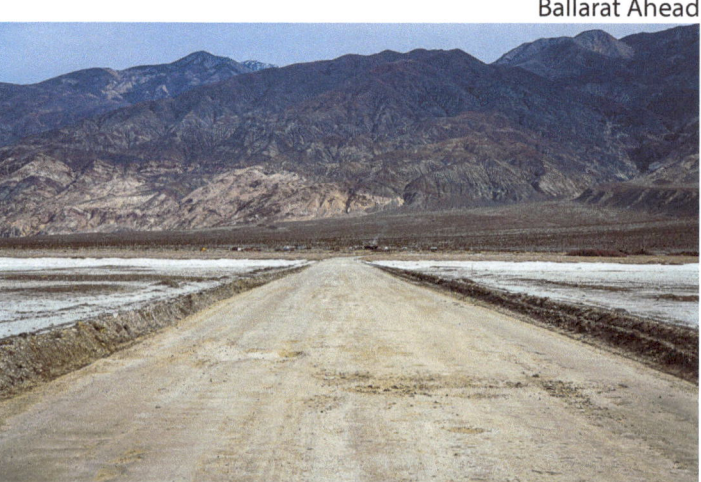

Ballarat Ahead

a dirt road leading away from the highway off into the distance. "Where does it go?" I idly wondered. Before I fully realized it, I was on that dirt road heading directly away from my intended destination. I saw nothing interesting ahead, as far as I could tell, but I spotted a distant hillside, so maybe it would prove interesting. It probably wouldn't be, but I never know. Ever onward, I continued.

Before long, the road headed straight to a collection of buildings, one of which had smoke rising from it. Either it was on fire, or far more likely, it had a chimney. I wagered, correctly, on the chimney option, mainly because it was a chilly January morning. I continued on the road, finally rolling into Ballarat. I didn't find much to see, just some rundown buildings, an aged truck parked prominently out front, and not much else. The door was open on one of the buildings, and its sign read Visitors Welcome, which was all the incentive I needed to walk in.

Inside were three men, all of whom looked like I would expect rugged miners to look. They were friendly, and I had a blast chatting with them. We passed the time swapping a few stories. They told me about Ballarat and its history. Like most mining camps, its story was predictable: the mine opened, and so did the town. Ballarat flourished along with the mine, and times were good. The mine played out, and the miners drifted away for better opportunities, and the desert began reclaiming the abandoned buildings. Unlike most such towns, some of Ballarat managed to survive, so its story does too. As might be expected, the old truck parked out front came up in conversation. In fact the men made sure of it.

"What do you think of the old truck?" one of the grizzled men asked me.

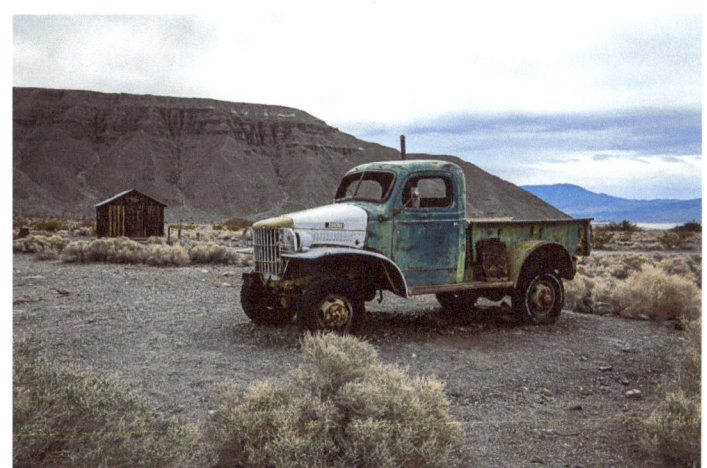

Aged Truck

I stuck my head outside the door and carefully regarded it. "Well," I said, "I'm guessing there is a story about that truck."

There was.

It turns out, and I have no reason to not believe it, that the Feds wanted an outlaw, the Feds being the FBI. The outlaw, Charles, knew the area intimately and decided to make his hideout in and around the old mine. He knew every rock on every hill and figured he would lay low until the heat was off. The plan was a good one and should have worked. He could live out there for years, if need be, and was prepared to do it. We were in the West, and hiding from the law in a desert is a time-honored tradition.

What Charles didn't account for, however, was the sheer relentlessness of the FBI. Agents were not going to let him go. Through good old-fashioned legwork, hard work, and sheer determination, agents tracked him to Ballarat. One morning they swept in to scoop Charles up. Charles had a brief moment's warning, and without a chance to come up with any better plan, he jumped into his truck to make his getaway. He sped across the desert, and he figured he might be able to evade capture.

Unfortunately for Charles it had rained the night before, and his truck unexpectedly mired down in the mud. The FBI agents surrounded him, and seeing no other option, Charles finally surrendered. His mired vehicle was left where it was, for the cops had their man, and that's all they wanted.

OK. So far, so good, and it was an entertaining story. The storyteller then told me Charles's last name: Manson.

Yeah. That Charles Manson.

The truck was Charles Manson's truck, the one he had for a good part of his adult life and the one he drove everywhere. The very one the FBI captured him in. No wonder the town had it prominently displayed. To say I was deeply surprised is an understatement. I had no idea, absolutely none, that I would hear such a story, and it floored me. After the field dried out, Charles's friends retrieved the truck and stored it for him in the event Charles came back. Over the years a few people have tried to purchase it, but it isn't for sale at any price, and some of the offers were well above six figures. It remains at Ballarat, stuck in time, but at least not stuck in the mud. I never know what I might find, even if the backstory is a bit gruesome.

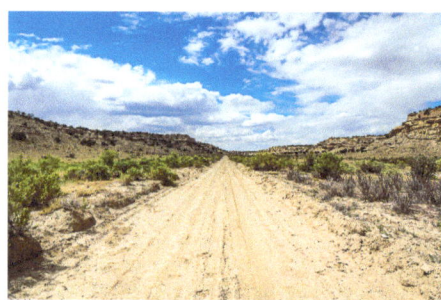
La Lena

To be fair the vast majority of dirt roads do not end in any story whatsoever, let alone an interesting one. My find was entirely accidental, not in any research I had read or heard about, and was a genuinely unexpected event. It's all part of exploring and uncovering stories. It may sound trite, but the journey is indeed the point of it all.

Most unnamed and unmarked dirt roads result in nothing more than a bumpy, jostling drive, and curiously, many terminate at a locked gate. Millions of gates locked with rusty padlocks must be littered across the countryside, and I often wonder if anyone has a key anymore or even remembers the gate is there. Some of the gates look like they haven't swung open in decades. Weeds, and sometimes even trees, have encrusted them. Each gate thwarts me, for I am sure the most remarkable photograph is ready to be made just out of sight beyond it, if only I could get past it. With a heavy sigh I turn around and remind myself that the journey is the thing, but I do get disappointed when an especially promising path doesn't pan out.

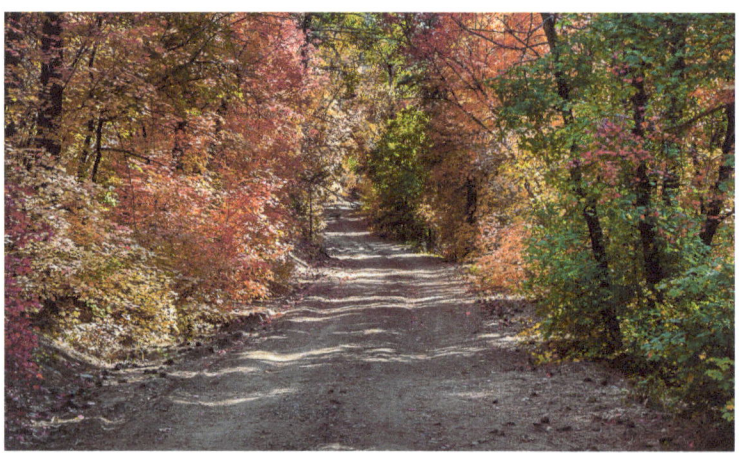
FR 55

I don't want to give the impression that I barrel headlong along an unexplored dirt road without a care in the world. That's far from the case. By definition I am going somewhere unknown to me, and sometimes surprises are not the welcome kind. The road could unexpectedly stop with no way to turn around, although I am well-practiced at turning my 4x4 around in tight places. The road could have a washout or rut that I do not see that could damage my vehicle. Flat tires I can, and have, handled, but who is to say that I don't have multiple flats in a lousy place? What if that innocuous section in front of my hood turns out to be deep sand or dirt so fine I sink in it? I am cautious as can be, and driving down some of the sketchy dirt roads I've been on is a slow, nerve-racking process. Should something go wrong, like I become stuck beyond my ability to recover or break something that requires a tow, the process is not quick or inexpensive. I treat each new road with respect and am as careful as can be. I've certainly had problems and will undoubtedly have more. The trick is avoiding serious issues as much as possible, and being mindful of the road ahead of me.

Sometimes I find a road that I just know, deep in my heart, has something exciting at the end of it. Once I get there, I look around, all the while wondering what I am missing. I get disappointed then, and head back the way I came, being mindful that the fact that I didn't see something while coming in didn't mean I wouldn't see something on the way out. Luckily for me, by the time I've found another possible path, I've convinced myself that the new one will indeed have something at the end, and the ever-optimistic cycle continues.

Now and then I turn out to be right. Or lucky. It's hard to say which. Let's go with "right," because it sounds better.

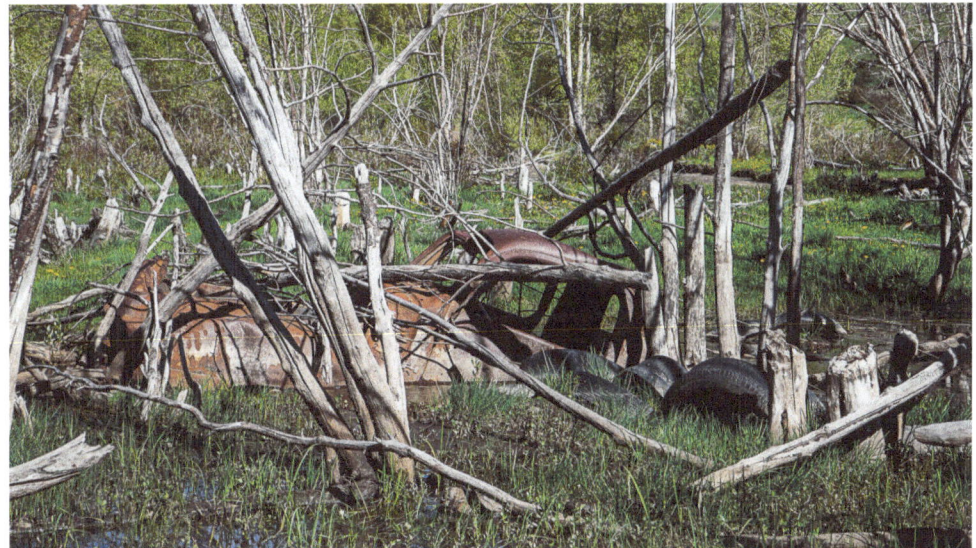

Reclaimed Car

Usually what I find tends to be slightly unusual, but not photogenic enough for anything other than a memory. That fact doesn't stop me from going down unknown roads, of course. A good case in point is this old car found on a branch off a small dirt road a few miles off a slightly larger dirt road, as the crow flies, from Ghost Ranch, New Mexico. I had been exploring myriad nameless "roads," to use a generous term, in the area, going down one after the other. While pretty, they all stopped at a dead end or faded into nothing. Off to the side of one of them, I spied this old car. Rusty old cars are not unusual, but old cars sinking into a small stream are. Sooner or later Mother Nature always gets her way, and in another few decades, the diminutive stream would swallow the car. The car was behind a rusty fence, which prevented me from walking right up to it. If it's not a gate in the way, it's a fence. I wandered up and down the fence line, looking at the car from every angle, before settling on this view. Even without the barrier, I would choose this view for this photograph anyway. It's just the point that the fence was there in the first place that made me want something different. Gates and fences are my archnemeses.

When exploring I need to keep an open mind about what I might discover, for it could be, and has been, anything from sinking old cars to newborn wildlife. I also get excited when I find interesting old houses along the dusty byways. Each abandoned house has a story to tell, although often no one is left to recount it. Every now then, though, the story finds its way to me. Such is the case of the old house in *Maybe Tomorrow*.

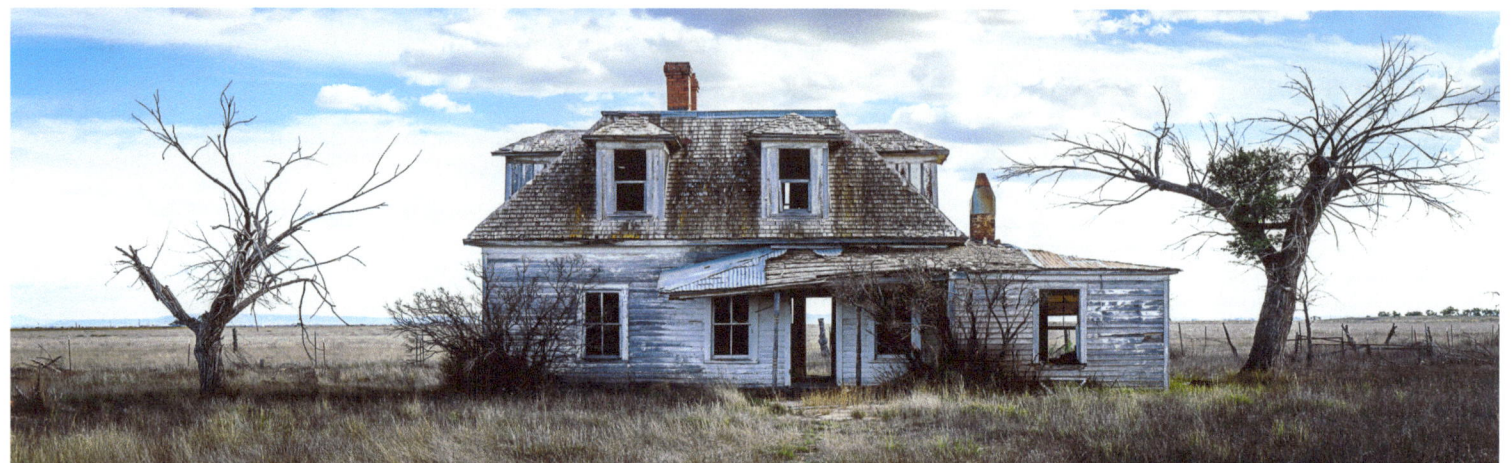

Maybe Tomorrow

At first glance this abandoned house near Estancia, New Mexico, is a run-of-the-mill lonely house. It sits alone in an empty field with nothing but distant memories and the howling wind to keep it company, so it's easy to envision all sorts of stories about who lived there. I can imagine a happy family in happier times, the kids running and playing in the yard, and the house full of love, laughter, and the sounds of joy. I hear Mom yelling, "Dinnertime!" out the door and the little feet scamper to the dinner table. Later, at night, the lights in the house went out one by one as darkness stole the daylight away. That is, all but one light in the upper window, which took its time before finally winking out. I later hear a distant rooster crowing when the next morning wins its battle against the night, and the cycle begins anew. Eventually, though, the children grew up and moved away, and Mom and Dad also faded away, leaving the house to embark on its lonely vigil, hoping for happier days again. Maybe tomorrow those days would come once more. Maybe tomorrow.

I wasn't far off the mark with my made-up story. By sheer happenstance I encountered a woman, Barbara, who lived in this house. We met in Colorado, struck up a conversation that ranged far and wide, and before I knew it, we ended up talking about this house. What a wild coincidence that was, and I am amazed by it even to this day. Somehow, I forget precisely how, the topic of old houses came up. I mentioned that I was quite fond of a good-looking old house near Estancia, New Mexico. Barbara said she knew where Estancia was, which was a coincidence, because it is not a large town. Before long we connected the dots and realized we were chatting about the same house. What are the odds of that happening?

The house itself is a Sears, Roebuck and Co. HonorBilt Modern Home kit house. Back then people could purchase the kit for a specific house through a catalog. You could flip through the pages, looking at the available house kits. You'd read all the text and dream of owning it. At night, after the lights went out, you'd toss and turn in your bed, wondering if that house was indeed the one for you. Finally you would purchase the house, sight unseen, and wait for your dream to arrive. Today we have the Internet and all manner of websites to help us select the perfect house, already built. We browse websites looking at all the houses until we find one we like. We look at the pictures and wonder if it is the house for us. We try to sleep on our decision, but toss and turn throughout the night, wondering if it is the right house. Finally we make our purchase, sometimes sight unseen, and we can't wait for move-in day and our dreams to become reality. Oddly enough, even though a century separates the kit houses from the houses for sale on websites, we've come full circle, yet folks claim we aren't making progress. In any event, the original owner purchased the kit house from Sears and had it delivered by railroad, as many kit houses were.

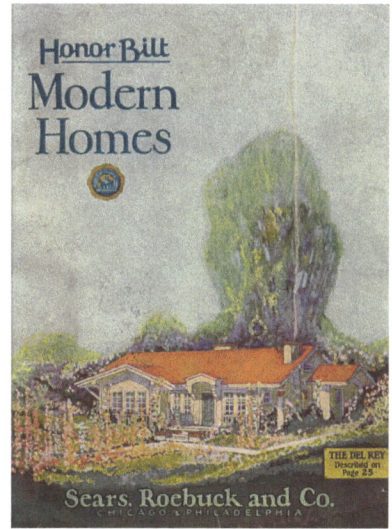

Of the first family who lived there, or the first families, Barbara had little information. Her family purchased the completed house in the early 1940s, and it remained in her family until 2017 or 2018, when it finally sold. Barbara grew up in that house, and she remembers her childhood well. Yes, she played outside, and yes, she was eager to get to the dinner table. Yes, it had happy memories, and yes, it had squeals of laughter and joy. She spoke of her home with longing and just the trace of a tear in her eye, although she tried to pass it off as allergies. I know she was sad to leave it, but it is nice to know it remains forever strong in her heart.

One interesting tidbit about the house came to light. Barbara's father worked with Robert Oppenheimer at Los Alamos, New Mexico, a scientist on the Manhattan Project. Although Estancia is far away from Los Alamos, even by today's standards, her father made the commute. Although I don't know why he chose to live so far from work, perhaps he was trying to keep his family safe and out of harm's way.

Today the house is in shambles and beyond repair. We have no idea what will become of it and its memories, but it is nice to know that sometimes my stories come close to the mark. I never know what I will find at the end of a road.

Some roads, however, come to an unmistakable and abrupt end. I had been poking around outside of Canyonlands National Park and Dead Horse Canyon State Park in Utah, chasing down some of the smaller roads and trails adjacent to the parks. Most were simply an enjoyable ride through the desert, but one was interesting. It started like many others, relatively smooth, graded sometime in the distant past, and easily passable in a passenger car. I expected it to end shortly, as most did. It had plenty of smaller side trails, though, best explored with a 4x4, and I eagerly explored them. One particular track didn't fade away or end at a locked gate, and I saw no fence in sight. It did, however, stop after a short distance. I can't complain about where it stopped, that's for sure. Continuing past the end of the trail, while an option, was one I chose not to exercise.

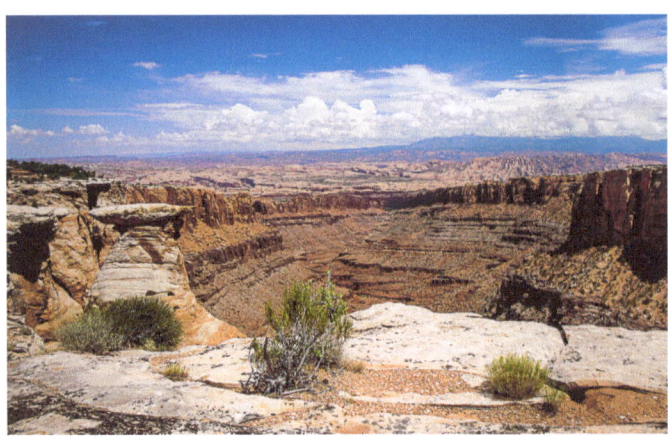

Long's Canyon

The gravel became rock, and a few feet beyond that point became thin air. I parked and hopped out of my 4x4 to enjoy the view over Long's Canyon. As I've mentioned, I need to pay close attention to where I was going, and I could not depend on the next pothole not being bottomless.

Not every byway is a dirt road or little-used highway. Some are not even on land at all. Such is the case of Caddo Lake, which straddles the Texas and Louisiana state line. Caddo Lake is a large, sprawling lake and a popular recreation area for boaters. A state park is on one of its shores. Its swampy edges, though, especially on the Texas side, present a different story and an entirely divergent world. The lake becomes less of a lake and more of a bayou. Far away from the speeding motorboats and sounds of families having picnics, the bayou is dark and quiet. Stillness and serenity held me fast, and even if I wanted to move quickly, I couldn't. The swamp moves at its own pace. It's easier to adjust to the swamp, for it will not adapt its ways to you.

In the swamp the difference between dry land and water is a murky one and difficult to discern. The water is shallow, Spanish moss drapes over the dense cypress trees, and the path is ambiguous. Slow-moving streams and rivers without borders freely flow at whim, creating the bayou. No roads go through there, no trails, and no paths. The only viable way to explore it is with a small rowboat or other small craft. As with all byways, it's best not to be in any hurry or have any set agenda. Whatever sunlight might be present above scarcely makes it down to the ground or water, and daylight ceases at the treetops, leaving only mysterious shadows below. The bayou is quiet too, save for the distant sounds of an occasional frog and an unidentifiable plop and

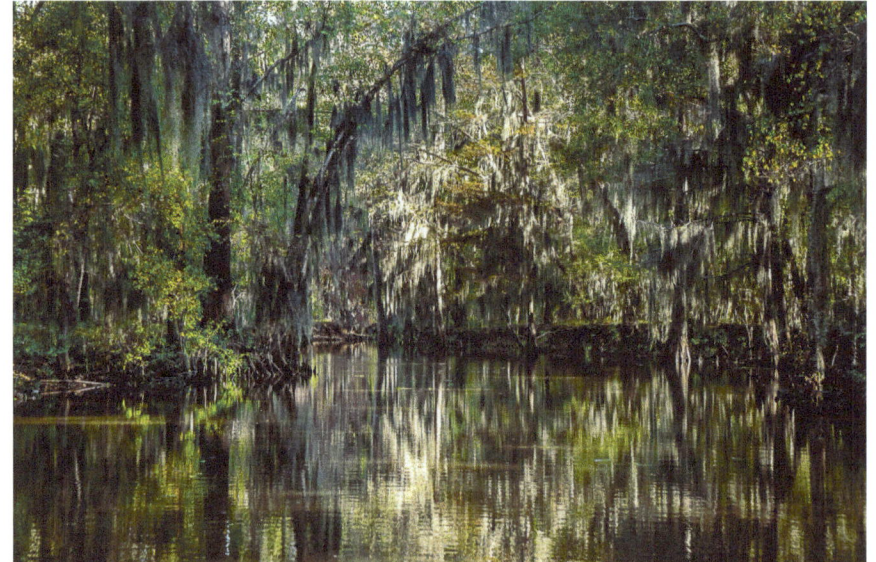

Bayou Way

gurgle as something enters the water. The bayou is not utterly silent, by any means. It has a gentle background noise, which quickly becomes comforting. Floating along the bayou's shallow byways allows me to slip effortlessly among the dense tree roots, weeds, and tangles of vegetation.

I spent the better part of a day exploring various paths through the swamp from the safety of my small boat. Alligators and all manner of snakes live there, both of which I prefer to avoid. In my rowboat I slipped quietly among the trees, taking in all the beauty. The deeper into the bayou I went, the more I became one with it. I felt a strong sense of peace there, and far from being spooky, the darker shadows held a great sense of mystery. Who needs bright daylight, anyway? In the more open areas of the swamp, I encountered white egrets fishing for their next meal. Now and then they were successful. Mostly they stood silent as I drifted along. Like the ocean, the gentle motion of

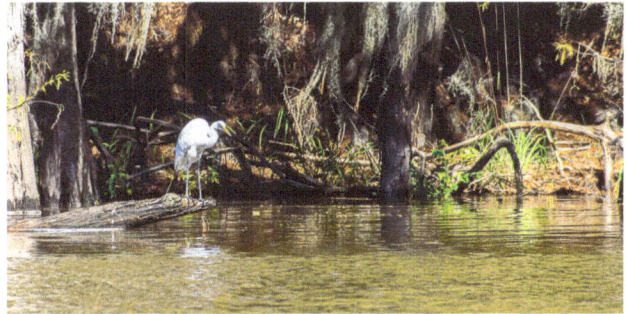
Hopefully Fishing

the boat was natural to me, but unlike the ocean, I had no sense that the bayou wanted me or even noticed I was there. I felt comfortable while I moved through the trees. I continued deeper into the bayou, exploring its secrets.

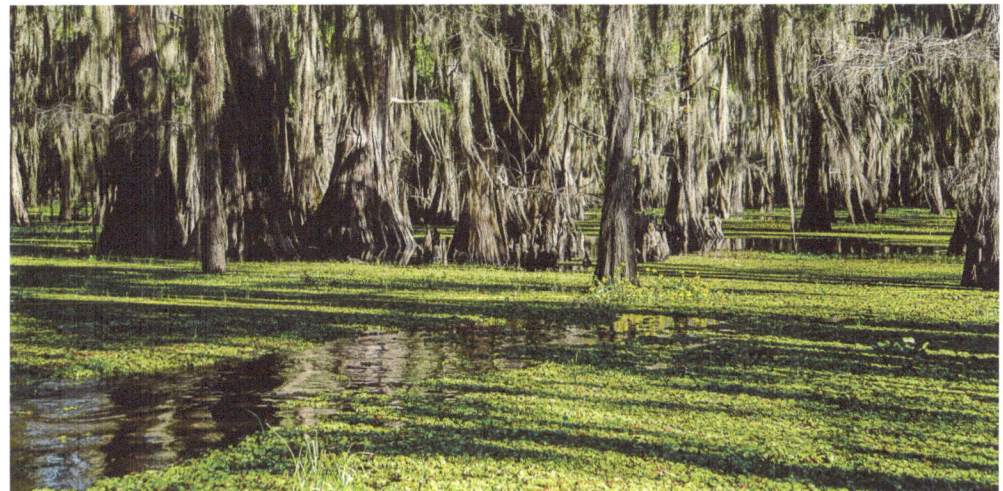
Bayou Color

Now and then I encountered a section with a break in the cypress canopy that allowed scraps of sunlight to reach the ground. If lucky, I saw a raft of flowers that provided a small pop of color to the scene. The flowers were likely growing in dirt, not on the water, which gave me a feel of how ill-defined the shoreline was. While the greenery in the foreground appears pretty in this photograph, it is an invasive species, giant salvinia, representing a severe problem for the lake's ecosystem. The conditions are ideal for giant salvinia, and it is quickly overtaking and choking off the native species. Scientists use chemical and biological means to control and eradicate it, although progress is slow. Some areas have seen significant improvement, so there is the hope of controlling it.

The bayou represents one great byway for me, and I enjoyed every moment I was in it. Even as I write this, I feel the sense of calm there and take comfort in that feeling.

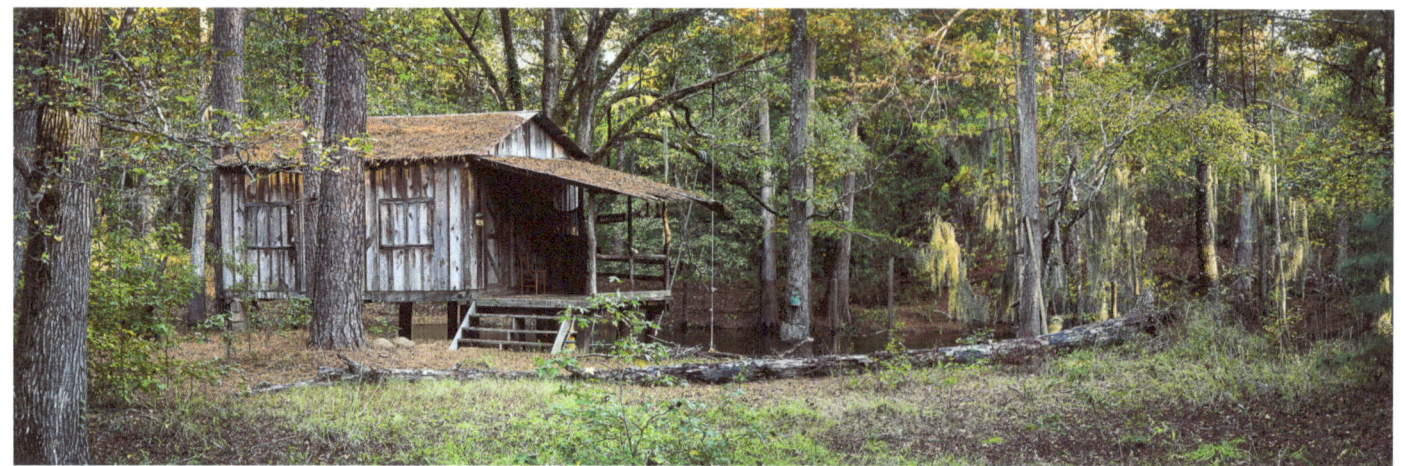
Marshy Reverie

Complementing that feeling is this old cabin on the shore of Big Cypress Bayou near Jefferson, Texas. The cottage sits next to Big Cypress Bayou, a stream or river by any other name, which feeds into Caddo Lake. I came across this scene while exploring the area on a chilly November day. It was late afternoon when I spotted the cabin, and the chills I felt were from excitement, not cold.

A few meager rays from the setting sun stole their way through the moss-draped trees and provided just enough light for me to make *Marshy Reverie*. I felt as if I was in a different, timeless era, and my thoughts drifted to what it was like to live there and how wonderful it would be to enjoy the calmness every day. The tranquility was absolute, and the only sounds I heard were the whispers of the bayou. The distant croak of a frog accompanied by a faint kerplop as some creature or other slipped into the water momentarily captured my attention, but the sounds quickly faded away.

The longer I lingered, the more the bayou wanted me to stay and become one of its permanent residents. It's hard to resist the allure of the swamp's calmness, and I was narrowly able to tear myself away and make my way back to the modern-day world.

Colorado Trail

Let's leave the swamp and go into the trees on dry land to finish this chapter. Central Colorado is one of my favorite places to head off-road and into the mountains, especially in the autumn. Some of the jeep trails can be challenging and yet rewarding, both to drive over and to make picturesque photographs. Other trails are easy enough for a passenger car. Some trails aren't official at all, just a pair of tracks where people have traveled before me. Many of the trails are lengthy, taking a full day to traverse, and others can be done end to end in a couple of hours or fewer. But sometimes I don't have to go very far off the highway to find something marvelous.

The season was fall, and I wandered through the central Colorado mountains seeking to make the perfect aspen photograph. I didn't have a specific location in mind but figured I would know it when I saw it. I knew I wanted plenty of aspens with the perfect mix of color, but beyond that, I was flexible and open to whatever I found. I had gone through Kebler Pass, one of my all-time favorite places, but nothing jumped out at me, which was unusual. I typically find a unique angle there, but this time it was not to be. I'll admit to feeling a sense of disappointment, but mostly I took it as a sign I needed to work harder. So I did.

I headed from Kebler Pass generally toward Carbondale and Glenwood Springs and then down through Aspen and over Independence

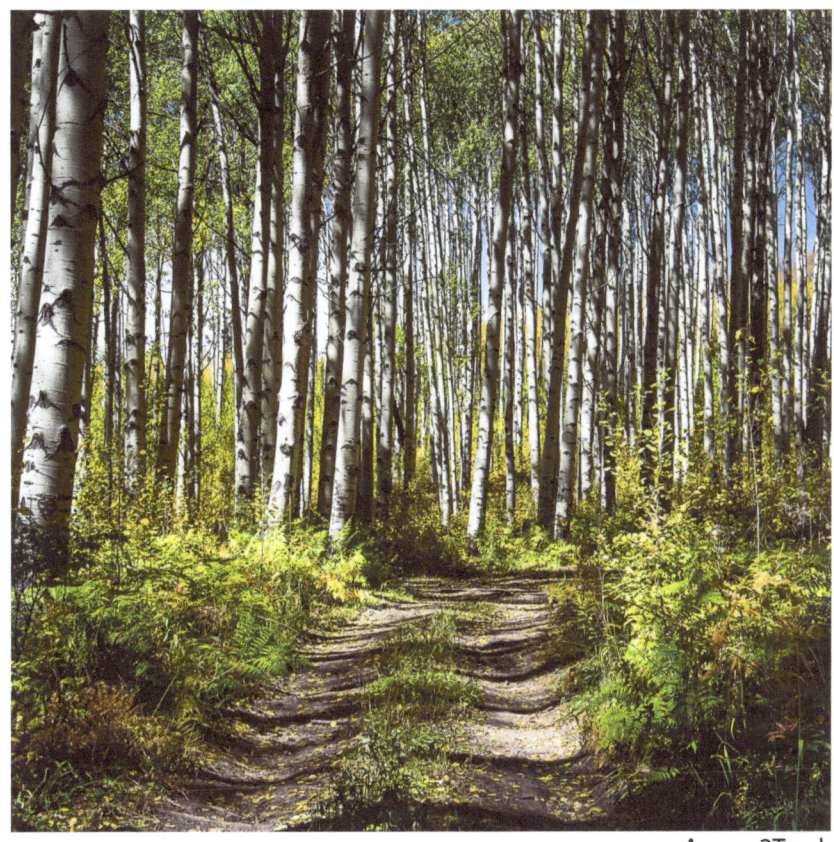
Aspen 2Track

Pass. Surely I would notice something there, but all of my go-to areas were not working out. Crud. I called it a day and found a nearby hotel room. The next day I headed out bright and early and this time went north and more westward. Again, try as I might, I couldn't find the perfect scene. No matter how hard I looked, I knew I didn't see "it." And I did try. I spied a small road or track and headed down it. I found several stands of aspens, but for whatever reason, they didn't sing to me. I knew I needed to stay confident, and I did, right up until I took another hotel room for the night. My plan was not working, and my hopes began to fade.

Morning dawned, and much to my surprise it was not bright and sunny. A front had moved in, and the day was drab and dreary. This development was not going to help matters, and I decided it was time to head to a completely different location. I headed south, back past Glenwood Springs and Carbondale. I didn't have an exact route planned and figured I would generally make my way southward and see what happened from there. I like to have a reasonable plan for each day, but sometimes I end up winging it and hoping for the best. I continued south, up to the top of McClure Pass. I'd been there two days earlier, so I wasn't looking hard, but a two-track near the top caught my eye. I'd seen it before on my travels and knew it didn't go far, but I figured why not see if anything might be different this year.

About this time, and so slowly it had escaped my conscious attention, the day had begun to clear. The light was gradually improving, bit by bit, and sparkles began to replace the dreariness. And wouldn't you know it, there at the end of the short track was the scene I had been waiting for: *McClure's Aspens*.

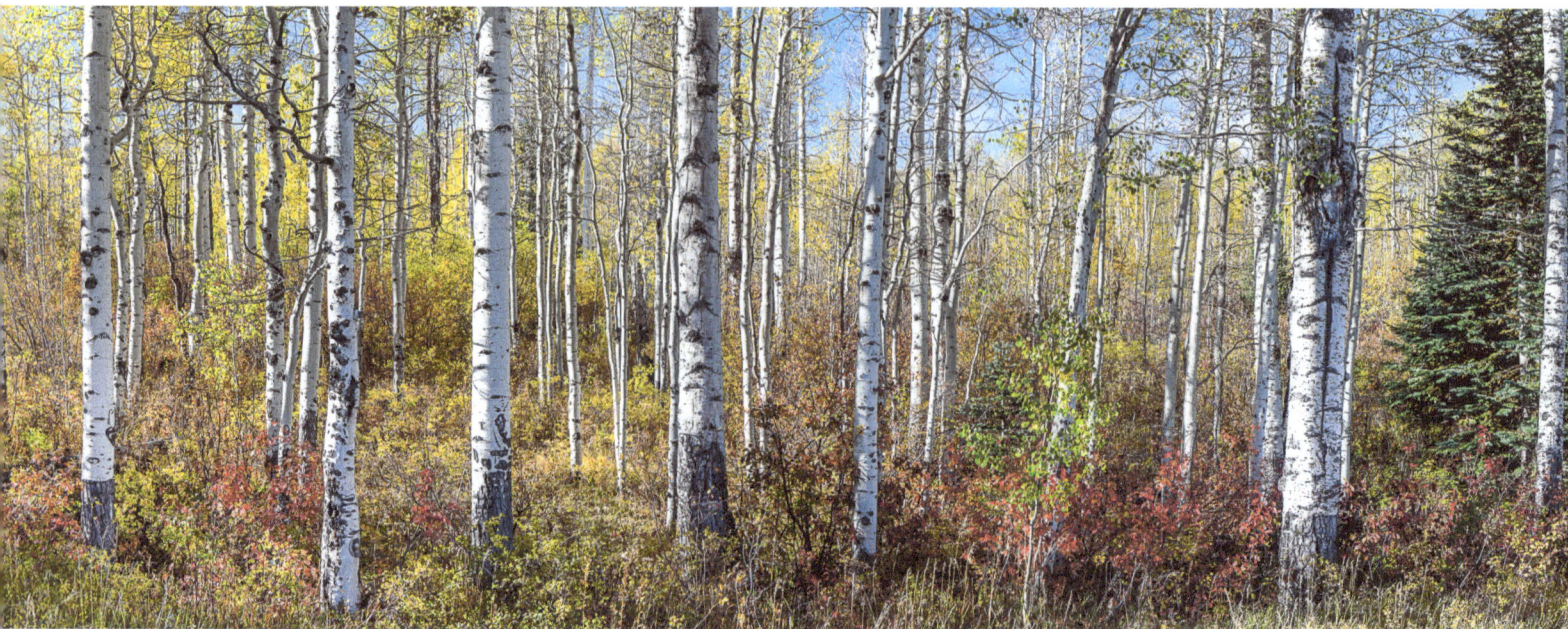

McClure's Aspens

I have made many aspen photographs over the years, and some of them are quite stunning, but *McClure's Aspens* is one of my favorites. Something about it, a light within it, jumps out of the photograph. It isn't that the aspens are particularly tall or big; they aren't. It isn't that the scene has the most color or the most leaves; it doesn't. But something about the way everything comes together and works as one creates this one dramatic moment in time.

These stories aren't about perseverance, per se, because underlying everything is my firm determination to keep moving ever onward, even when things are not working. These stories don't imply that at the end of every out-of-the-way road or byway something photo-worthy awaits. It doesn't. It is hard work to find what I am looking for and then create a stunning photograph, even if I don't always know what I am looking for until I see it. I go and go and go until it works out or I've exhausted all the possibilities. But sometimes fortuity finds me.

I had been poking around Red Mountain Pass in Colorado one late September day, and nothing had jumped out at me as the perfect opportunity. I poked around a little too long, though, and ran out of time to make it home that evening, since I still had an eight-hour drive ahead of me. I'd done that drive at night before, but there was no hurry or need this time. I decided to drive home the next day and found a nearby hotel. The next morning, and much to my surprise, I woke up to the season's first snowfall. I hadn't been expecting it, although had I bothered to check the weather the

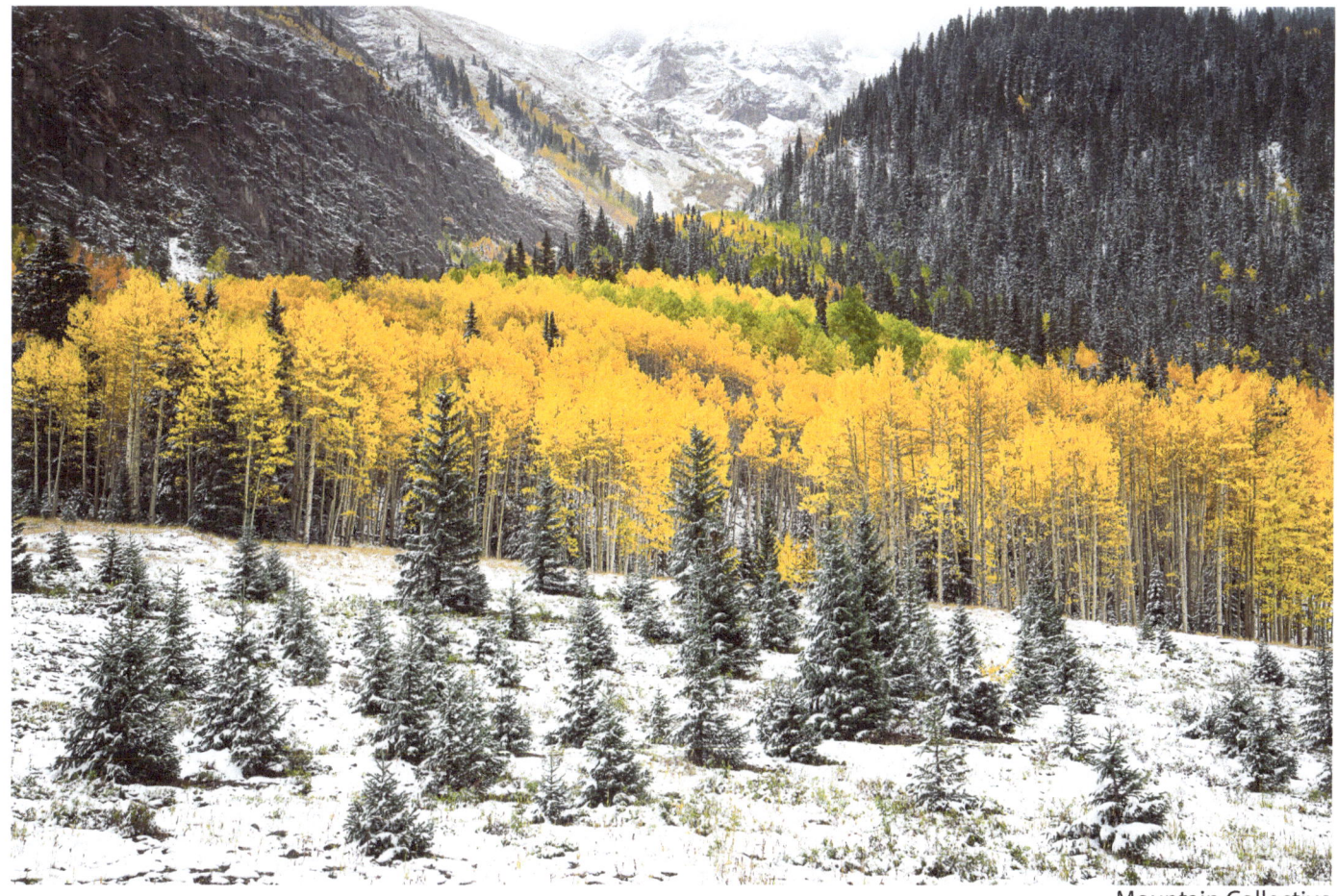

Mountain Collective

night before, I would have been. The change was an unexpected treat, and I wanted to make the most of it. Rather than heading straight home, I went back onto some of the smaller side roads on the pass. *Mountain Collective* is the result of one of those byways. I adore how the light snow and lingering fog provides the perfect setting for the aspens in full fall color. Most of all, I love how the snow flocked the scattered pine trees, which completes the scene. I'm glad I stayed the extra night.

These stories are a long way of saying that if there is a little, seldom-used road, you'll likely see my taillights up ahead.

Parks Redux

Our national parks continually draw me back to them with their gentle lure. How can I not respond to their call? Let's continue with more national parks on a coast-to-coast whirlwind tour and see if I manage to keep avoiding the ocean's wrath and becoming lunch.

My heart belongs to the National Park System. You didn't think I could stay away from our parks for more than a chapter, did you? Let's explore a few other favorite parks, starting with Yosemite National Park in California.

Yosemite is one of our National Park System's crown jewels, and with good reason. It's hard to find anywhere inside Yosemite that isn't gorgeous. Although most visitors stay inside the centrally located Yosemite Valley, wonders abound throughout the park, and visual delights are everywhere. Yes, it is that kind of national park, and like so many other topics, I could devote an entire book to it. Selecting these few highlights was not an easy decision. Let's start with one of the most recognized mountains anywhere: Half Dome.

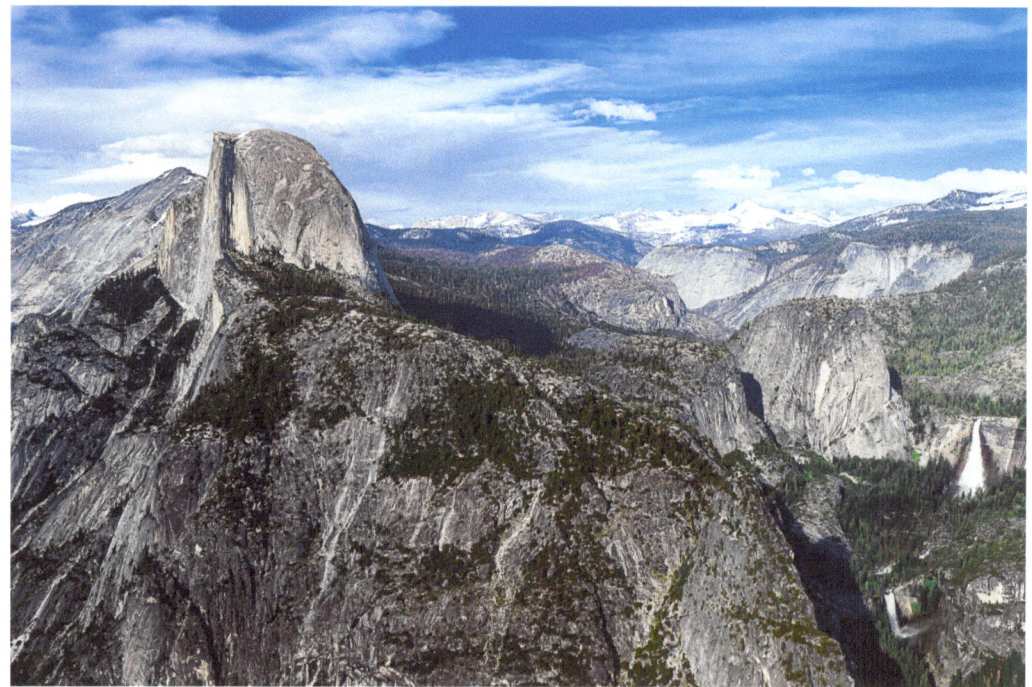

Dome View

Half Dome, the mountain that looks precisely like one half of a dome, is a standout iconic feature in a park full of them. This grand scene shows Half Dome and the surrounding and equally alluring countryside, including the Merced River surging over the Nevada and Vernal waterfalls. I love how the scene at first is dominated by Half Dome, but as you look at it and into it, you discover the other details it holds, making it a photograph of discovery. I can easily see myself walking into the far mountains of the Sierra Nevada range to see what might be there, for that trek is the sort I adore. It was hard not to head that way immediately after making *Dome View*, but somehow I managed not to.

Another view containing Half Dome is *Yosemite's Valley*. This view showcases some of Yosemite's more notable features, include El Capitan on the left and Bridal View Falls on the right. It's an iconic scene because it is the first view

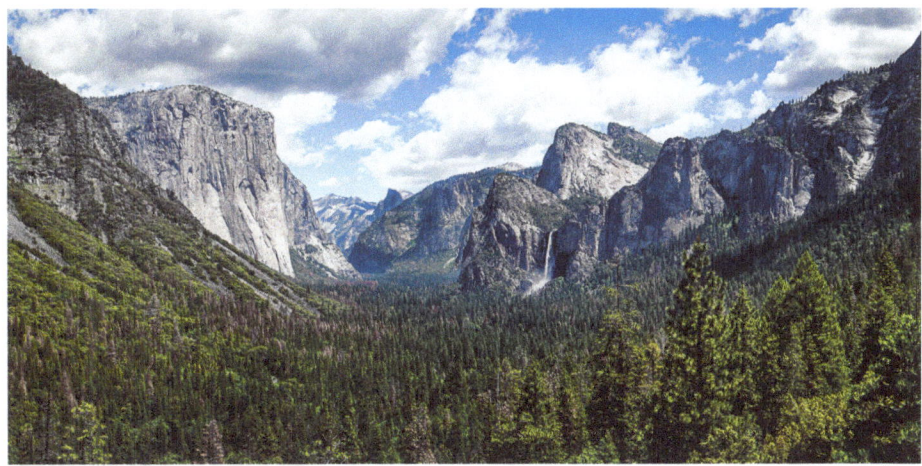
Yosemite's Valley

people have of the valley when they come by way of the common Highway 41 route. Up until that point, after you enter the park, you've been driving through forests and woodlands. You know you're in the park, of course, but for an hour, you've seen naught but trees. You go through a tunnel, and there, on the other side, this viewpoint awaits you, making the transition from woods to valley all the more jarring and stunning. Like *Dome View* above, it's hard to take in everything at once, and the more you look, the more you find. I adore these extensive, expansive views and delight in making them. Locations like Yosemite give me the perfect opportunity.

I delight in the smaller vignettes the park holds too. A view doesn't have to be vast to be scenic. I spend day after day exploring, looking for more intimate settings. It's easy to become carried away looking at the impressive, and often crowded, overlooks and viewpoints. Make no mistake: I enjoy them and stop at every one, but I truly revel in the extensive exploration of an area and delight in the results.

Lupine's Day

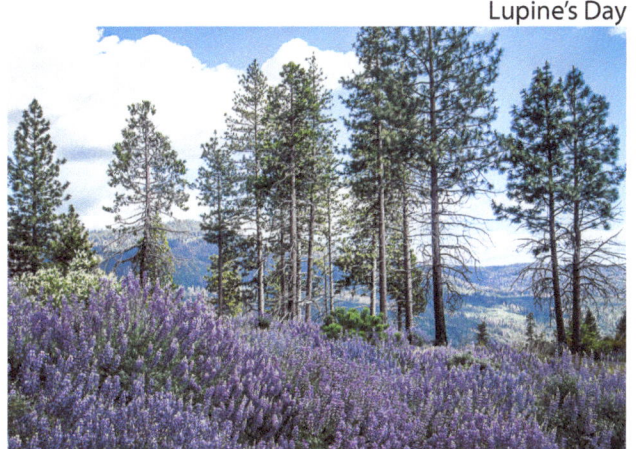

Lupine's Day is an excellent example of my reconnaissance. I was on the western side of the park, far from the main valley and the bulk of the crowds, on a lovely spring day. The lupine were blooming, and now and then I found substantial patches of them. It took me a long while to find just the right cluster of them. I drove and drove, searching high and low, and true to form, even took all the small side roads I could find. I searched across fields and meadows, all to no avail. Eventually, though, I located precisely the spot I was looking for, replete with scattered trees behind the lupine, and made *Lupine's Day.* My perseverance paid off again, for I knew a photograph awaited me if only I could find it.

The mighty Merced River slices through the park and is a central feature of Yosemite. In my journeys I often looked for bridges, because what I wanted seemed always to be "just on the other side." The Merced River looks calm in most places, but it's deceptive. A staggering amount of water flows in the Merced, and it will carry the unwary away. As we've already seen in *Dome View*, the river is capable of generating strong forces in the form of mighty waterfalls. I made plenty of photographs of the Merced, but *Merced Glow* is my favorite. I made it late in the day, with barely any light, but what little light there was gave the young dogwoods a glow that caught my eye. I was walking along the shoreline looking for whatever I would encounter, when I glanced up and saw

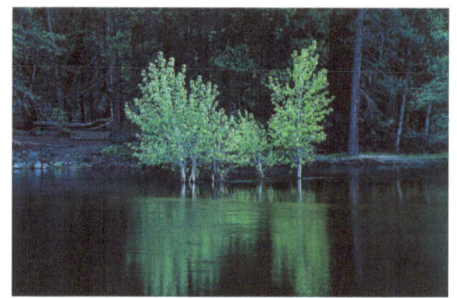
Merced Glow

this small scene. How could I not photograph it? I laugh at myself sometimes. There I am, in Yosemite National Park, among some of the most photogenic mountains and grand views anywhere, yet I find myself captivated by and photographing young trees submerged in a river.

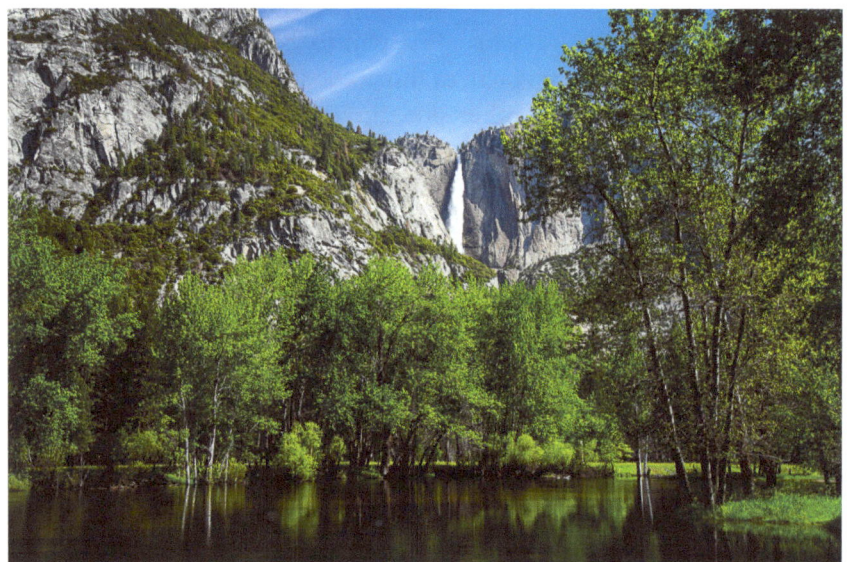
Merced View

We'll leave Yosemite for now with one more favorite view from the Merced, *Merced View*. I had to bushwhack a little to find a location I liked for this setting, especially since I wanted to put Yosemite Falls in the background. I could isolate the falls alone, and I could effortlessly photograph the river by itself, but I couldn't find the perfect location where they both came together for me. I went all along the riverbank until I found the perfect view, avoiding the underbrush when I could, and pushing through it when forced to. I spent the better part of an afternoon searching for this spot, and I am glad I did. Not all of my searches for the ideal scene work out, but I appreciate them all the more when they do.

Other national parks also feature water too. Let's head north to the state of Washington and another jewel of the park system: Olympic National Park.

Olympic National Park covers a broad and diverse range of ecosystems, putting it mildly. Many parks encompass a single, or perhaps two, cardinal features, protecting them, but Olympic National Park has everything from soaring mountain ranges to ocean coastlines to temperate rainforests. It has so much to explore that it's hard to know where to begin or end, and I could spend a lifetime in this one park. Let's visit a few of my favorite highlights, starting at the top of the park and Hurricane Ridge.

Hurricane Ridge is easily accessible; all you have to do is drive to the top of the mountain, provided, of course, that the road is open. The snows there are significant, and the mountains don't let go of their snowpack quickly. Like most mountains, they are moody, so different days yield wildly divergent photographs, depending on the weather. Many, if not most, and maybe even all, of my days in Olympic have had rain in them. Rain follows me around, so it is hard to say if this is the natural state of affairs or unique to me. Rain means clouds, and clouds make for dramatic photographs, as *Cloudy Hurricane* aptly illustrates.

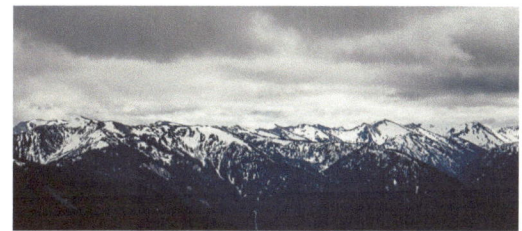

Cloudy Hurricane

To be fair, I've been at Hurricane Ridge when it wasn't snowing, raining, or even had any clouds. When I made *Hurricane Deer,* I spent the afternoon there, mostly watching the deer grazing peacefully on hillsides greening up after the long winter, while I waited for sunset. The sun, not being quite as patient as I, decided to pack it in and call it a night, leaving only the deer and me. Eventually even the deer concluded the day was done and headed downslope to where they spent the night. Before the sun and the deer could slip away, however, I made the photograph that shows an unusual lack of clouds. Not to worry, though, because the clouds would be with me again. Aside from this one brief moment, the rest of my time in Olympic has been cloudy and rainy. Let's drive out of the mountains and down to the shoreline.

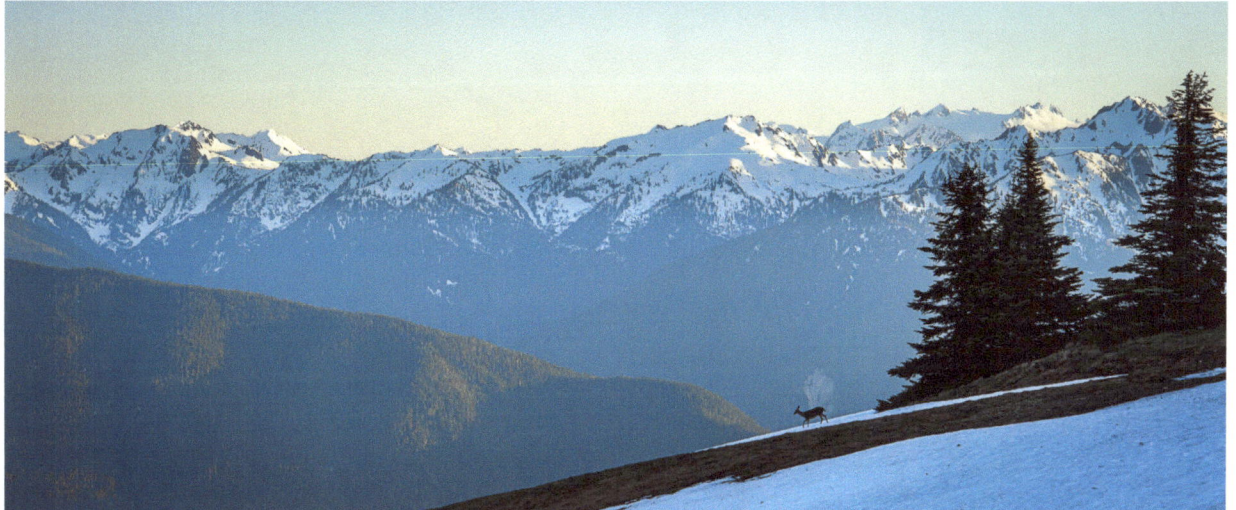

Hurricane Deer

Olympic abuts the Pacific Ocean and has an abundance of coastline to explore, including iconic beaches. Most of the beaches are easy enough to reach, but Second Beach requires a bit more effort. I parked along a road, hiked through the woods, including up and over a steep hill, and then descended a steep slope to the beach. There's a trail of sorts, although mostly it is just a "find your way through the woods, what can go wrong?" kind of approach. As I hiked, the dull roar of the beach intruded into my consciousness so slowly I wondered when I first heard the waves' distant crash. Although the half-mile hike certainly isn't difficult, carrying heavy gear makes it challenging, and I was happy to tumble down the slope and safely onto the beach.

Sunsets are my favorite time to make photographs on the Pacific Ocean beaches, and *Second Sunset* is no exception. Like the mountains, and really, like everywhere, each evening is entirely different from the one before. Sometimes the scene dramatically changes from one moment to the next. For example, I made *Second Flares* eight minutes after *Second Sunset*, but what a change happened in that short time! The sun momentarily broke through the clouds and celebrated a brief freedom. I like how the golden

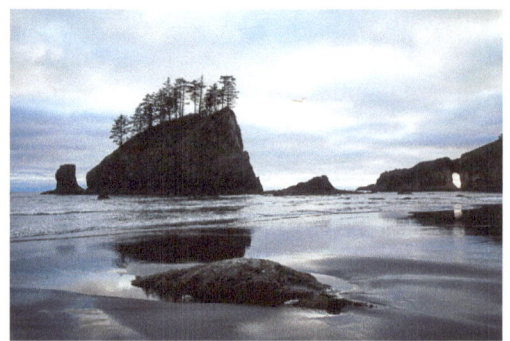

Second Sunset

Second Flares

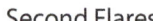

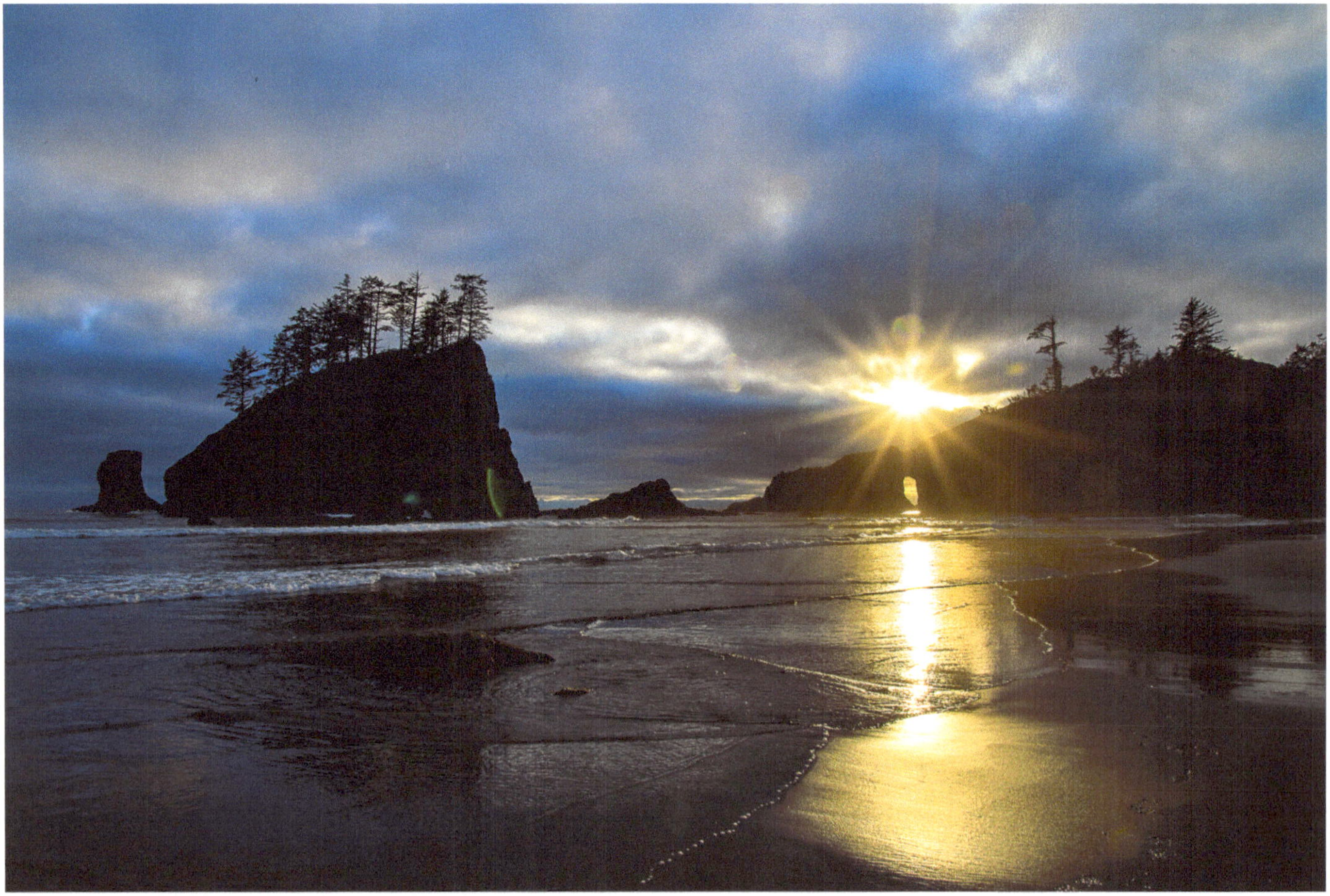

light complements the blue tones of the evening, creating a startling and dramatic contrast. After I made *Second Flares*, though, and before I could create any more photographs, the sun disappeared behind the clouds for the rest of the evening. I packed up my gear in the last of the light and headed back up the trail. That trail was quite a bit more difficult in the dark, and it was no fun to pick my way through to make it back to the road. There's nothing quite like carrying a heavy pack of gear while finding my way through the thick woods with nothing but a small headlamp for light. The once-lovely woods became dark and conspiratorial, and I wondered what creatures of the night watched me hungrily. In comparison to some of my other park adventures, though, it was no problem at all. I found my way back to the car without incident, and elated with the evening's results.

Unlike some of the other parks, I haven't had any "big adventures" in Olympic, which is probably a good thing. I did have some profound quiet moments, though, especially in the rain forests.

Olympic boasts two temperate rain forests, the Hoh and the Quinault. If I found myself randomly placed in either one, I could not tell them apart; their flora and fauna and the ecology of each of them are identical to my eyes. They have minor differences, but for my purposes, they are much the same. Despite the similarity, I immensely enjoyed my time in each of them, and they each hold separate and distinct memories for me.

The Hoh Rain Forest is memorable because it is the first bona fide rain forest I have entered and photographed. Stepping into it is like stepping into a whole new, magical wonderland. Even a few feet inside of it is enough to notice the change. The world is quieter there, if possible, and like the bayou, time moves at a slower pace. Because of the dense canopy of tree leaves, the lighting is softer and dimmer. Even at midday, the rain forest is quiet and shaded. Rain falling doesn't hit the ground directly, either; instead it is slowly dispersed by the trees, making for a steady and seemingly constant drip-drop of water. The fact that the world was quieter, though, doesn't mean it was silent. The steady plip-plop of abundant water globules striking the ground surrounded me, and I can still hear that ethereal sound as I write these words. The drops hit me on the head, plopped onto the ground next to me, dripped a few feet from me, and so

Hoh's Elms

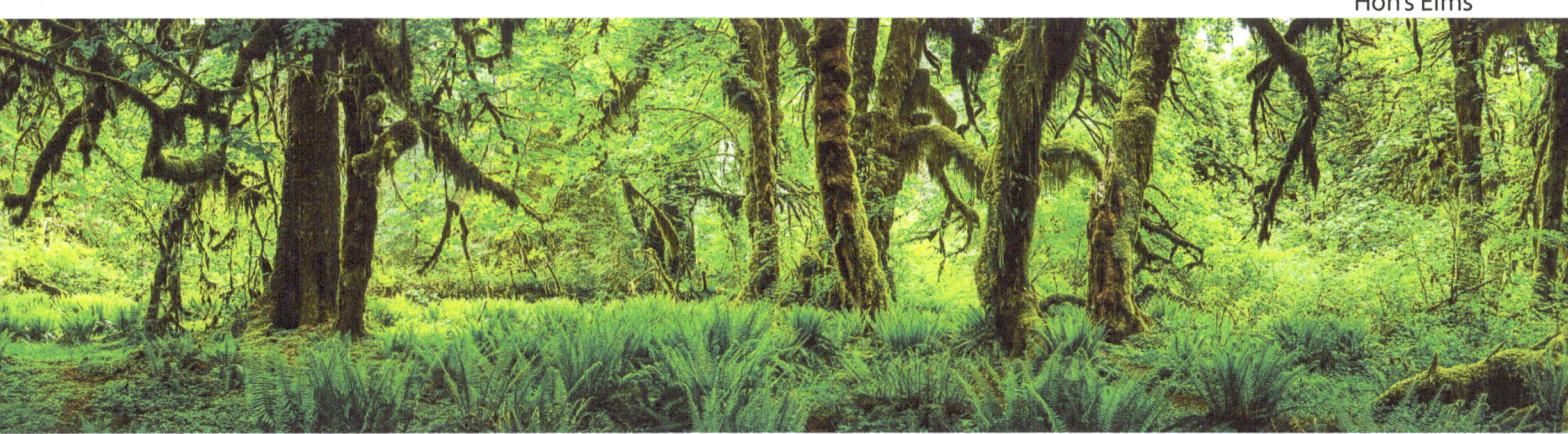

on, well into the forest's far reaches. The sound is, and I use the present tense because I can still hear it, comforting, and although this trek wasn't challenging, it was an adventure all the same. The lonely call of a single bird echoed in the distance, mirrored by a closer bird. A rustling behind me startled me for a moment. A squirrel, perhaps? A rabbit? Something bigger, maybe, like Bigfoot? Whatever it was, by the time I turned around, all was still again. The rain forest is alive, from top to bottom, front to back, and side to side, and it is one of the most tranquil places I have ever visited.

The trees were all moss-covered, and the only question was whether I could see any bark on them. Moss draped every branch, and spots had so much moss that it touched the ground. Grasses and ferns covered the forest floor, and some ferns were gigantic. Most striking of all was the amount of green.

Everywhere I looked, it was green, green, and more green. Bright and vibrant, even in the dim light, the verdant forest glowed with an inner light. In places it was hard to tell what was dry land and what was waterway. Shallow, slow-moving streams meandered through the rain forest, and especially in the Quinault. It was easy enough to walk through the forest, but I had to pay close attention lest I suddenly find myself walking in the water.

Rainforest Way

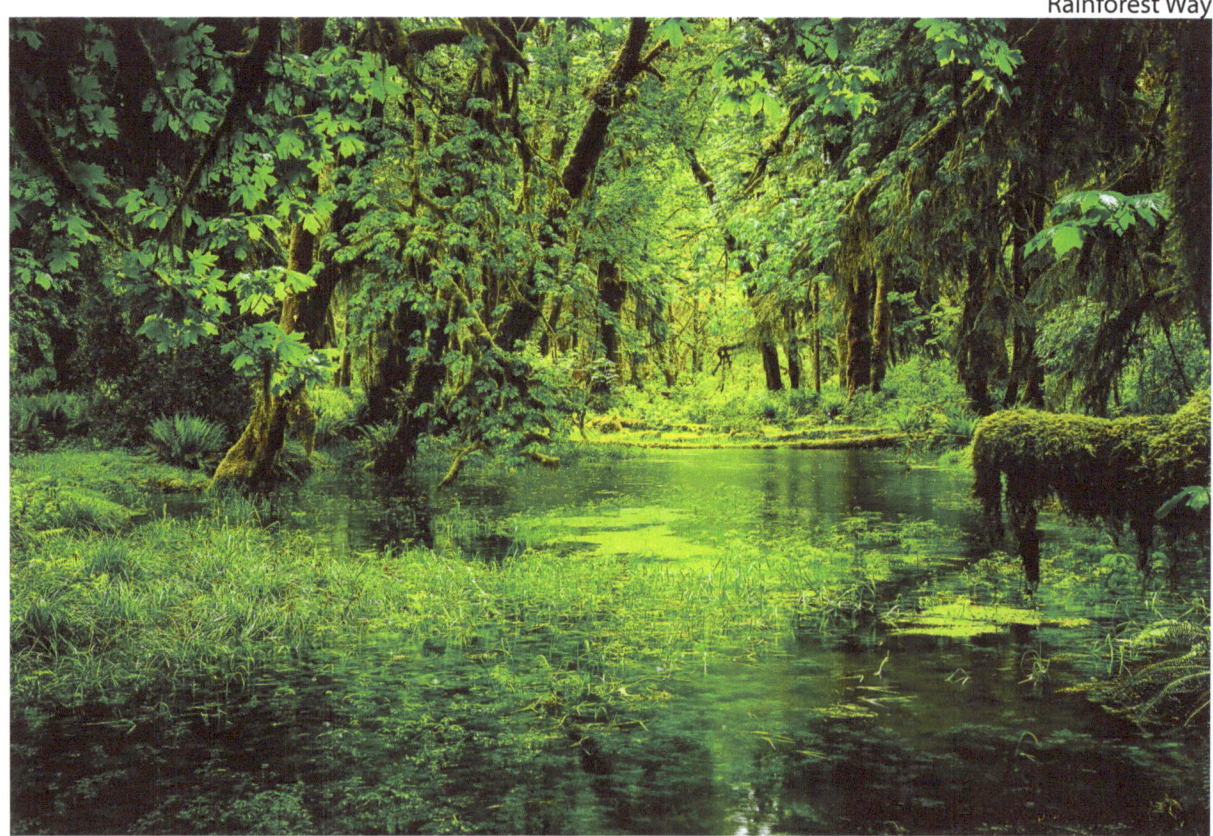

In thinking through it, my impression of the Quinault Rain Forest involves the presence of more water. While the Hoh, at least the sections I was in, had its share of streams, they were easily walked or jumped over. The Quinault tends to have broader streams that are not possible to jump across. The rain forests are extensive, though, and I explored only a fraction of each, so take my impressions for what they are worth.

We should visit some waterfalls before leaving Olympic. The water there is not slow-moving, meandering streams. Instead it rushes headlong over waterfalls, large and small, plunging down into a roiling maelstrom below.

Olympic has myriad waterfalls, each more picturesque than the one before. It's hard to select one waterfall over the others for this chapter, but I've settled on two that I especially like: Madison Creek Falls and Sol Duc Falls.

It's easy to visit Madison Falls, mainly because it is at the end of a short, paved trail. Typically I look for out-of-the-way places and scenes that few people visit, but I cannot overlook Madison Creek Falls. The falls aren't tall, no more than fifty feet, but the sight is captivating because it's tucked into the foliage. I'm a sucker for waterfalls, especially ones with a splendid view.

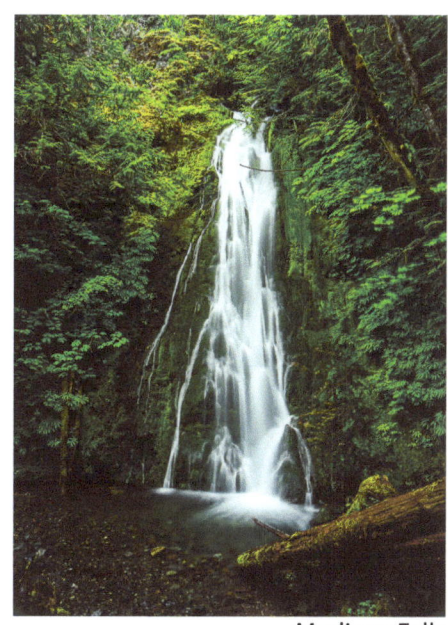
Madison Falls

Sol Duc Falls is another beauty in the park. This waterfall is a little harder to get to, but a well-marked trail leads there. What better way to prepare for a waterfall than a mile hike through the forest? Sol Duc Falls is another compact waterfall, also around fifty feet high, but the amount of water roaring through it makes it an phenomenal sight. At first glance it appears to be a triple waterfall, but to me, it looks like more a single waterfall with a couple of well-defined channels.

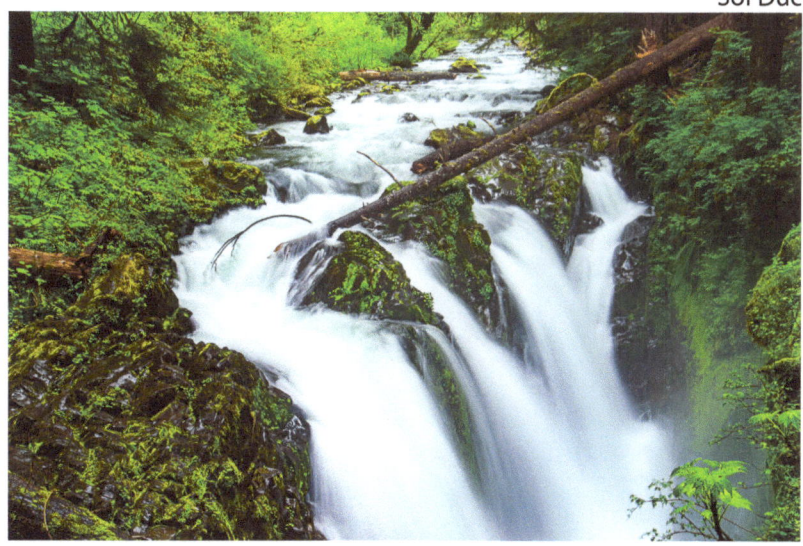
Sol Duc

Wildlife, mountains, beaches, rain forests, waterfalls, and more make Olympic National Park an extraordinary park to investigate, but it is far from the only park that captures my attention. For our next stop, let's travel diagonally across the entire country and delve deep into another park with significant water: Everglades National Park in Florida.

The Everglades encompasses and protects significant wetlands; it's another place where the difference between wet and dry land is slim to nonexistent. As with the rain forests, you need to be careful where you walk, because while you may think you are walking on dry land, you'll find yourself walking in the swamp before you know it. While turning a corner might not yield a bear, it will undoubtedly produce an alligator, and they are far less afraid of you than bears are. I've never quite felt like I was about to be lunch as much as in the Florida wetlands, but I'm getting ahead of myself.

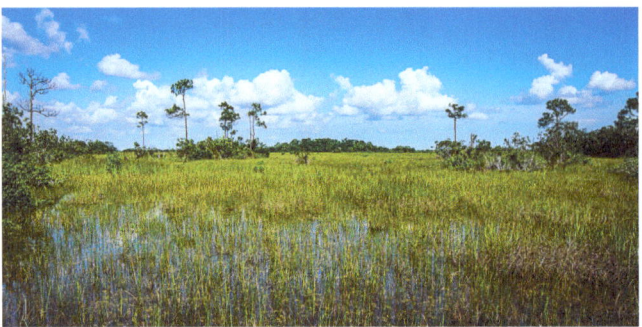

Everglade Wetlands

Unlike many of the other national parks, no extensive road system crisscrosses the Everglades. A solitary two-lane road wends through the park to the main visitor center complex, and the park has a few short side roads. Exploring the park by car isn't the best option, which leaves hiking and boating. Despite my trepidation about boats, I decided that a boat was the best way to get into some of the inaccessible backcountry. The way into the backcountry involves heading out into the ocean, motoring along the coastline, and going back to the shore when you get where you need to be. Once again I found myself watching the shoreline recede, although I was never out of sight of land and always close enough to swim to what passed as a shore. The boat was small enough—a rowboat with a motor—that I figured my odds were pretty good. I could have chosen an airboat, but they are noisy, and for photographing birds, I needed silence in my arsenal. A small rowboat it was, and once again I was at the ocean's mercy. It wasn't the best feeling, but the results were worth it.

Everglade Calm

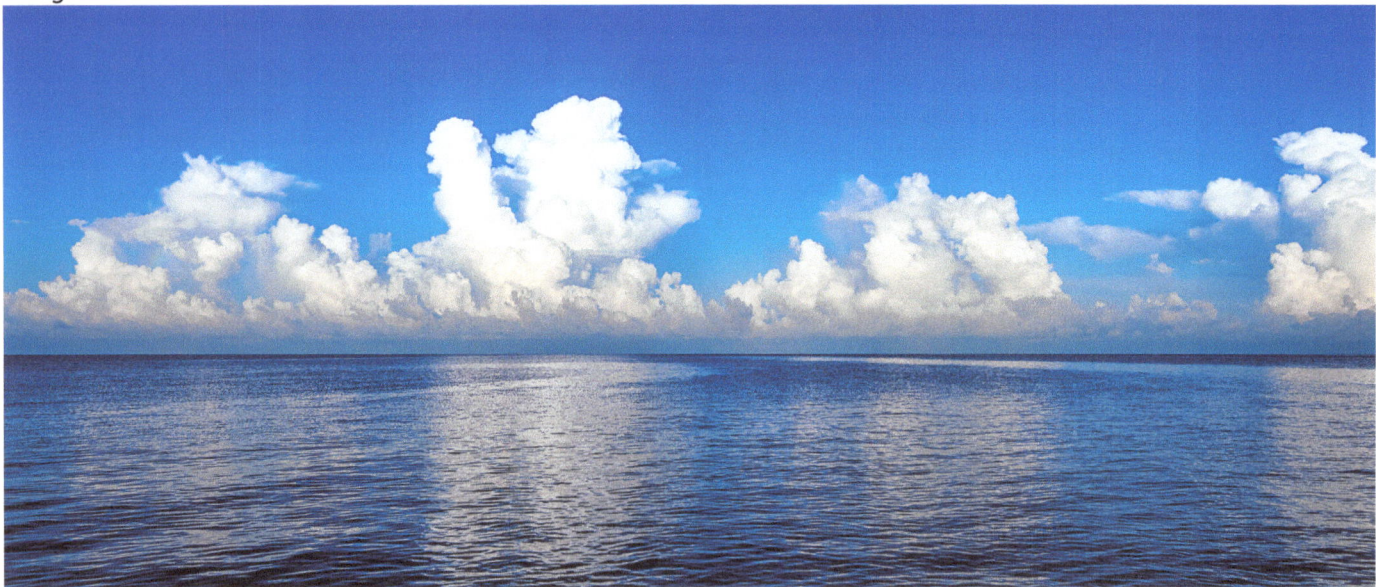

Despite my trepidation, the views from the boat were spectacular. I made *Everglade Calm* on a calm, bright morning. The ocean was as flat as could be, almost welcoming me, but it wasn't fooling me. Although I never drop my guard when it comes to the ocean, I'm not opposed to making beautiful photographs on it. I continued on my way, again looking out for any one-hundred-foot rogue waves and stealing glances at the beauty around me. Far from any road, and with the freedom the boat offered me, I headed deeper into the park.

I quietly motored into some of the park's backcountry, where I hoped to spot some of the birds I wanted to photograph. The Everglades is a bird-watchers paradise and hotspot; my adventure would not disappoint. Before long I spotted a roseate spoonbill perched in a low tree. As stealthily and quietly as I could, I readied my camera, and with a soft snick of the shutter release, created one of the photographs I was hoping for: *Roseate Spoonbill*. The bright-pink bird merely looked at me and watched me float by. Like the flamingo, the roseate spoonbill's pink coloration is a result of high levels of carotene in its freshwater shrimp diet. Regardless of the color source, though, it is an attractive bird, and I am glad I had the chance to photograph it.

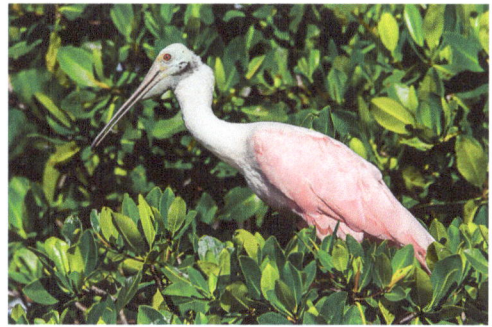

Roseate Spoonbill

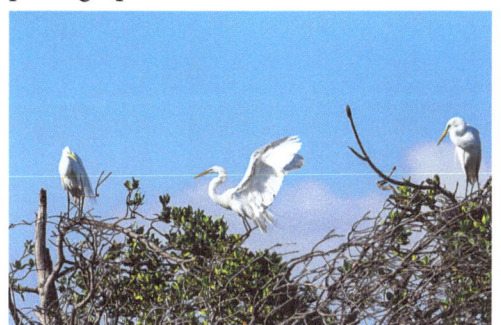
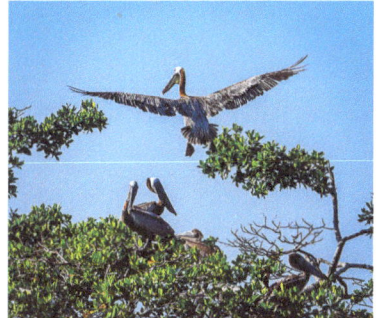
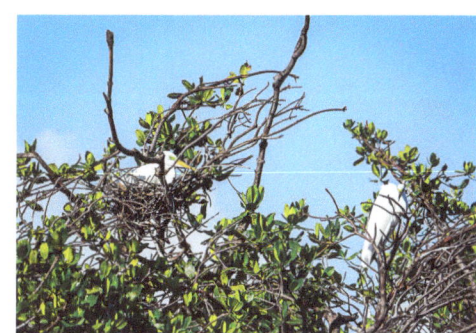

Egret Rookery

Another of my destinations was a bird rookery that supposedly hosted great egrets. I love seeing egrets. Their snow-white color, hair-like plumage, and overall behavior make them a joy to observe, and I take the opportunity any chance I get. I was able to get the inside scoop on a rookery location and had to try to find it. The site wasn't easy to locate, since it is nothing more than a clump of low trees in the middle of water deep in the park, but time and effort yielded results. Whew! I thought only one type of bird used the rookery, but much to my surprise, many species shared the same site and build nests almost next to each other. The calls and cacophony overlaying the gentle cooing were wondrous to listen to, and I can still hear them today, the same as I can still hear the sounds of the rain forests in Olympic. I floated alongside the rookery and created this sequence of photographs.

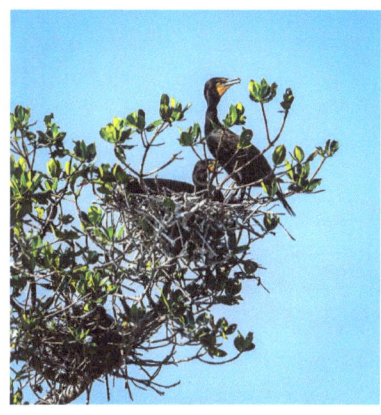

The birds came and went, sometimes quietly and sometimes loudly announcing their intentions. Some stayed on a nest while others switched out so their partners could head out. The commotion was something to behold, and I was able to observe double-crested cormorants, pelicans, and great egrets all nesting within a few branches of each other. I floated quietly nearby, observing and photographing. That one clump of trees turned out to be my favorite encounter in all of the Everglades. Of course, I say the same about every encounter, but I hope you get the idea.

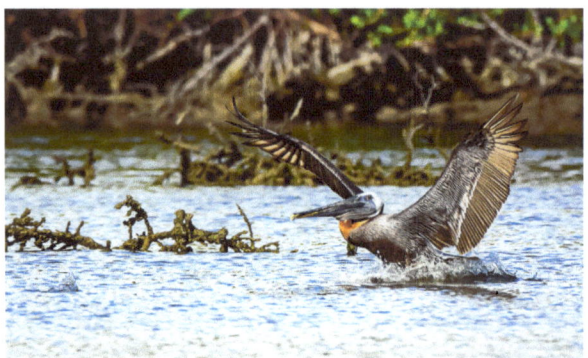

Pelican Takeoff

As with so many other subjects, I could write extensively about the Everglades birds, but I'll leave with one of my favorite bird photographs from there. I'm proud of these photographs because creating them wasn't simple. I was on a boat in the water, which is far from a stable photographic platform. I was using a long lens, which requires pinpoint focusing and precision, and I was in shadowed areas with challenging lighting conditions. With the constant and slightly unpredictable motion of the waves continually moving me, each photograph was challenging. I overcame those obstacles to create *Pelican Takeoff*. What makes it even more special to me is the pelican was aware I was there and was looking right at me as it took off. It was a brief connection, but you can feel it in this photograph.

I successfully motored back to the boat dock and once again reached terra firma. As before, nothing untoward befell me while I was on the ocean, although the sea had plenty of opportunity to have its way with me. And as before, I left the boat with a sense of sadness I can't explain. Perhaps, then, the ocean truly is home for me, and it knows no other way to tell me.

Although this chapter focuses on national parks, I'm going to detour a bit and take us to Big Cypress National Preserve. Mary Beth is well used to me starting in one place and ending up in somewhere completely different, so I thought I'd give you the same experience. Big Cypress abuts Everglades National Park, and unless you are using a GPS, you have no idea you went from one to the other. If I had to describe Big Cypress, I would say "dryer," but make no mistake: we're still in swampy and marshy areas. Big Cypress is where I encountered most of the alligators, all of which were unnerving experiences.

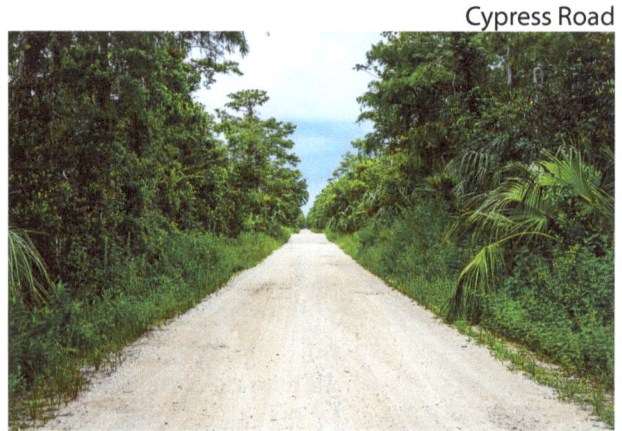

Cypress Road

A paved road slices through Big Cypress, along with a few dirt side roads. By now I don't have to mention whether I took the dirt roads or the paved roads. As dirt roads go, this one was an absolute pleasure to drive on. It was wide, reasonably flat, and had very few potholes. I almost didn't know how to drive on it. It led me through what passes for a forest.

Off to the side of the road, the forest was thick, dense, and not something I wanted to attempt to pass through. My hat goes off to the first people through there, because they cut their way through, with no idea of what lay before them except alligators. You will find alligators here.

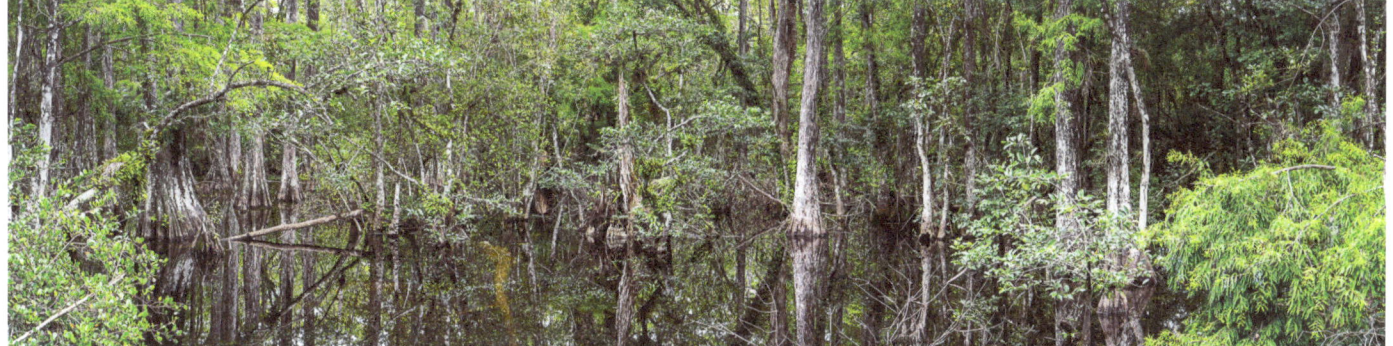

Cypress Secrets

After a while the jungle opened up and turned into a swamp. The swamp was more like what I expected. Small ponds were everywhere, with cypress trees clogging the shoreline. The foliage was so dense that light breezes were blocked, leaving perfect mirror reflections. This photograph is a typical small pond, and it is hard, if even possible, to find the shoreline.

As I was making this photograph, I kept feeling like someone was watching me. I looked all around but didn't see anyone, so I went back to making the photograph. Still, the feeling persisted, so I carefully looked around again. Finally, after scanning all through the trees, I looked into a small pond behind me. There, looking back at me, was a pair of eyes. Yikes! It gave me quite the start, and I instantly felt a little like lunch. Not having lunch, mind you, but being lunch. The feeling was not one I cared to have.

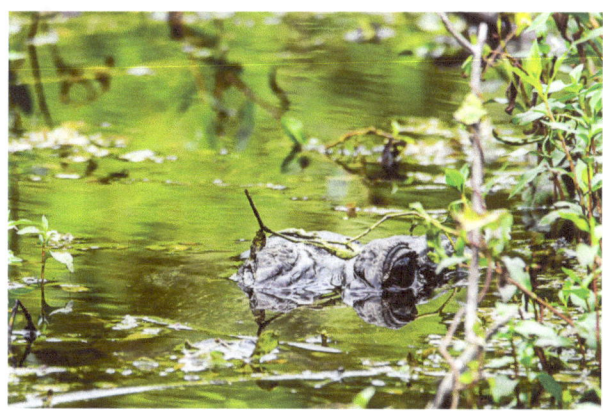

Alligator Eyes

I've been by myself in the wilderness long enough to have a basic understanding of what an animal, especially a large animal like a bear, is likely to do. I never know for sure, of course, but generally, animals follow the same basic behaviors. By carefully watching the animal and knowing what to do, such as puff up, back down, or move away, you can increase your odds of not having any problems. There are no guarantees, as each animal is an individual who may or may not be having a bad day, but you can tilt the odds in your favor.

The alligator stirred and lumbered up and out of the pond, and I realized I had no idea what it would likely do next. My uncertainty was deeply unsettling, but by then I was up on the hood of my 4x4, deciding that discretion was indeed

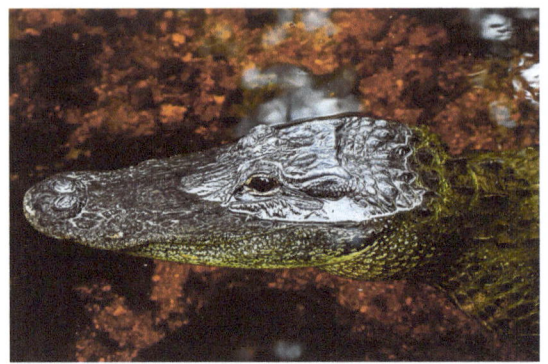
Gator Stare

the better part of valor. As it turned out, the gator wasn't interested in me and went to the far side of the pond, sliding into the water without making a ripple. I stayed on the hood a while, just in case. I thought about staying on top of my 4x4 permanently, but in the end I decided to be brave and made a mad dash for the 4x4 interior. I made it, barely, panting and winded. The alligator had no idea about my courageousness and was nowhere in sight, which didn't do a thing to calm my nerves. I spent the rest of the day being extra vigilant.

I had plenty more alligator encounters, although none were quite like the first one. What an introduction to the wetlands! I never did figure out what those huge scaly creatures would do next. I'll continue to give them a healthy distance. I think they are impressive creatures, but they still make me nervous.

Let's end *Parks Redux* in our newest national park, White Sands National Park in New Mexico. Luckily for me, New Mexico is not noted for its alligators, so I figured I would be safe.

Originally established as a national monument in 1933, its designation changed to a national park on December 20, 2019. Our federal lands are a complicated, loose hierarchy, with each unit having a titular designation, such as national park or national monument. Most of the time the unit stays with its original designation, and it takes an act of Congress to change it, but now and then a case is made to alter a unit's designation. National parks offer the most protection, so it is comforting to see a home-state national monument become a national park.

White Sands in New Mexico gets its name from the white gypsum crystals—sand—that pile into mile after mile of dunes. The stark white dune field is an impressive sight, especially knowing that it goes on for 115 square miles. The dunes are not wholly barren, however. Yuccas and even a few brave cottonwood trees somehow establish a toehold and do their best to survive. Their survival is no simple task in an ever-shifting sand field, and their only hope is to grow tall enough fast enough to remain above the sand. Plants face a constant struggle to survive, but life is tenacious and finds a way.

I love to create photographs in White Sands, and we've been here before in previous books. I wanted to return to it briefly and celebrate our newest national park with *White Storm*.

The summer monsoons bring much-needed moisture into the desert southwest. Each day starts sunny and bright, but by afternoon clouds fill the sky. Sometimes storm cells form, and some become impressive supercells. I was fortunate enough to be in White Sands when one of those cells appeared. The fading evening light left the sands in shadow, but the sun lit up the cell with a fiery display. *White Storm* celebrates that moment in our newest park.

Speaking of fading evening light, let's see what happens when the sun goes down.

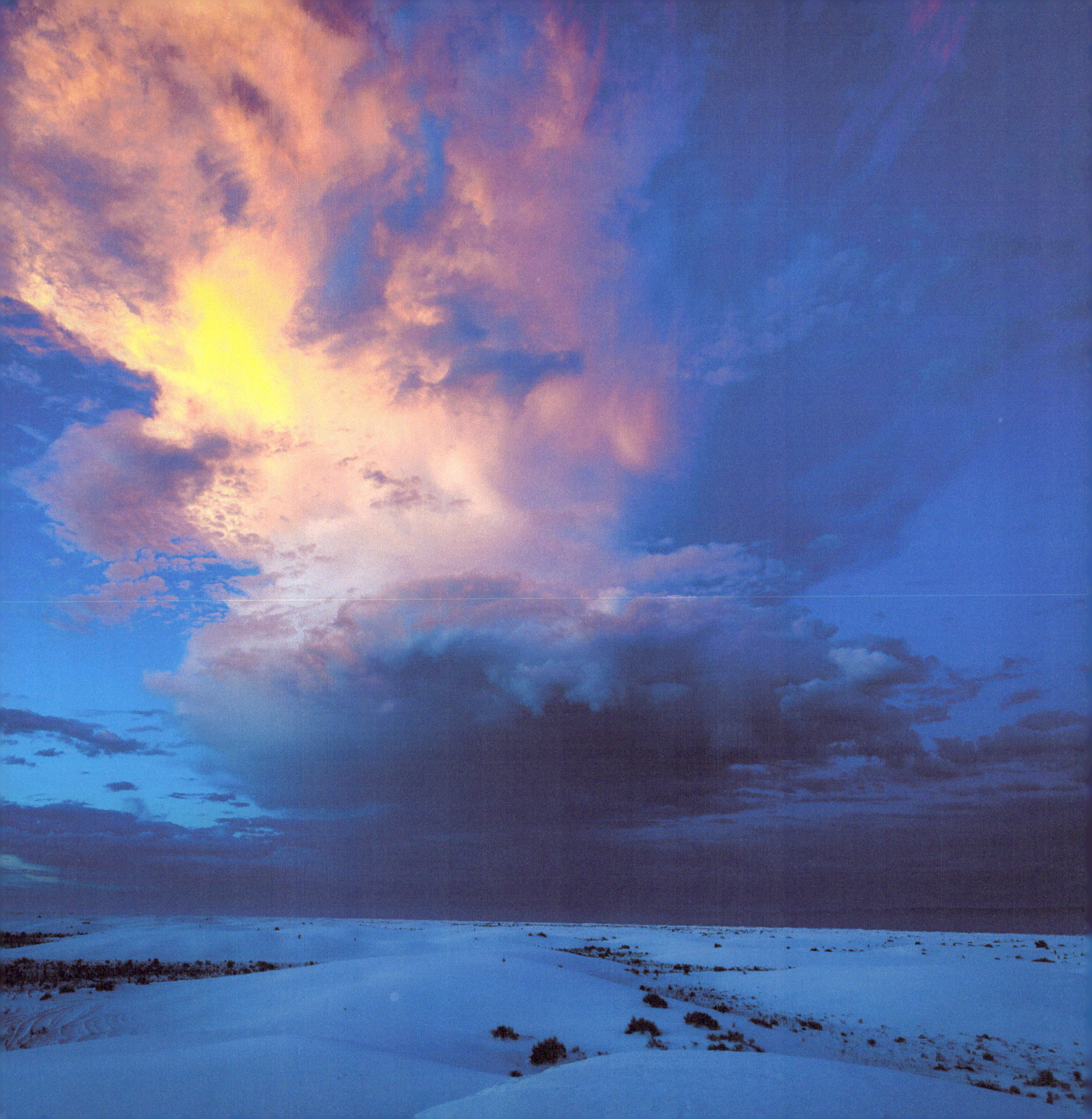

After Dark

The fact that the sun disappears from the sky doesn't mean we can't continue our explorations. Nighttime opens up new vistas and new worlds for us, and we peer into and beyond the heavens to glimpse the vast infinity of our universe. Dimming suns, twinkling stars, and interstellar visitors share their stories with us.

I always look forward to the end of the day. It's nice to have a good dinner, curl up with a book, or perhaps watch a little TV. Being home is delightful. I enjoy the quiet evening routines as daylight fades and nighttime sweeps in. Finally I settle into a toasty bed, all snuggled up, and drift off into a peaceful night full of sweet dreams.

Who am I kidding? Once that pesky sun gets out of the way, the moon and the stars come out to play, and I go outside after dark and have a ton of fun. Nighttime is a land of mystery and magic, a land where moonlit shadows dance across the ground, and I get a chance to see the night sky in all its glory. Once I get away from the city, it's staggering to realize how bright the evening is and how many stars are above me. Standing alone in the darkness with nothing but the infinite sky makes me realize how vast the universe is. Is there life out there? Perhaps there is, or maybe we are alone. Either way, I love to explore the night and see what it has to offer.

First, though, we'll explore nighttime during the day, a phenomenon otherwise known as a total solar eclipse.

There are two primary types of eclipses: lunar and solar, although each has variations and nuances. Regardless of the type, they are all fascinating to see, if you are lucky enough to be able to see it. In August 2017 a total solar eclipse covered a large swath of North America. Total solar eclipses are the most dramatic, and I wasn't going to miss it for anything.

I began my preparations long before the eclipse arrived. I made sure I had all of the specialty gear I would need. Quite the understatement, pointing your camera straight at the sun is a terrible idea. You need camera filters designed for photographing the sun, and you need to understand how to capture the image of the sun without directly looking at it with your naked eye. Achieving results is easy. Achieving good results is much harder. Well before the date of the eclipse, I took the time to prepare and practice, which was a good thing too, because as the eclipse drew near, the items I needed sold out.

Fortunately for me the eclipse would make a rare wide arc across the entire continent, giving a broad range of locations for the best outcome. I was grateful for all the possibilities. I had an excellent chance of avoiding worrisome weather and clouds, as long as I could make a successful forecast. When the day grew near, I obsessed over the forecasting, checking, rechecking, and then starting all over again. I didn't have to travel far from where I live in Albuquerque, New Mexico, to be successful, so I looked for suitable locations in Wyoming and Nebraska. I searched for smaller cities with major highways into them. My theory was that smaller cities meant fewer people, not that I was expecting all that many people to watch the eclipse. All the targets in those two states were well within a day's drive for me, making for a quick journey. I checked everything, packed, and readied myself. I knew I wouldn't have another opportunity at an eclipse for years, and I wasn't going to leave anything to chance.

I finally settled on a forecast I believed in at a location that suited my needs: Casper, Wyoming. Casper would be an easy drive, and I would take the interstate the whole way there. Food, gas, and lodging would be plentiful, and I would have options for whatever I needed. Like everyone else, I was getting progressively excited. The country was working itself in a fever pitch. That fact should have set off alarms bells for me, and I failed to consider the implications of every person in America wanting to experience the eclipse. Sometimes I think I am the only person, ever, to come up with an idea.

The day before the eclipse, I rechecked all my preparations and hit the open road. I especially liked my plan because I could go quite a way north before I needed to commit to Casper fully. Up until Denver, I had the option to divert to Nebraska, and I prepared for that eventuality. I can make contingency plans with the best of them.

I excitedly headed north, stopping every few hours so I could double check the forecast. All was going according to plan. I made one final check in Denver, since it was my last opportunity for a major course correction. As with many best-laid plans, mine suddenly was in jeopardy. Nebraska was showing a chance of rain, and even Casper had a chance of precipitation. Rain isn't a big deal normally, but rain means clouds, and clouds mean trouble. Uh-oh. Despite all my planning and forecasting, I was faced with the possibility of failure. I decided to continue to Casper; it remained the better choice, although not without a good deal of variability. I drove northward to Cheyenne, where I decided to spend the night and make a fresh and early start the next day.

Pulling into the hotel, I noticed it was far more crowded than I expected. In hindsight I know why, but at the moment I was not picking up on the fact that everyone from the surrounding states had the same plan I did. Before going to bed I worked out the mileage and the timing for the next day and then gave myself plenty of leeway in case of something unforeseen. I called it a night. I slept so-so, tossing and turning, continuously wondering if the clouds were going to steal the show. I spent quite a lot of time wondering how I could tell the clouds to go away without offending them, because almost always I want them around to help me make better photographs. In the end I fell into a fitful sleep, which was something, at least.

The next morning the shrill of the alarm woke me with a start. Like a flash I was out of the hotel room. As I was checking out, the clerk wished me good luck with the traffic. "Traffic?" I thought. "That shouldn't be a problem." I was just under two hundred miles from Casper, which wouldn't take long. I was awake super early and would surely beat whatever congestion might occur later, I naively thought at the time. My grand adventure in traffic was just beginning.

I took off north on the interstate, and the miles whizzed by. At least the first couple of miles did. Almost immediately after leaving Cheyenne I noticed brake lights up ahead. "Uh-oh," I thought. "Must be an accident up ahead." I slowed to a crawl, figuring I would pass the accident in a moment and then be zooming on my merry way. After a few miles I started thinking the accident was a major one. After a few more miles, for the first time, I wondered if the traffic might be because of people headed to see the eclipse. As the miles dragged on, my impatience grew and I realized that yes, I was indeed in a traffic jam. Finally, at last, I recognized that everyone ahead of me, which must have been everyone else who had the same idea as me, was going to the same place I was. People from Denver and eastern Colorado, everyone from New Mexico, and plenty of folks from Texas and Arizona funneled up Interstate 25 ahead of me.

Yuck. My sure-thing eclipse opportunity could go poorly.

I checked my watch every thirty seconds. Sometimes I managed to hold out for forty-five seconds before checking. One time I made it to sixty. At least I was creeping along and not at a complete standstill. I was making progress, however painstakingly slow. I was in a race against the clock, because I was pretty confident the eclipse would not wait for me.

In all my preparations, I had never imagined such traffic, but I had thought of other ways the trip could go sideways and brought plenty of maps. The total eclipse would be visible over a wide band, and Casper was at the exact center. Anywhere in that band would produce the same results, but the closer to the edge of the cutoff point I was, the shorter the total eclipse time would be. I pulled off the road, broke out my maps, and worked out Plans B, C, and D. As the morning agonizingly crept by, I became resigned to the fact I was not going to make it to Casper, but armed with my map, I was able to work out another location that put me dead center of the eclipse: the small town of Glendo, Wyoming. Best of all, I was there already. I exited the interstate and looked for a suitable place to set up. If I thought traffic was horrific on the interstate, the sheer congestion on Glendo's small and thoroughly clogged roads exasperated me. I doubted I would be able to move more than a few feet from where I exited, so I looked for a place I could pull off the road. I do what I have to do.

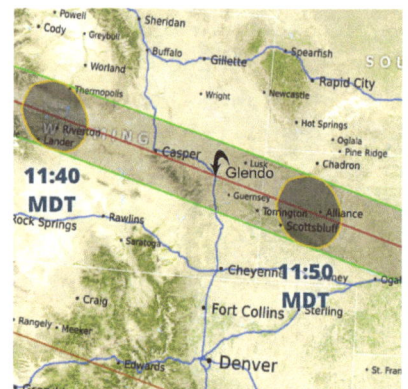

As luck would have it, an enterprising farmer, who was far better at understanding traffic than I, had opened one of his fields for parking. Even better, he had the foresight to bring in portable toilets. That heaven-sent oasis was perfect and well worth the twenty-five dollars I paid to get in. I was far from alone, for plenty of people entered behind me. The field was large enough to accommodate everyone, and it allowed room to spread out, which I promptly did. I didn't make it to Casper, but neither did I need to. The field took on a party atmosphere, and while I am not used to photographing amid other people, I enjoyed the camaraderie.

From there everything went smoothly. The clouds I earlier feared failed to materialize, and the sky was clear from horizon to horizon. I was within the total eclipse zone and would have a couple minutes of total eclipse. I set up all my gear without incident and even had a moment to compose my thoughts and ready myself. I started well before the eclipse began and ended after it stopped, allowing me to create this magnificent composite panorama, *Eclipse Panorama*.

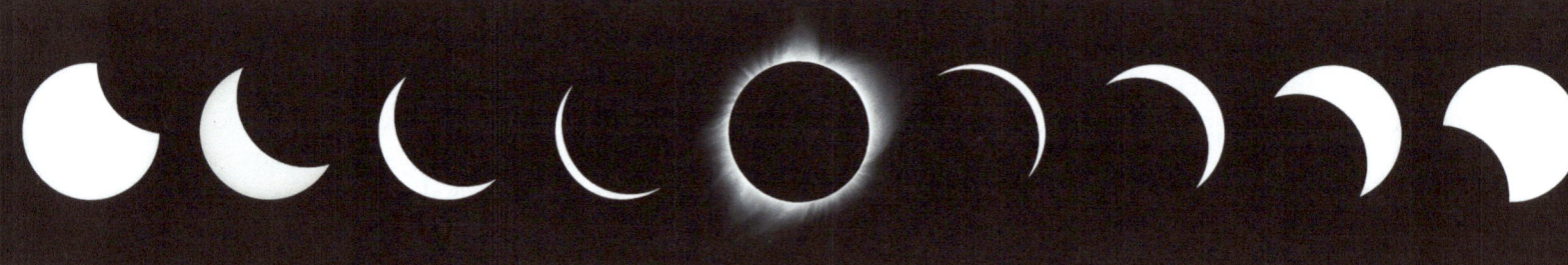

Eclipse Panorama

During totality, or the magical time when the moon hid the entire sun, I made *Eclipse Totality*, which thrilled me to create. As totality neared, the world around me grew increasingly darker, and all sounds, natural and human alike, faded away. Immediately before it happened, I could have heard a pin drop onto a pillow from miles away; the silence

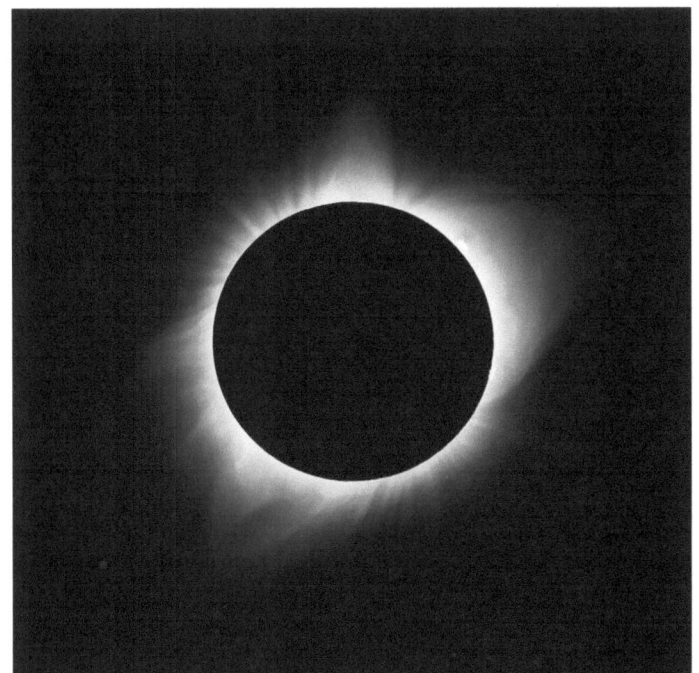

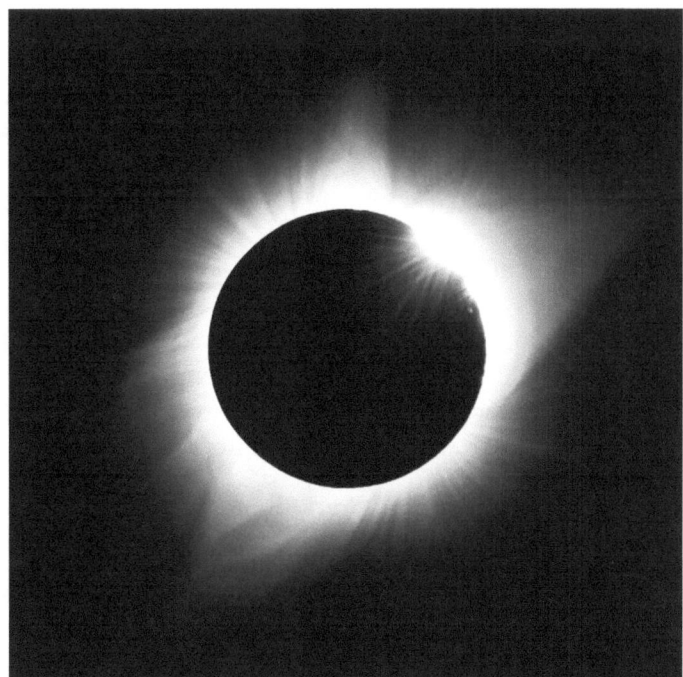

Eclipse Totality · Diamond Ring

was that complete. Totality was an otherworldly experience; everything was dark but ordinary, and everything was as different as could be. It was hard to remember to breathe during that time and harder still to remember to create the photographs I wanted. Lots of people cheered and hollered the moment totality happened, and in that heartbeat, I was glad for the people surrounding me and sharing the experience with me.

I was also able to make *Diamond Ring*, which is the effect that happens in the split-second the moon crosses the outer edge of the sun. The mountains of the moon create a flare, and the result is that of a diamond ring. Another flare happens when the edge of the moon again touches the edge of the sun as totality ends. This effect lasts for only a brief moment; I needed to be ready and focused on making a photograph at the exact instant it happened.

As soon as totality ended, the vast majority of people in the field packed up and headed out. I stayed until the bitter end, and I was almost the last person out. I was pleased and content and looking forward to a quick and easy drive home, knowing that all my planning paid off, and none of my worst fears, such as clouds ruining the view, came true. I exited the field, turned left on the road to head home, and came face-to-face with yet more traffic.

Remember a moment ago when I was complaining about the traffic while getting to the eclipse? That traffic was, as it turns out, a mere slowdown barely worth mentioning. After the event, I entered a monumental traffic jam. Before, everyone trickled toward the eclipse car by car, but afterward, everyone leaving at once created a traffic nightmare. On the way there I crept along, but on the way home I spent most of the time at a standstill, able to move a car length every few minutes or so. Each movement felt like a hard-won victory and was worth a celebration. Several times I thought I was cunning and exited onto a side road no one else thought about using. Each time I was proven unequivocally wrong and somehow made it back to the interstate. I stopped to eat at a taco place, but once inside, it looked like a scene from an apocalyptic movie. The employees, dead tired on the feet, had thousand-yard glassy-eyed stares. Most items on the menu were long gone, and one barely lucid employee mentioned the place had served more food in the last couple of hours than in the previous weeks. Somehow, after a thirty-minute wait, I managed to score a snack and a table, and I figured that traffic would taper off while I ate. It didn't.

Traffic had gotten worse. Far worse. I'll spare you the sordid details, but the congestion finally broke free a little south of downtown Denver, Colorado. I, and undoubtedly the rest of the entire country, went through a two-hundred-mile bumper-to-bumper traffic jam. Later, however, after talking to people from across the nation who saw the eclipse, I realized my experience was typical. Funny how everyone had the same idea I did.

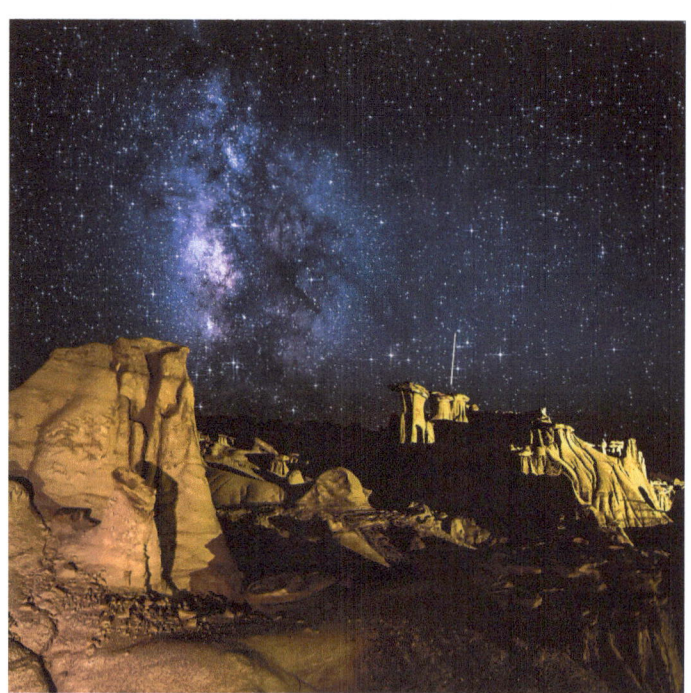

Ah-Shi-Sle-Pah's Night

Usually I strive to make my after dark photographs alone, in actual nighttime, in a far off wilderness without another human for miles in any direction. Such was the case of *Ah-Shi-Sle-Pah's Night*, which I created in the Ah-Shi-Sle-Pah Wilderness in New Mexico.

The Ah-Shi-Sle-Pah Wilderness is only a few miles north of Chaco Canyon in central New Mexico as the crow flies. As the car drives and the photographer hikes, however, it is quite a bit farther. The wilderness is small and little-visited; most people who are inclined to see its hoodoos and fantastical rock formations visit the far more well-known nearby Bisti Badlands or its connected cousin, the De-Na-Zin Wilderness. I adore the Ah-Shi-Sle-Pah for the simple reason that I am highly unlikely to encounter anyone else. I know of a series of back roads that are two-tracks through the weeds more than they are roads in the traditional sense. Those roads get me close to the wilderness. They can't get me into the wilderness, because no motorized vehicles are allowed in wilderness areas, so "close" is as good as it gets.

At any rate, I parked, loaded my gear, and hiked the rest of the way. I scouted the area in the daylight and found several ideal places. Although it was hard to choose, I selected the one I liked best and set up. It was just a matter of waiting for the sun to go down and the Milky Way to come out. I had plenty of time to set up my lights to illuminate the scene exactly as I wanted and then made *Ah-Shi-Sle-Pah's Night*. A meteor even streaked straight down through the frame, seen as the very small line just right of the middle and barely above the rocks, which delighted me. I take credit for the timing, but truly, it was by happenstance.

I couldn't see a darned thing after I turned off the last light and stood still, waiting for my eyes to adjust to the darkness. I think I can see perfectly well in the dark. I can't, but I think I can. This belief has caused me countless trips, spills, skinned knees, and various other bumps and bruises as reality let me know otherwise, but I still think I can see well enough in the dark to move around, and even jog, without a light. In any event, while I was standing in the dark, something large with wings that made a wholly unsettling "whooshing" sound flapped around my head a couple of times. I flailed my arms but didn't touch it, which is probably a good thing. I have no idea what it was, because despite my wishing otherwise, I actually can't see in the dark. I think it was big, about the size of a school bus; probably bigger. Most likely it was hungry and ready to carry me off to feed its young. It was enough to convince me that my time alone in the wilderness was at an end, so I turned on the lights, packed up, and made my way back to the 4x4 to get home. Even as I write I can hear those wings and their "whooshing." I wonder what it was that decided not to eat me that night. Probably aliens or a giant raptor or something. Yeah, that had to be it.

Sometimes, however, a nighttime photograph attempt goes as planned, without any traffic, unidentifiable things trying to devour me, or other unforeseen events. I like when that happens. *Galactic Spill* is one of those times. The Quarai unit of the Salinas Pueblo Missions National Monument in New Mexico hosted a dark-sky event, and I didn't want to miss it. As with the Abo unit, which we visited earlier in *Southwest Expeditions*, Quarai features an old Spanish mission and its attendant pueblo, both long past their prime. The mission and pueblo were active in 1678 and briefly again in the early 1800s. We're fortunate anything is left to study and learn from there, and Quarai keeps its history protected for us.

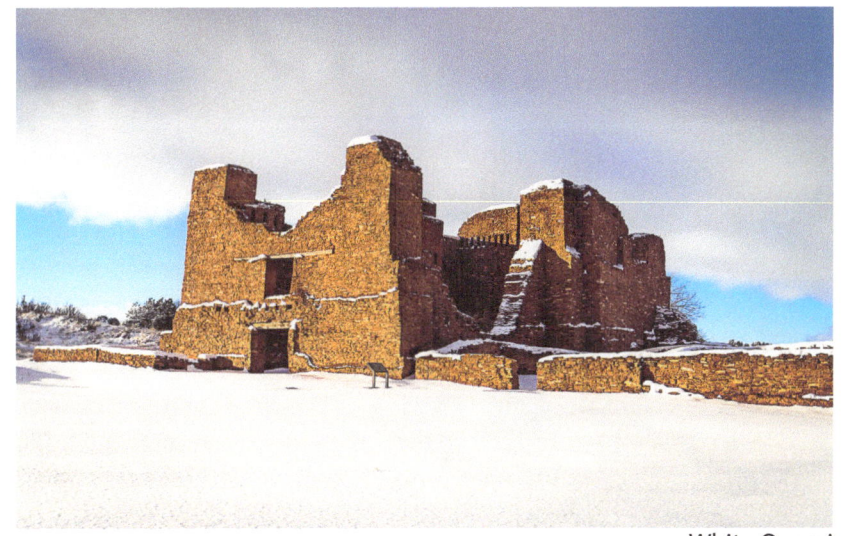

White Quarai

Even though Quarai is a small unit, it one of my favorite places, and over the years I've come to know the rangers there. The event celebrated the National Monument obtaining Dark Sky status, which is a big deal. This coveted status means that the park controls light emissions at night and doesn't add to light pollution; it is not an easy designation to achieve. In a time when cities are growing and humans are lighting up the night everywhere, we need more dedicated dark-sky places. It was a celebration I couldn't miss and a chance to be in the unit after dark. I was confident I could make an after-dark photograph or two and was excited at the prospect.

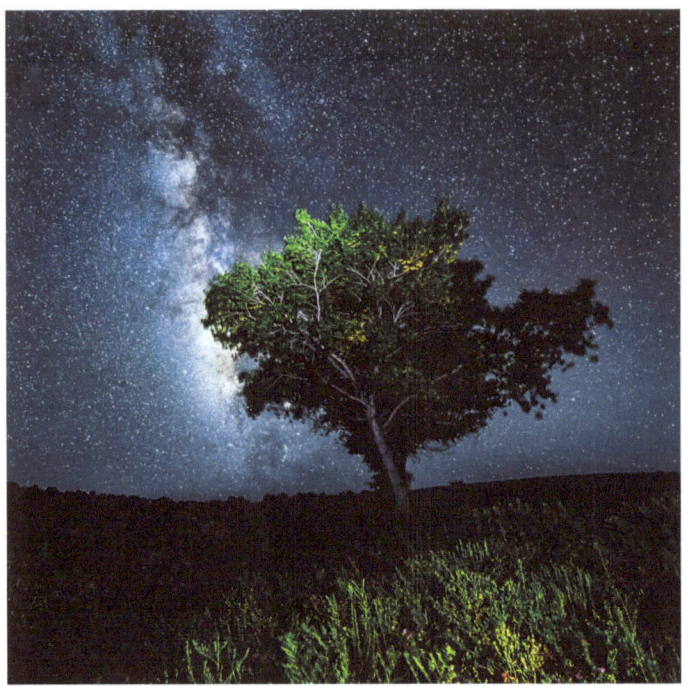
Galactic Spill

After the gathering, the rangers let me linger for a few moments. I admired the brightly glowing Milky Way, which seemed unusually bright, or rather it would have been if a cottonwood tree were not right in the middle of my view. Instead of moving to the left or right, as most sensible people would do, I had Mary Beth hold a light, lighting the tree perfectly, while I made *Galactic Spill*. It was terrific to have the time and space to myself and be able to create the photograph I imagined.

I adore the effect of the Milky Way seemingly "spilling" into the tree and from there, casting its light on the foreground. It is easy to imagine that the light of the distant stars nourishes the tree and the grasses and reminds me that everything is connected, no matter how far away they are from each other. Thanks to the dark skies of the park and some understanding rangers, I was able to pull this photograph off.

I was hustling by some of the low pueblo walls earlier in the evening. Since the park was pitch black, I was going by memory of where the walls were, but even if I couldn't quite remember. You'll recall my belief that I can see in the dark. Luckily that very darkness prevented anyone from seeing me go end over teakettle, when a wall was not where I thought it was. Mary Beth heard the commotion and asked what happened, and I, as nonchalant as could be, answered, "Oh, nothing." That low wall accounted for one of several skinned knees I've picked up in the dark. Worse, because I had already said nothing happened, I couldn't acknowledge or comment on it later, no matter how much that knee bothered me. Covering up the limp for a few days wasn't easy. When Mary Beth reads this, she'll remember that incident, and now I have some explaining to do.

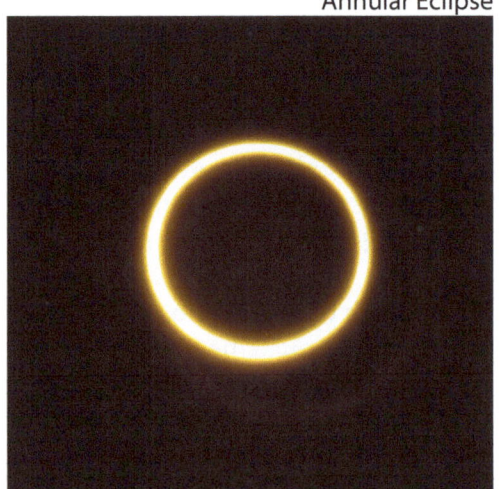
Annular Eclipse

I would be remiss if I didn't mention the last unit of Salinas, Gran Quivira. It was at Gran Quivira that I saw my first annular eclipse, known as the Ring of Fire, in 2012. As with the previous eclipse, the moon obscured the sun. The moon was farther away, though, which meant it didn't cover the sun completely. It came close, though, and the annular eclipse is as stunning and almost as dark as a total eclipse. As before, when the eclipse is at its maximum, it is a breathtaking sight that makes it hard to remember to create the photograph.

Although an annular eclipse is a rare event, this one didn't attract nearly the amount of attention that the total eclipse did. I didn't have any traffic to contend with or crowds of people or any other problems, which explains why I didn't properly consider the traffic implications of the total eclipse. Instead a few of us were at Gran Quivira, and together we waited patiently for the main event. As fabulous as it was to share the total eclipse with lots of other humans, it was equally powerful to share this eclipse with just a few others. As with the total eclipse, the entire world gradually darkened and quieted when the eclipse reached its zenith, with nary a word said during it. Afterward the world brightened again, and we went our separate ways, all the better for the experience.

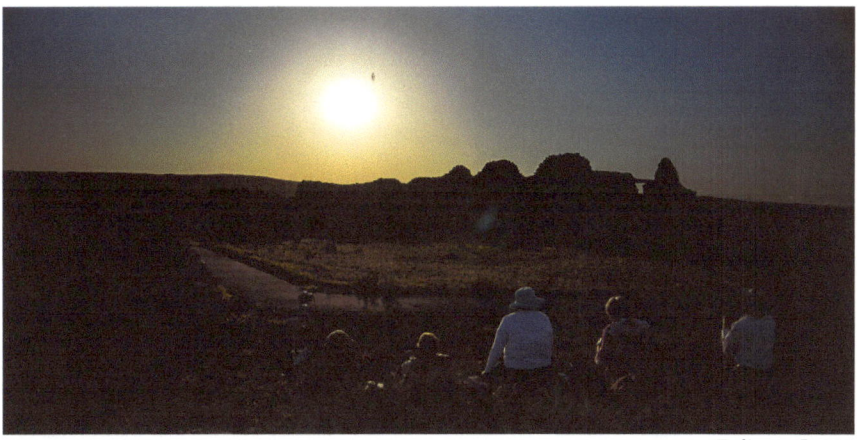

Eclipse Party

While I enjoy eclipses—they are extraordinary events—much of my night work involves the stars and the Milky Way. As much as I enjoy it, photographing the Milky Way is a time-consuming and slow process. It takes time to get everything set up in the first place. It takes time to make the test exposures. Creating the final photograph is not quick and requires me to find patience. It takes a lot of waiting followed by still more waiting and looking at the stars—not that I mind, of course. The more time I spent looking at the Milky Way, the more I pondered the sky itself, and especially deep space. What would I find if I focused on individual galaxies? How could I image the nebulas in the reaches of infinity? I figured if the Hubble Space Telescope could do it, so can I. It then became a question of "How can I make it happen?" It is not a simple question to answer. I thought about calling NASA, but the folks there wouldn't be too keen on me using the Hubble, so I had to find a different way.

I had a couple options, all involving a telescope. After much thought, I ended up renting time on large telescopes, the kind through which much professional modern-day astronomy is accomplished. For the past few hundred years, astronomers have had to travel to dark skies and set up their telescopes. In more modern times they can go to observatories that house larger telescopes. Times change and progress marches on, and instead of astronomers looking through eyepieces, the telescopes now record the observations on cameras. Astronomers no longer have to peer through the telescopes and no longer need to travel to observatories. More importantly to me, though, is that I too can use telescopes to explore the universe at my own pace and schedule. The hardest part, which quickly became an overwhelming problem, was working out what targets I wanted to image. The more I looked at the night sky, the more outstanding opportunities presented themselves, and before I knew it, my target list had more than a hundred entries on it, with more added each day. The night has only so many hours, and the Earth's rotation means not everything is viewable precisely when I want it to be. Storms, clouds, and other weather events can ruin a perfect opportunity. I know, I know; we should all have such problems.

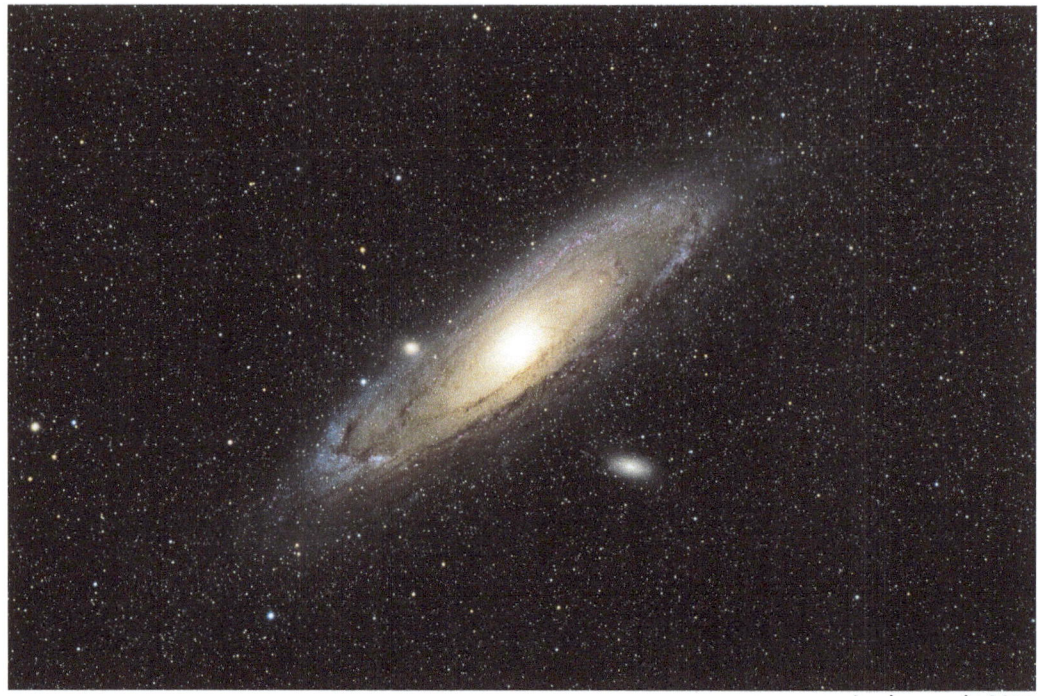

Andromeda M31

First on my list was the Andromeda galaxy, also known as Messier 31, or M31 for short. Andromeda is "just" 2.5 million light-years from us, which in the relative terms of the universe means it is in our backyard. It is also the farthest galaxy that we can see with our unaided eyes, meaning you do not need binoculars or a telescope to view it. Most importantly, it is a stunningly picturesque spiral galaxy. When I think of galaxies other than our own, I think of Andromeda. I quickly succumbed to its call and pointed the telescope toward it to make this photograph.

Photographing objects in deep space is fundamentally different from photographing scenic locations on our planet's surface. For a typical terrestrial scene, I need to work out the best time to photograph it, which means paying attention to the time of day and the weather. As the sun moves across the sky, the shadows move with it, enhancing or hindering a particular subject. Photographing in the early morning or late evening creates an immensely different photograph than one made at high noon with the sun overhead. I also need to get to the location, but I don't need to worry about the location moving. It always stays in the same place, every moment of every day. I need to control the time of day and pay attention to weather, but I don't need to account for the subject moving.

Charles Messier was a French astronomer whose passion was detecting and cataloging comets. From his point of view, quite a few objects in the sky were perpetually in his way, so to help other astronomers, he identified and inventoried forty-five of them in 1774. His collection became known as the Messier Objects and slowly grew to 110. Today we still refer to them by their object number. Andromeda was the thirty-first object he cataloged, or M31.

On the other hand, deep space objects can be photographed only at night. The bigger challenge, however, is the Earth's rotation. Because our round blue ball is rapidly spinning, the deep space object's apparent position is continually moving. Worse, not every target is visible every night, and even if it is visible on a particular night, it might not be visible for all of it. If those issues aren't enough, the object must be high enough in the sky to image successfully. Finally, to top it off, I need clear and calm skies. Clouds, of course, will prevent photographing, but so will a turbulent atmosphere. Even the smoke from forest fires, a typical summer occurrence in the Southwest and West, can prevent success. In short, photographing galaxies and nebulas is an entirely different process than photographing an Earth-bound scene.

There's another fundamental difference too. When making a photograph in the daytime, the camera shutter will typically be open for a fraction of a second. The fast shutter speed makes sense because the sun provides plenty of light. Space, however, has the polar opposite issue. Exposing a deep-space object means the shutter has to be open for an extended time. A typical exposure might well be three hundred seconds, provided you can move the telescope perfectly with the Earth's rotation.

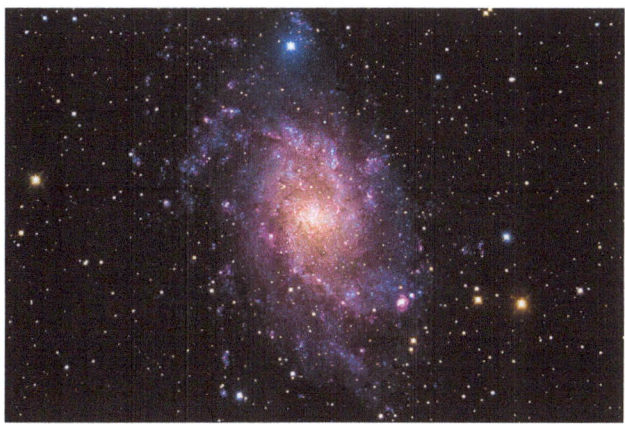
Triangulum M33

Even three hundred seconds, though, is not enough exposure time to create a stunning image. The solution is to create more than one photograph and then stack, or layer, each on top of the other, which effectively increases the total exposure time. The cumulative effect of stacked images adds detail, resolution, and color to the final result. Almost every space photograph you have seen is a result of stacking, including *M31 Andromeda*, which has several hours of cumulative exposure. All the plotting and planning to photograph a deep sky object does wonders for my patience, for sure. At least I don't have to contend with any traffic.

Another nearby spiral galaxy, the Triangulum Galaxy, also makes a heavenly photograph. Triangulum might now be, or might previously have been, a companion to Andromeda, and astronomers believe the two have passed close to each other in the distant past. Triangulum has active star-forming regions in it. They show up as the larger magenta areas on its edges. Star-forming regions are full of the gases and materials necessary to create stars, and we believe that more will be born there in time. Triangulum is in Charles Messier's collection as M33, and it is also known as NGC 598.

In 1888 John Louis Emil Dreyer created another, more comprehensive catalog of deep-sky objects, a list called the New General Catalogue of Nebulae and Clusters of Stars, abbreviated NGC. Like the Messier Objects, this list is still expanding today and inventories more than 3,600 objects. It is one of many such catalogs, and figuring out these lists has been another exercise in patience. I still don't know all of them. Maybe there is a catalog of the catalogs somewhere.

Now that we've wandered deep into the weeds chatting about lists and catalogs, let's use those lists to find more targets. Barnard 33, the Horsehead Nebula, is located in the Orion Constellation, to the east of the easternmost star, Alnitak, in Orion's Belt. It is an easy nebula to find, although you can't discern any of the details with your naked eye. Through a telescope it is an entirely different story, and the nebula and the surrounding region reveal all their glory.

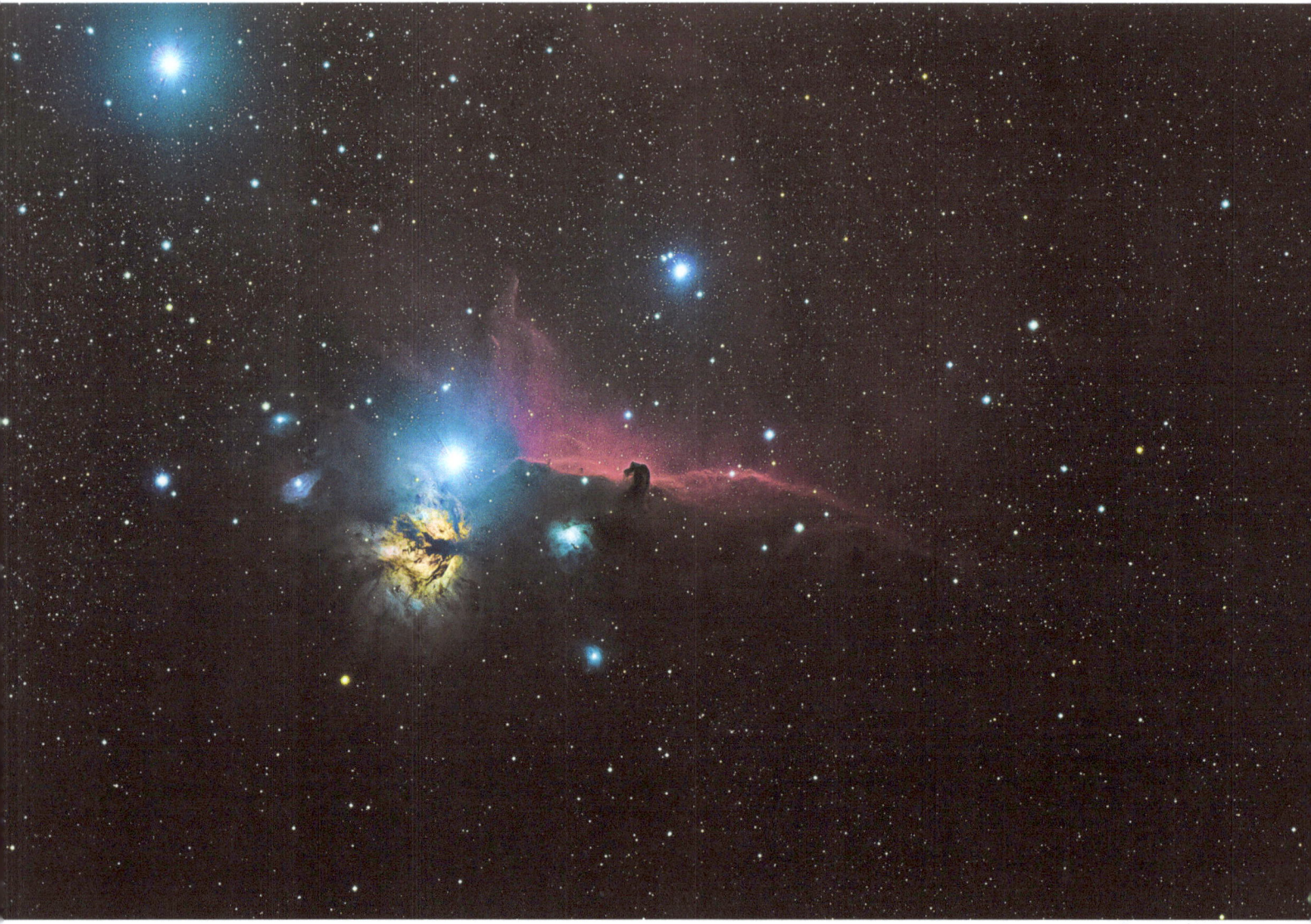

Barnard 33

This composite photograph features the Horsehead Nebula in the center of the image. The Flame Nebula is to the lower left, and Alnitak is in the far upper left. The Horsehead Nebula features a large dust cloud in the vague shape of a horse head, which gives rise to its name. This region of space strikes me as one of the most alluring. If I could go anywhere, I would head there first, because it offers so much to explore. As extraordinary as it looks in this photograph, I'll wager it is even more so up close.

Are the fantastic colors in this photograph real? The answer is not as straightforward as you might expect. First off, yes, they are authentic. Our eyes can see reds, greens, and blues just fine, and those three primary colors make up all the other colors we see. Photographing the Andromeda and Triangulum galaxies in visible light makes the most sense, but nebulas, in addition to starlight, also have gases such as hydrogen, oxygen, and sulfur, none of which we humans can see. The solution to photographing invisible gases is called Narrow Band Imaging.

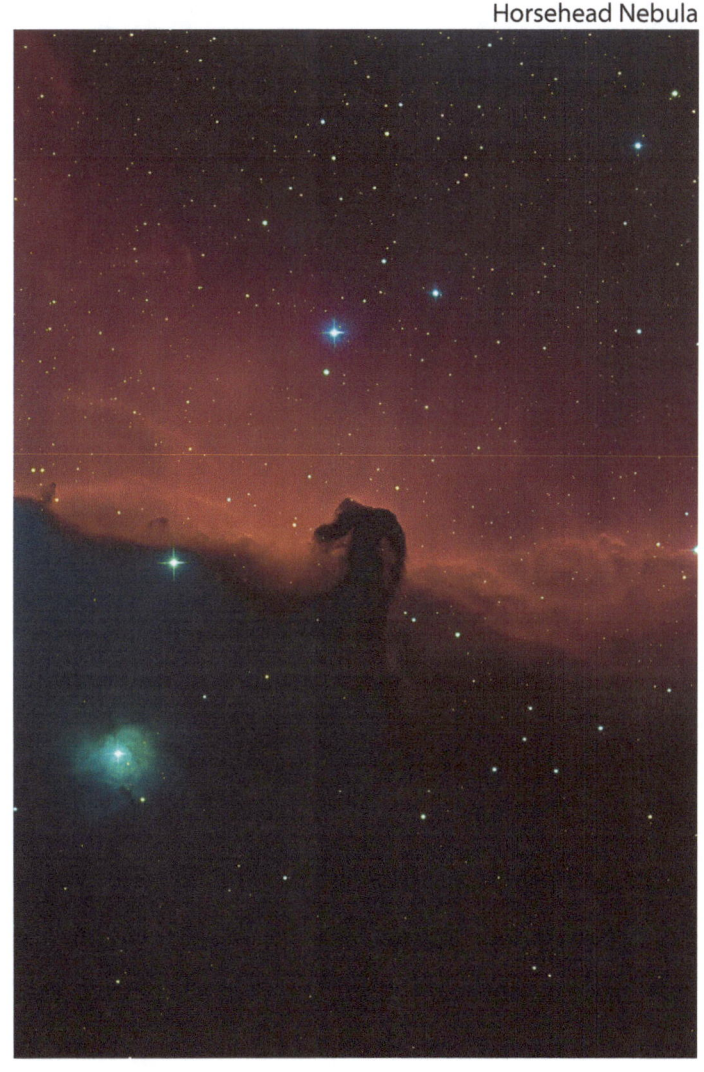

Using a filter that passes only the spectral wavelength for hydrogen and blocks all others, another for oxygen, and a third for sulfur, we can create a black-and-white image that contains only one component.

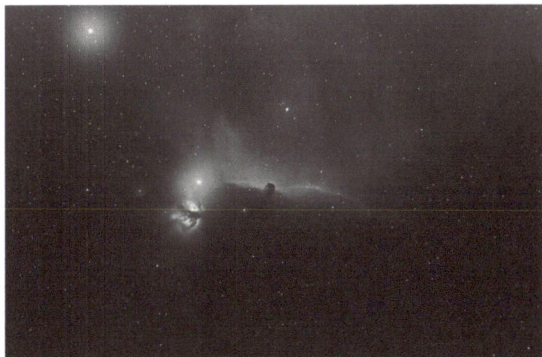

When looking at the picture, what we're seeing is only the light representing that specific gas. We then assign that image to a particular color. For example, green is used for hydrogen, blue for oxygen, and red for sulfur, commonly known as the "Hubble Pallet." The images are then combined to create a full-color image. To complete the final photograph, another set of true-color images were made and combined with the narrowband images. Don't forget that we need to layer many of the same images to increase the total exposure time, so each color needs many exposures. The final result is a single stunning image that lets us see the gases of the nebula.

In the case of Barnard 33, I made several hours of images in red, green, blue, hydrogen, oxygen, and sulfur, and then combined them into the final composite image. So yes, the colors are "real," but we are using some techniques to help us visualize them.

Photographing deep-space objects is quite different from photographing earthly ones, that's for sure!

Another favorite example of narrowband imaging is found in *Cygnus Wall*. The predominant gas, oxygen, is mapped

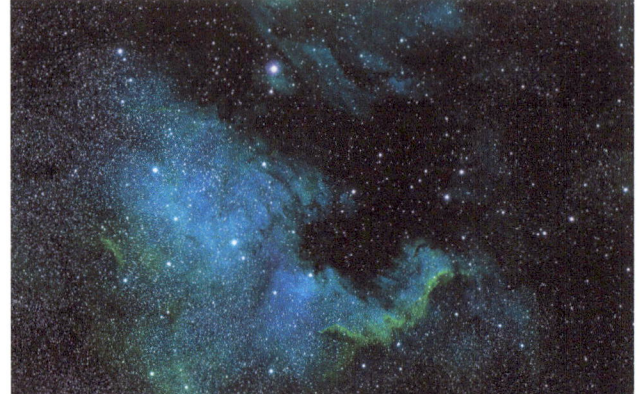
Cygnus Wall

to blue, with sulfur, appearing primarily around the edges, in green. The large, cross-shaped void in the middle is an opaque cloud of dust, and the stars that appear to be in it are actually between us and the dust cloud. The Cygnus Wall, in green, is found in the North American Nebula, NGC 7000, and is one small part of the vast and sprawling nebula.

We'll leave outer space with the gigantic Carina Nebula, NGC 3372, located in southern hemisphere skies. *Carina Nebula* is another narrowband image composited with visible light. In this photograph, however, hydrogen has been mapped to red, as is commonly done with this nebula.

Carina Nebula

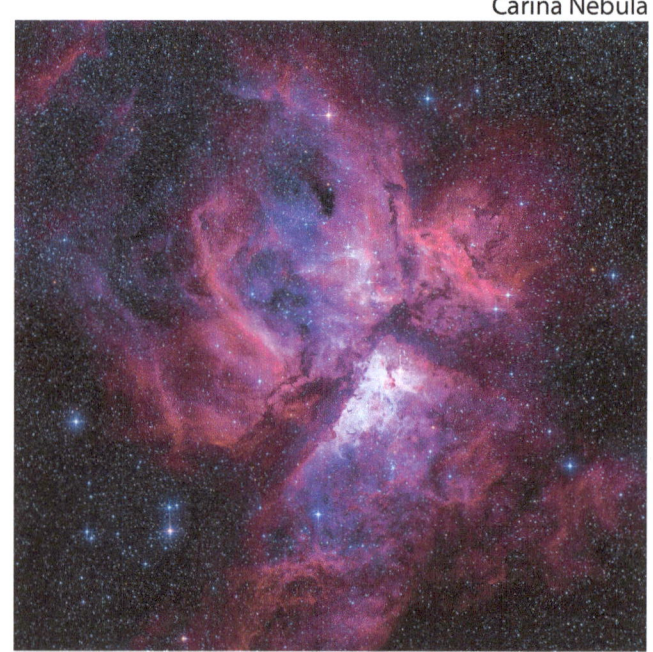

The large Carina Nebula is three thousand light-years away and lies in the Sagittarius Arm of the Milky Way. Barely visible with the naked eye, it is home to several star-forming regions and clusters. The gases and dust clouds swirl and twist together, forming a tangled knot of color. Bear in mind that nebulas aren't flat, as shown in the photographs, but are vast, sprawling three-dimensional structures.

Not all telescopes use visible light to search the skies. Some, like those found at the Very Large Array—the VLA—just outside of Socorro, New Mexico, capture radio waves. Let's come back to Earth while we continue to explore our night skies.

The VLA incorporates twenty-seven identical radio telescopes that operate together to form a single, larger telescope. It constantly searches the heavens for radio waves and signals and has made several important discoveries. The search continues, even after hours, when the scientists have headed home. This photograph of a single telescope with the Milky Way behind

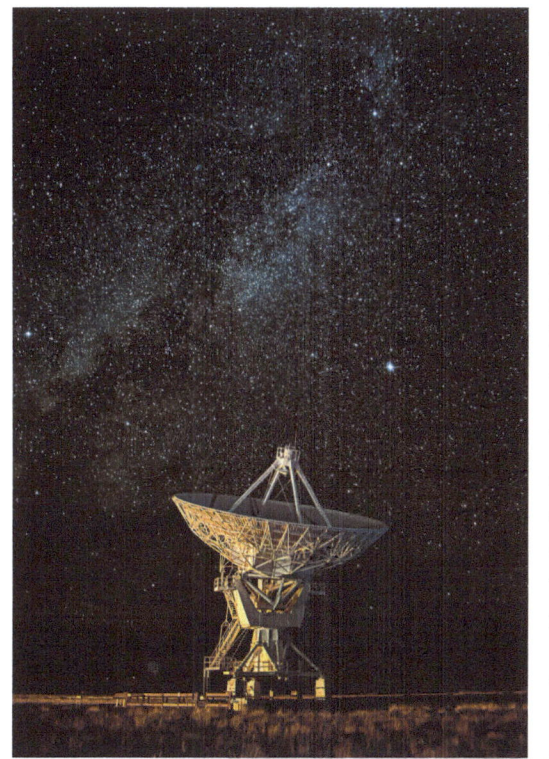

VLA Night

it captures the loneliness, yet mightiness, of the vigil. I wonder what the telescope was hearing at the time I was making this photograph. While I stood there straining to hear what the VLA did, the silence was broken only by a gentle hum and the occasional "click-clack" as the telescope made a fine adjustment. Try as I might, my human ears failed me, and whatever signals were beaming to Earth eluded me. I wondered if the mysteries of the universe were being revealed or if someone was signaling us, waiting for our answer. I thought of many questions, yet no answers came. Perhaps in time the answers will come to us, but in the here and now, we continue our search. I continued to listen, alone in the dark, and then quietly packed up my gear for another time.

We'll leave our brief visit to the VLA with *The Search*, depicting a row of telescopes seeking answers on a moonlit night. As powerful an image a single telescope is, multiple telescopes straining to hear the universe creates an even more awe-inspiring image. Maybe all of them together will capture the answer hiding among the zeroes and ones they faithfully record.

We've got one more nighttime jewel to see.

Charles Messier was on to something when he was scanning the skies for comets. Seeing one of those celestial visitors is an addictive experience, and once you see one, you'll have a deep hunger to see more. I can readily imagine Charles searching the skies and becoming frustrated by finding the same objects repeatedly, only to realize they were not comets after all. That exciting momentary pause after he saw something, but before he had confirmed it, had to have been thrilling and full of trepidation at the same time.

In mid July 2020, Comet NEOWISE paid a visit to us, and I was finally able to photograph a comet of my very own. I was standing in an empty field photographing the comet when I briefly thought of Charles, and at that moment, connected to his quest. Seeing a comet is quite the experience.

Many of the most famous comets, such as Halley's Comet, have well-known and well-established orbits. We discovered them long ago, and we know when they will visit next. Now

The Search

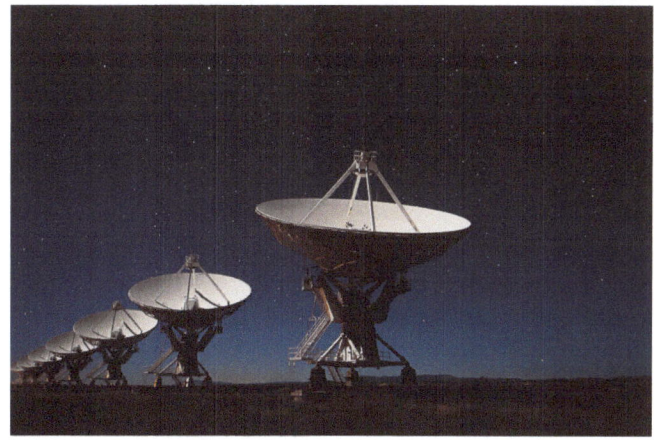

and then a new, unknown visitor appears in our skies. Even more rarely, its orbit lets us catch a glimpse of it with a telescope. Even more unusually, we can sometimes see them with our unaided eyes. Comet NEOWISE was one of those infrequent visitors.

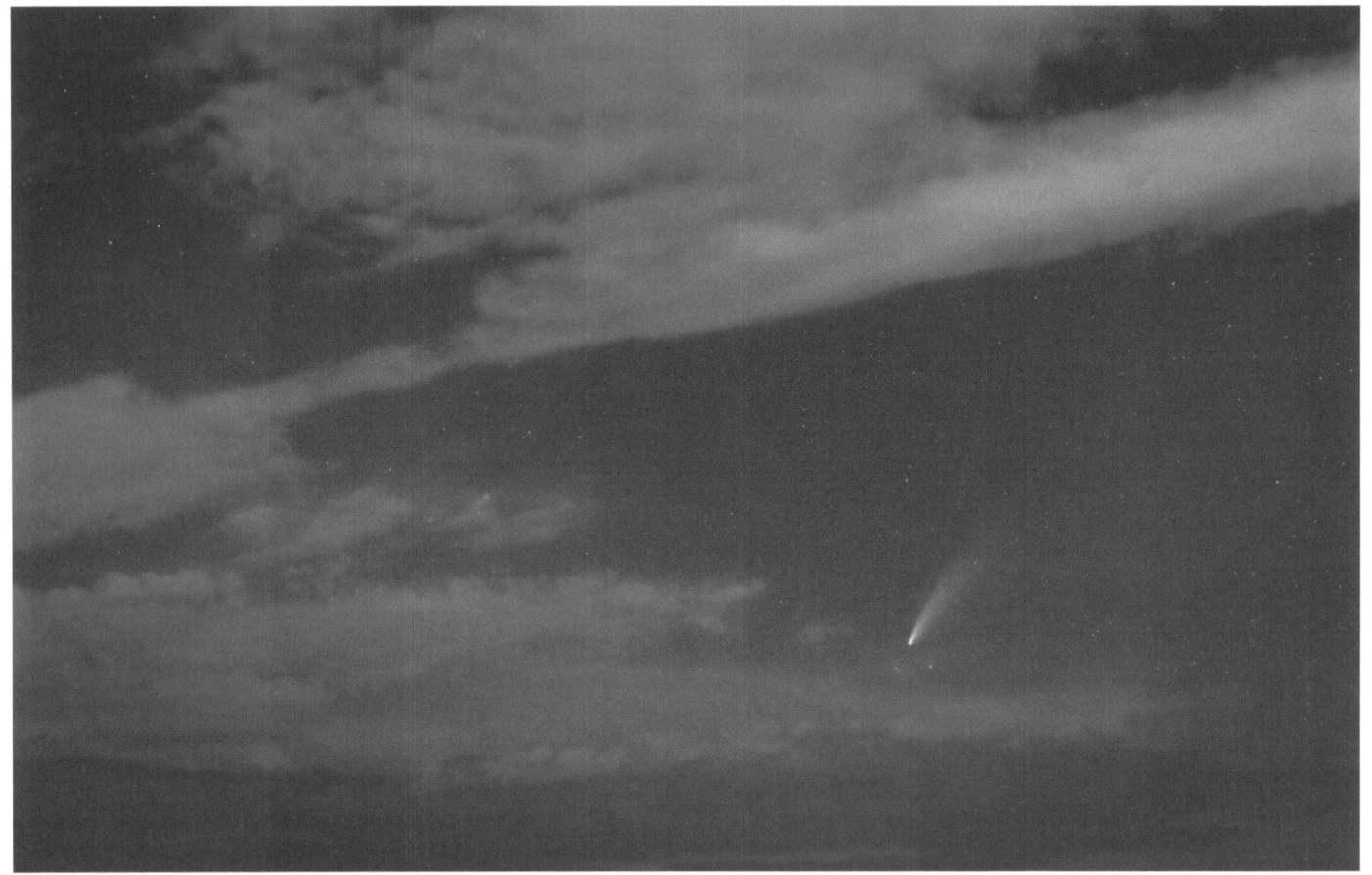
Comet NEOWISE

Astronomers discovered the flying object as part of the mission of the Near-Earth Orbit Wide-field Infrared Survey Explorer (NEOWISE) space telescope and were thrilled when they realized they were looking at a new comet. Even more astonishing was the comet's orbit, which would take it close enough to Earth so us Earthlings could see it. Whether the comet's approach to the sun would disrupt it remained an open question, though, because comets often break up from the sun's heat. As it turned out, the comet remained intact after its closest approach to the sun, and as it swung by the Earth, it provided us with spectacular views. NEOWISE was visible across much of the entire planet.

For me, though, the sighting was problematic. Because of the COVID-19 virus, I had curtailed my summer travels and stayed safe at home. Under normal circumstances I would have found an excellent location with a fantastic foreground to create the best photograph I could, but the times were far from normal, so that option was out. That's OK, though, I told myself. I said I had plenty of opportunities around New Mexico, except, as fate would have it, July is right in the middle of monsoon season, so clear skies do not usually happen in the evenings.

One night, though, offered a break from the cloudy skies, and I could see the comet. It wasn't much of a break, but I had enough time to reach a nearby field away from the majority of Albuquerque's light pollution. To be sure, right behind me, a summer storm replete with crashing lightning was brewing over the city and threatening to take my view away. I had just enough time to create a photograph, though, for which I am eternally grateful. I located the Big Dipper, Ursa Major, and then let my gaze drift down. There it was! At first I thought it was my imagination, but after a moment I knew I was looking directly at NEOWISE. I stood awestruck at being able to see a comet with my own eyes and nothing else. All in all I am quite pleased with how the photograph turned out.

Who knows? Perhaps one day I'll create my own catalog of objects in the skies. Comet NEOWISE will henceforth be known as Schneider 1 or S1. I completely understand, Charles.

Alas, it's time for our journey to wrap up, although my photographs and stories will continue.

The emotions I felt when seeing the Northern Lights for the first time will never leave me, nor will the feeling of elation when I heard whales breathe across the Alaskan waters. The feeling of being next to a tornado is not one I'll ever forget, nor I will I forget my lessons learned trying to catch lightning. I'll always remember the feeling of encountering the moss-draped trees and holding my breath as the sunrise ascended over the orange rocks of the desert southwest yet again. I'll always be awed when I gaze at and through stars into the unknown beyond.

Where will I go from here? It's hard to say, but I do know I'll continue adventuring, delving into our national lands and country as a whole, from coast to coast and everywhere in between, exploring dirt roads and two-tracks, making my own trails in the frontier and pondering the uncountable lights of the universe. I'll also continue communing with our past, for we've barely scratched the surface of its rich tapestry.

I'll also spend time with the ocean. I've dwelled on my relationship with it, and with good reason. Although I live in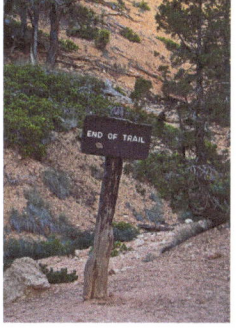
the desert, the ocean somehow defines me. I've always thought that it was "out to get me," but in recent years my feeling has morphed into the thought that it is "calling me home." Perhaps these feelings are one and the same. My answers are hazy. I am aware that "calling me home" doesn't always equate to longevity. I intend to spend more time with the seas, and maybe clarity will come with time.

In any event, I'll discover more magnificent scenes, for we are surrounded by a world full of light, beauty, mystery, magic, and hope. I know I'll meet more interesting people and hear their stories, because "hello" is one of my favorite words. I'll continue chronicling my sojourns, wherever my footsteps might lead. As always, I'll go ever onward.

About the Author

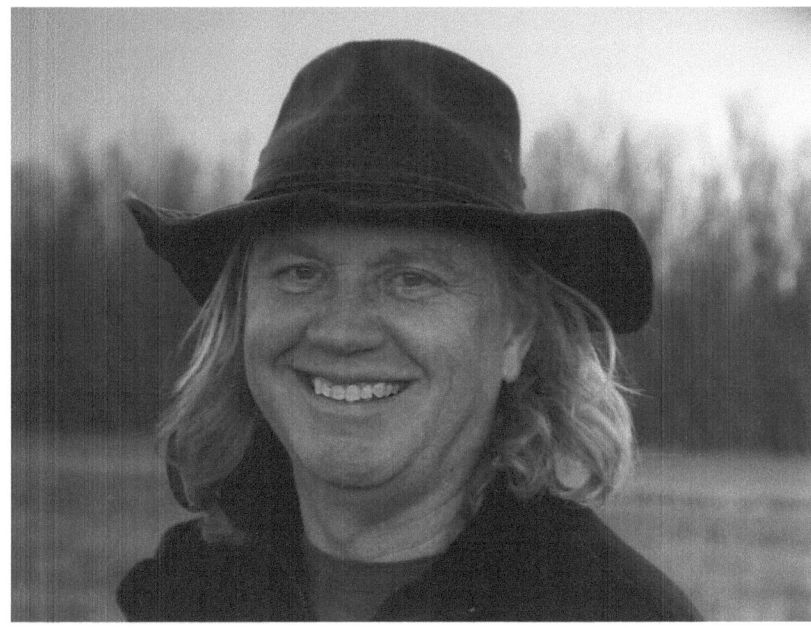

The sun sleeps on, not even thinking about rising yet. David, already standing out in a cold, wet field, waits for the sun and the wildlife to come alive. Seemingly the last place anyone else would want to be, this field springs to life with the dawn, and so does David's camera. Only the shot matters, in spite of toes threatening to move to the equator and fingers looking for a cup of coffee instead of wanting to hold the camera. He waits for exactly the right moment and then ... click. He has it.

David Schneider, a nature and wildlife photographer, focuses on bringing alive each scene and creature his camera sees. With a unique point of view and style, his prints capture the color, beauty, and soul of his subjects. His affinity for nature extends into the scenic arena as well. His landscapes bring out the incredible emotion, beauty, and grandeur of the Southwest and beyond; his photographs will take you from the tops of misty mountains to the shifting sands of the deep desert, letting you always be in the moment.

David lives in Albuquerque, New Mexico. He prefers to be outside whenever possible, in his "studio"—the great out-doors. He believes in being one with nature, and not a day goes by that he doesn't find something new to be amazed and delighted by. David has had a lifelong interest in photography and nature, and his passions combine, providing arresting photographs for everyone.

Photo by M.B. McClean